D1528863

Hannah Arendt and International Relations

HANNAH ARENDT AND INTERNATIONAL RELATIONS

READINGS ACROSS THE LINES

Edited by

Anthony F. Lang, Jr.
John Williams

palgrave
macmillan

First published in 2005 by
PALGRAVE MACMILLAN™
175 Fifth Avenue, New York, N.Y. 10010 and
Houndmills, Basingstoke, Hampshire, England RG21 6XS
Companies and representatives throughout the world.

PALGRAVE MACMILLAN is the global academic imprint of the Palgrave Macmillan division of St. Martin's Press, LLC and of Palgrave Macmillan Ltd. Macmillan® is a registered trademark in the United States, United Kingdom and other countries. Palgrave is a registered trademark in the European Union and other countries.

ISBN 1–4039–6783–0

Library of Congress Cataloging-in-Publication Data

Hannah Arendt and international relations : readings across the lines / edited by Anthony F. Lang, Jr., John Williams.
      p. cm.
Includes bibliographical references and index.
ISBN 1–4039–6783–0
  1. Arendt, Hannah. 2. International relations. I. Lang, Anthony F., 1968– II. Williams, John, 1969–

JC251.A74H326 2005
327.1′01—dc22   2004061823

A catalogue record for this book is available from the British Library.

Design by Newgen Imaging Systems (P) Ltd., Chennai, India.

First edition: July 2005

10 9 8 7 6 5 4 3 2 1

Printed in the United States of America.

CONTENTS

ACKNOWLEDGMENTS

This book was conceived, as with more academic projects than most are prepared to admit, in a bar. A chance introduction over a drink in the Chicago Hilton during the 2001 ISA Convention resulted in each of the editors discovering that they were not, as they had tended to think, the only person in International Relations (IR) with an interest in Hannah Arendt. The first vote of thanks therefore goes to our mutual friend, William Bain, who effected the introduction.

From these chance and unlikely beginnings, we embarked on a project to put together a panel on Hannah Arendt for the 2002 ISA Convention. Given our impression that we were the only people in IR with such an interest, this looked like a tall order. We could provide two papers, but looking for two more, a chair and a discussant would, we thought, be pretty difficult. However, this insular impression was soon revealed to be wholly false and we easily established two panels on Arendt as there turned out to be many people who shared such an interest. Thanks therefore must go to those who helped us find our panelists, especially Andy Schaap and Patricia Owens for their suggestions on participants, and to the discussants, Kim Hutchings and Molly Cochran, who did that job with their characteristic good humor, good grace, and intellectual insight. Both wished us well as we declared our intention to develop the papers on those panels into a book, and have expressed supportive interest in its progress ever since. John Williams would like to thank the British Academy who supported financially the presentation at the 2002 ISA Convention of the paper that has become the chapter on an international in-between.

Our next vote of thanks goes to Toby Wahl at Palgrave, who agreed with a surprising readiness to take on a book on Arendt and international relations. He has been very helpful throughout the somewhat protracted process of putting it together, showing understanding and encouragement through some difficult stages of developing the final version. We would also like to acknowledge that an earlier version of the chapter by Andrew Schaap appeared as "Forgiveness, Reconciliation, and Transitional Justice," in *Contemporary Political Theory* 2, no. 1: 77–88 and is included here by permission of Palgrave Macmillan.

Our families have also provided a great deal of support during this process, too, and their contribution deserves recognition and our very considerable thanks.

Finally, these acknowledgments began with the metaphor of conception and they finish with the reality of death. The project of putting this book together has covered a period marked by the death of John Williams's father in November 2001 and Tony Lang's mother in December 2003. They never met or knew one another but both played similar roles in providing the encouragement, support, love, and companionship that helped us, and continues to help us after they have gone, to pursue intellectual and personal fulfilment. We would thus like to dedicate this book to their memory.

CHAPTER 1

INTRODUCTION

John Williams with Anthony F. Lang, Jr.

WHY HANNAH ARENDT?

International Relations (IR) theory has benefited greatly from a growing interaction with political theory and philosophy over the last 20 years.[1] Via postmodernism and the work of Foucault, Derrida, Rorty, and Lyotard continental theory has become an accepted part of theoretical discourse.[2] The Frankfurt School Critical Theory, exemplified by the work of Habermas, has also carved out a significant niche.[3] In International Political Economy (IPE), the work of Antonio Gramsci has inspired perhaps the most dynamic analysis of economic globalization, and certainly one with a powerful critical voice.[4] Traditional stalwarts of political theory courses, such as Kant, Mill, and Bentham, have regained prominence via the democratic peace literature and issues such as cosmopolitan democracy and global citizenship.[5] The revival of normative theory also owes a great deal to political theory and philosophy with both cosmopolitan and communitarian camps often identifying themselves with Kant and Hegel, respectively.[6] Even realism, often seen as lacking in philosophical sophistication, has looked to its theoretical roots. This is most obvious in the use of neoclassical economic analogies and rational choice theory in neorealism, but has also involved a consideration of thinkers such as Carl Schmitt—adding the, admittedly problematic, weapon of the twentieth century's most trenchant critic of liberalism to the armory of policy-oriented, problem-solving pragmatism.[7]

The process, hopefully, is becoming increasingly two-way with political theorists waking up to the eroding credibility of a basic distinction between domestic and international politics and the need for two different sorts of theory. Martin Wight's famous account of why there is no international theory of comparable sophistication to domestic political theory is less and less persuasive, both as a description of the situation and as a justification for it.[8]

One significant absentee from these interactions is Hannah Arendt.[9] This book is a first effort at highlighting ways in which her rich and rewarding, if also sometimes frustrating, political thought can be used to enhance and stimulate our understanding of aspects of international politics. This book's chapters look at issues ranging from Douglas Klusmeyer's Arendtian take on classical realism—Arendt was a close friend of Hans Morgenthau—to contemporary international political issues such as Anthony Lang's look at the antiglobalization movement and Andrew Schaap's analysis of post-conflict justice. There is also a diversity of approaches, with chapters such as Bridget Cotter's on human rights and Patricia Owens' on the public sphere paying close attention to Arendt's texts and standing as considerable works of Arendt scholarship. John Williams, on the other hand, draws inspiration from Arendt's ideas and categories, but asks for more license in their use in his account of an emerging international space "in-between."

This may suggest that Arendt is a theorist of almost limitless applicability, making her relative obscurity in IR's return to political theory especially striking. However, the chapters are united by a recognition that Arendt's is a very individual politics, not just in its distinctiveness, but in its focus upon individuals as political agents, acting within specific circumstances, but always retaining a unique character and capable of unpredictable and surprising acts of great political significance. Individuals have tended to fare badly in international relations, with its focus on states and institutions and the great, impersonal forces of anarchy, war, balance of power, and the movements of capital. Thus, Arendt is not a solution to the problems of IR theory in any and all of its guises. However, while the contributors make good cases for her special applicability in their areas, this chapter hopes to show that she can be a stimulating read for a wider variety of IR theorists.

The chapter is thus divided into three main sections: First is Arendt's radical attack on the failures of most traditional political thought and the development of a distinctive approach of her own. Second, this introduction touches on the issue of plurality and its political ramifications. Finally, it considers her thought about institutions, including the law.

Additionally, this introduction serves as something of a "primer" for those unfamiliar with her work. This is not a comprehensive covering of all Arendt's contributions, but it should prove helpful in getting the most from subsequent chapters.[10] Where possible, we highlight contrasts or illuminate points by drawing examples from International Relations, hopefully helping orientate those coming to the book from IR. Those familiar with Arendt's work may find these choices unusual or somewhat forced, but we ask their forbearance.

HANNAH ARENDT AND THE FAILURE OF POLITICAL THEORY

Hans Morgenthau: What are you? Are you a conservative? Are you a liberal? Where is your position within the contemporary possibilities? *Hannah Arendt*: I don't know. I really don't know and I've never known. And I suppose I never had any such position. You know the left think I am a conservative, and the conservatives sometimes think I am of the left or I am a maverick or God knows what. And I must say I couldn't care less.[11]

Arendt's frustration with the limits of standard political categories, whether in day-to-day political debate or in political theory was significant.[12] Her cavalier attitude to such conventions rests ultimately on a bold, even chilling, assertion. The vast majority of the political philosophy of the last 2,500 years is nothing of the sort.[13]

Arendt asserts that we have been obsessed by "ruling" and not by politics in our thinking.[14] While she has nothing directly to say about IR theory, she would doubtless regard international relations as guilty of the same charge. "Ruling" is about relieving the mass of the population from the need to engage in politics via grand schemes and plans, concentrated on institutions. The goal of this approach is to rid us of the need for participatory politics and to concentrate responsibility for managing these schemes and institutions in the hands of a small, professional class of political "craftsmen."[15]

Arendt argues that the modern version of this move is rooted in the Enlightenment search for Archimedean points as the basis of universal categories and truths, something of which she is highly critical—"neither truth nor reality is given. . . ."[16] Such a search is one of the principal reasons for the lack of true political philosophy in the modern world.[17] Arendt attacks the consequent imposition of human schemes upon the natural world via the generation of facts.[18] She refers approvingly to Heisenberg's remark that the natural sciences are now so tied up in a web of human making that via science, "instead of nature or the universe . . . man encounters only himself."[19] Politics has also become too much about trying to identify universally true and applicable political categories, institutions, and mechanisms. We are thus dealing with a theorist interested in "social facts"—facts only by human agreement.[20] She thus has little time for the objectivism of modern liberal economics, behaviorist sociology, and rational choice politics with their emphasis on the quantification, homogenization, and statistical modeling of human experiences.[21]

Arendt argues that this Enlightenment approach robs politics of its nobility. For her, real politics is the highest form of human action, the noblest pursuit in which people can engage and the realm in which they can discover and display their truly human character.[22] Reducing it to the job of a skilled but small minority, therefore, denigrates politics and with it human beings. Indeed, "ruling" is a form of "work"—political craftsmanship—which is unpolitical and which consigns most of us to a world of "labor," which is antipolitical.[23]

Arendt's approach to politics stresses "action," understood as freedom, participation, and discourse. "Wherever the relevance of speech is at stake, matters become political by definition, for speech is what makes man a political being."[24] Therefore, Arendt's account of politics is profoundly intersubjective and concerned with choices and alternative courses of action. This helps explain her dissatisfaction with the ruling approach that she identifies in most political theory.

> [T]he impossibility . . . to solidify in words the living essence of the person as it shows itself in the flux of action and speech, has great bearing upon the whole realm of human affairs, where we exist primarily as acting and speaking beings. It excludes in principle our ever being able to handle these affairs as we handle those whose nature is at our disposal because we can name them.[25]

Arendt's ontology of politics is therefore concerned with plurality, unpredictability, uniqueness, and other elements that do not fit well into grand schemes predicated upon the homogeneity of political subjectivity. "Whatever touches or enters into a sustained relationship with human life immediately assumes the character of a condition of human existence. This is why men, no matter what they do, are always conditioned beings."[26] People thus make the world, rather than vice versa, within the confines of the natural environment and the limitations of previous actions, and they are unable to do so in isolation. Arendt is a social theorist not just in the sense of concerning herself with the study of society but also in the sense of an ontological assumption about the sociability of human beings. Humans, who become "lonely" in Arendt's term, are deprived of the ability to act and thus deprived of the ability to be properly human. The political manifestation of loneliness is isolation, "Action . . . is never possible in isolation; to be isolated is to be deprived of the capacity to act."[27]

Arendt thus moves away from the state as the principal political actor that is a characteristic of so much of International Relations theorizing. It is the socially conditioned and located individual who is the focus of politics and the essential political agent. While Arendt, like Morgenthau, recognizes the centrality of power to politics, and the ethically laden character of political action, she does not see the state as capable of being a proper political actor. As argued below, agency cannot, for Arendt, be incorporated into an artificial political institution like the state. The state is vitally important. A good deal of books such as *On Revolution* and *Origins of Totalitarianism* emphasize the state as a necessary condition for the fulfillment of human agency, and the potential for its perversion into the nemesis of a proper human life. However, Arendt does not allow the state to acquire agency. Morgenthau, along with other classical U.S. realist theorists of IR, such as Kissinger, Lippman, Kennan, and Wolfers, entrust the state with a degree of agency that Arendt cannot.[28] Their state-focused approach, as Klusmeyer argues in this book, results in their failing to appreciate the full political significance of the Holocaust as a political act in the sense of an effort to remake the nature of politics, and not just to contribute to an institutional project of power-maximization.

Drawing again on IR, we can contrast Arendt with a writer such as Hedley Bull. He argues that the existence of states is the essential condition for international relations, placing the state at the very heart of the ontology of IR.[29] This is a position that Arendt would reject because human beings are the condition of politics, all politics, and efforts to separate off a branch of human activity, like international relations, on the basis that it is populated by a different sort of political actor is to try to separate it from politics properly understood. The English School may appeal to the legacy of the Western tradition of political thought, via the works of Hobbes, Grotius, and Kant most prominently, but there is little meaningful overlap with the theory of politics developed by Arendt.[30] Bull's focus on the institutions of a rule- and norm-regulated society of sovereign states renders him subject to the accusation of discussing "ruling," rather than politics properly understood.[31]

Arendt's critique of ruling also points to her likely dissatisfaction with currently dominant, strongly positivistic, approaches to theorizing international relations, and the policy conclusions derived from them. Arendt would be deeply critical of the kind of near deterministic structural theory represented by neo-Realism. Its view of a virtually eternal and almost immutable anarchy generating imperatives that are nearly impossible to resist and transcend contradicts the kind of political theory Arendt develops. Its policy implications are also incompatible with an Arendtian approach. They stress the need for small, skilful political elites conducting politics within the limited confines of agency left open to them. The notions governing political action, like national interest, national security and the balance of power, are fundamentally exogenous and the result of structural circumstances and the luck of the draw in terms of state attributes. They are not made as a result of political action stemming from a discourse among human beings possessing the ability to make and unmake their political circumstances. Instead, international political action is about "statecraft": the ability of professionals to maneuver their way through the difficult, dangerous, and complicated terrain of the world political landscape.[32]

A similar problem of accepting the exogenous nature of the basic constraints of the international system, adding the market forces of globalizing capitalism to the anarchic structure of the international system, afflicts liberal institutionalism. IR theory may recognize choice, but this choice is not action in the sense Arendt means, because it does not unavoidably incorporate a challenge to the prevailing order of the system and the limitations upon choice it is assumed to create. Instead these are accepted, respected, and entrenched through the choices that are made.

Thus, whether it is wealth or security that is being pursued, mainstream international relations is about ruling. This can almost hardly be otherwise, given the way in which the methodological refinement of these theories over the last 25 years has attempted to root them more deeply in mainstream, Enlightenment notions about the philosophy of social science.[33]

Arendt's methodology asserts the indeterminate intersubjectivity of social and political experience. This is summed up in one of her most distinctive notions—the idea of "natality"—". . . the birth of new men and the new beginning, the action they are capable of by virtue of being born."[34] Natality, as an example of Arendt's distinctive approach to political thought, appeals to the limitless potential and diversity that springs from every human birth, challenging the exogenous limiting frameworks of conventional approaches.

> [T]he new beginning inherent in birth can make itself felt in the world only because the newcomer possesses the capacity of beginning

something anew, that is, of acting. In this sense of initiative, an element of action, and therefore of natality, is inherent in all human activities.[35]

Thus unpredictability, the emphasis on immanent potential for innovation, even revolution, stands in contrast to dominant strands of international relations that are often distrustful of change. This distrust is deepest in the sort of change that is not directed toward clear institutional reform, focused on the resolution of specific and practical political problems. An Arendtian sensibility about the nature of political thought contributes to resisting what Ruggie calls the "neo-utilitarianism" that characterizes the major approaches to international relations theory and that constrains international political thought within the limits of policy specificity and relevance.[36] Rethinking the situation within such work is a goal aspired to but very rarely achieved in the sense Arendt intends by the idea of natality. She wants political thought to challenge framing discourses, to value unpredictability, and to open channels for new ideas and voices to gain access to political space. Thus, Arendt can be seen to be partially in line with post-positivism's concern with ideational structures, language, and normative vision, but Arendt retains a rootedness in time, place, and community that sees these as real and valuable. They matter because they reflect previous political actions imbued with the spirit of natality. Much of politics and our political structures are not like this, but some are. The immanent potential for change, via action, exists within a politics focused on ruling, and as a reaction must be against it, we cannot ignore it or dismiss it as worthless. Action cannot take place in a vacuum, it needs things and people to work with and against, often in the most unpredictable ways.

Arendt's approach to political philosophy is thus unusual and without clear parallel in IR. For those unconvinced by a politics of "ruling" focused on institutions and structures she offers an understanding of the role of ideas via her account of the way in which ruling has come to dominate political thought and conduct. Going further than this, she critiques such processes. At one level this critique is in terms of the way processes have entrenched certain sites of power and privileged certain groups. Arendt goes further by challenging the political nature of what IR takes for granted to be politics. However, she always takes the present situation very seriously as a political reality that is always contingent and mutable, but whose ontological power should not be underestimated, even if its unpolitical and antipolitical effects must be challenged.[37]

The politics of action, as opposed to ruling through the making of institutions, produces a bold vision of how ideational as well as institutional structures might be challenged and changed. Rather than restricting herself to an account of the possibilities of making what exists better, as Alexander Wendt does in his account of the development of Kantian cultures of anarchy,[38] Arendt's idealized politics would leave little left of the existing social and political order. However, she avoids a dichotomization of the real and the ideal via notions like natality and her radical intersubjectivity that stresses the elements of the ideal to be found in the real and especially in the interaction of human beings. The ideal is not an institutional project—the utopian dream of a perfect political system replacing one form of ruling with another— but an ephemeral and intersubjective moment, never static and always to be re-created through the actions of real people living real lives. Its manifestation is often fleeting, but its consequences are both unpredictable and potentially limitless, reflecting the idea of an element of natality being present in all true political action.

Therefore, Arendt cannot be subsumed into one of the versions of postpositivism on offer in IR.[39] Arendt's emphasis on the importance of discourse suggests that it is to postmodern and Critical approaches to IR that Arendt speaks most directly. Indeed, it is unsurprising that it is work in these areas that Lang and Owens appeal to most in their chapters. This is not to say we can assume Arendt's insights have been distilled into contemporary Critical Theory, meaning we need not delay ourselves with the way station of her work. There are important differences between Arendt and the sort of Critical Theory in IR exemplified by Andrew Linklater, as Owens in particular emphasizes.[40] Arendt's emphasis on speech in politics is nevertheless striking.

> [W]hatever men do or know or experience can make sense only to the extent that it can be spoken about. There may be truths beyond speech, and they may be of great relevance to man in the singular, that is, to man in so far as he is not a political being, whatever else he may be. Men in the plural, that is men in so far as they live and move and act in this world, can experience meaningfulness only because they can talk with and make sense to each other and to themselves.[41]

This reinforces Arendt's concern with the nonmaterial, ideational, world as much as with the material. In particular, her concept of politics, properly understood, relies very heavily upon a theorization of transitory, ephemeral, intersubjective, and institutionally fragile processes. These have to operate within a really existing world of industrial and postindustrial capitalism but this "social world," as Arendt refers to it, is at odds with the "political world."[42]

However, powerful though it may be, Arendt's critique of the notion of politics as ruling that dominates IR is not without problems. Her categories and concepts are not only individual but also somewhat cavalier. At a time of growing methodological care and precision among almost all IR theorists, this is a substantial weakness, even if we accept her rejection of the rigor necessary to the ruling approach of most political theory. Her emphasis on transitory, intersubjective, and highly contextualized phenomena requires a more hermeneutic and impressionistic approach. Even within these confines, we may well find her categories too vague and her concepts lacking adequate definition to contribute effectively. In particular, key categories such as "politics," "the social world," "work," "labor," and "action" are open to varying interpretations. As Hansen notes, "Few contemporary thinkers have been so difficult to pin down. . . . [W]hat is most important about Arendt is less the development of a specific theoretical stance and more the attempt to capture the 'temper' of political life."[43] Even when dealing with more specific and concrete examples, such as revolution and totalitarianism, Arendt is woolly and sometimes contradictory. Alternatively, she can be overly specific, such as her analysis of totalitarianism that is much more of an analysis of Nazism than it is of Stalinist communism.[44]

These are, of course, substantial and significant weaknesses in a social and political theorist, and they should not be overlooked. However, the immanent potential within Arendt's thought and the sheer originality and vitality of her approach, predicated upon the breathtaking claim of the failure of the overwhelming majority of Western political thought to be properly political, deserves consideration.

HANNAH ARENDT AND PLURALITY

At the core of Arendt's political thought is her account of and emphasis on the plurality of human beings. Plurality presents international relations with some of its greatest and most pressing challenges. For Arendt the plurality of humanity is its most fundamentally important feature. Indeed, Arendt argues it is humanity's only common feature: "Plurality is the condition of human action because we are all the same, that is, human, in such a way that nobody is ever the same as anyone else who ever lived, lives or will live."[45]

> Human plurality . . . has the twofold character of equality and distinction. If men were not equal, they could neither understand each other and those who came before them nor plan for the future and foresee

the needs of those who will come after them. If men were not distinct, they would need neither speech nor action to make themselves understood. Signs and sounds to communicate immediate, identical needs and wants would be enough.[46]

Arendt's plurality is nevertheless clearly distinct from crude nationalism and the idea of humanity divided into distinct and homogeneous nations that are mutually incomprehensible and incompatible. She regards such an approach as part of the homogenizing and antipolitical operation of the social world that dominates so much of contemporary life. Arendt argues that nationalism, particularly in its organic, ethno-nationalist forms, marks an important stage in the alienation of people from the world that she regards as so characteristic of the triumph of the social world. Nation becomes a substitute for family, preventing the operation of proper political relationships among equal but distinctive human beings because of the hierarchical nature of familial relationships and their rootedness in an essentially private world.[47]

Nationalism and the idealized nation-state play an enormous role in the study of international relations. Many state-centric theories of IR tend to assume that the state is the institutional manifestation of a largely homogeneous national community, or, to the extent that it is not, this is a source of weakness or potential trouble. For a theorist like Hedley Bull, for example, this nation-state ideal also establishes the principal manifestation of difference in international relations, subsuming what Arendt sees as a foundational element of the human condition to the homogenized and institutionalized "pluralism" of states as manifestations of nation. Arendt's pluralism clearly goes much deeper than this and is of an altogether more sophisticated kind.

A similar contrast could be drawn between the understanding of pluralism developed by Arendt, and that lying behind an approach such as Samuel Huntington's *Clash of Civilizations* in which he, too, homogenizes and amalgamates the distinctiveness and difference of individuals into crude facsimiles.[48] His postulation of an inherently conflictual relationship between civilizations would also be challenged by Arendt, who sees no basis for such certainty in the relationship between any individuals or political communities, given the inherent unpredictability in human political relationships.

Thus universal plurality does not preclude potential comprehensibility and understanding. This points to the way Arendt tries to distinguish between the distinctness of individuals and the "otherness" of objects, offering, by extension, a critique of the objectification of nation and civilization. Otherness, or *alteritas*, transcends every particular quality, whereas distinctness reflects variations on the common theme of humanity.[49] This distinctness, and the commensurate ability of human beings to distinguish themselves from one another, is rooted in speech and action through which people exercise their unique ability to take the initiative, to launch themselves into the political world.

Arendt's appeal to a universal feature of humanity arguably makes her a cosmopolitan, but that feature is plurality, rather than the more common ideas of universal human rights, universal human reason or a universal humanity as the basis for utilitarian calculation. Plurality is both predetermined and unpredictable. We have no choice about it because it is a fundamental feature of human existence, yet the forms such plurality takes and the way it manifests itself are not easily predicted. Therefore, Arendt does not possess a theory of social determinism, whether via culture or class.

This is not to say she dismisses these features of human life. Arendt places great emphasis upon the importance of class, nation, and community to understand the human condition in general and particular features of its politics, especially in the social world, but also in an ideally political one.[50] Plurality is not simply individualism. Individuals are rooted and conditioned creatures, and Arendt is a theorist of the bounded community. Intersubjectivity is not universal and yet it is not permanently constrained either. Arendt's account of history stresses that the idea of separate, national teleological histories and an objectivity of the fixed and final destinations they prescribe are a modern aberration.[51] However, the power of the idea of fixed and permanent boundaries is considerable, and thus has to be included in any account of politics. Plurality cannot be transcended, yet the forms it takes are constructed, flexible, and conditioned by human action and discourse. The homogenization and reification of human communities through notions such as nation-state and civilization in international relations tells us something about the way the world works but more important things about how it is that plurality, as Arendt understands it, has had its inherent transformative potential neutered by the political construct of the idealized nation-state and the homogeneous and static civilization.

This insight is reinforced by her emphasis on the fundamental sociability of human beings—a "lonely" human being ceases to be fully human. This connectedness, essential to the intersubjective nature of the world, means Arendt cannot be regarded as an individualist, marking her out from a liberal alternative to the theories of Huntington and deterministic nationalists. The sovereign individual is an impossibility for her.[52] Community and identity with the community are vital for individuals because they can only know themselves and act in the world in relation to others. However, these others are not universal because of the need for shared identity in order to recognize one another and to act as a basis for speech and discourse. History has importantly shaped and molded communities into distinctive identities that do not easily come together.[53] The boundaries of the past, reinforced by the modern approach to telling the story of history, are the product of human beings attempts to manufacture the world as a human artifice.[54]

Community is thus significant, and more than the sum of individuals, for practical reasons to do with the way the world is, and also for principled reasons to do with the nature of an ideal politics as community politics. The world is a human artifice, an artificial place, and this both limits and renders limitless the potential for human beings to act. It is limited by the legacy of the past and its importance to the present; it is limitless because, as an artifice, the world can be remade.

We can thus see how Arendt is distinguishable from a theorist such as Linklater who also has a strong concern for diversity. Linklater's international theory draws inspiration from the critical tradition associated most strongly with the Frankfurt School. His account of political community stresses the role that it has played in the construction of international relations as power politics, and that this is not immutable. He draws on a range of postpositivist thought to argue for the political nature of community, most especially those like the nation that have become so important to the conduct of international relations, and to stress that these forms of community and the associated forms of politics are not immutable. Indeed, under pressure from globalization, the failures of the nation-state ideal within a troubled Enlightenment project means that Linklater stresses transformation. The urgent need for human beings to address resulting political problems and forms requires us to think outside the states-systemic straitjacket. The sort of transformation of political community that he sees happening, though patchy and inconsistent, has the potential to produce a world that is more peaceful, where wealth is distributed more justly and where the diversity of different people and peoples is better protected. This contributes to the guiding normative goal of the critical theoretical project—the emancipation of individuals from the threats and circumstances that preclude them from living the sorts of lives that they would freely choose to lead, up to the point where their choices have consequences for the life choices of others. The negotiation of such a position, via the mechanism of discourse ethics as developed by Habermas, provides the central normative theoretical framework of Linklater's project, although it is developed in ways that move outside those suggested by Habermas.[55]

At heart, though, Linklater appeals to individualism—freedom and emancipation are judged in relation to individuals.[56] Hence his emphasis on citizenship as a means of securing individual rights and as a contribution to the goal of the universal communication community as a means of establishing a cosmopolitan ethic. Culture and community in this account are therefore overlays, which constitute the distinctiveness and difference of human beings, but rest on a fundamental unity of humanity, potentially actualized via communication. Arendt, on the other hand, cannot remove specific community from her individuals, even in her ideal political world, because of the essential nature of community to freedom. Her attack on the sovereignty of individuals means freedom cannot be about individuals because individuals removed from the community are not free but suffer the terror of loneliness. They are in pursuit of an unachievable control over the world, a control that cannot exist when one is compelled to live in the company of others. Arendt shares Linklater's goal of freedom, but this is freedom into politics and politics can only take place within a community.[57]

Thus specific identity plays a prominent role in Arendt's account of politics. In her account of an ideal politics, community is flexible, fragile, and impermanent, reflecting her dissatisfaction with institutions as the focus of the politics of ruling and marking a further distinction from Linklater, who offers an institutionally richly populated ideal world. However, her analysis of the nonideal world requires a more restrictive coming to terms with the sorts of political communities at work in the world.

This latter approach can be seen in her account of totalitarianism and the ways in which it can be resisted. She dismisses appeals to a common humanity as being the means to resist totalitarianism, instead insisting on the vital importance of maintaining individuals' rootedness in their communities. "Those who reject such identifications may feel wonderfully superior to the world . . . but their superiority . . . is the superiority of a more or less well-equipped cloud-cuckoo-land."[58] It is this sense of identity and place that resists the loneliness of life in a totalitarian society which attempts to destroy the bonds of community and identity.

> What makes loneliness so unbearable is the loss of one's own self which can be realized in solitude, but confirmed in its identity only by the trusting and trustworthy company of my equals. In this situation, man

loses trust in himself as the partner of his thoughts and that elementary confidence in the world which is necessary to make experience at all.[59]

The diversity of communities is therefore an essential part of a proper political environment and these communities possess durability across time.[60] This renders their existence valuable and at least partially independent of the individuals inhabiting them at any one time. Community cannot thus be regarded as an overlay on top of an essential humanity; it must be recognized as part of the essential plurality of each individual.

Here, too, there are differences with postmodern ethics, which attempt to explore ethical potential within an ontologically minimalist environment. Cochran's Rorty-inspired pragmatism, for example, emphasizes the opportunities of holding as few ontological assumptions as weakly as possible and recognizing the contingency of all ethical conclusions.[61] Arendt would dismiss the possibility of such a sparsely populated ontological world, as it requires us to adopt positions equally as abstract as those that underpin the Archimedean point of a more conventional liberal individualist ethic. Instead, there is a need to recognize the power of community and the rootedness and sedimentation of identity in ethics. These are not permanent and unchanging, and thus ontologically uninteresting. Indeed, the opposite is true, but they have great power in locating individuals, sparing them from loneliness and are thus of considerable ethical value. A normative vision of international relations is better served by a coming to terms with the ontological sedimentation of notions like community and the need for the plurality of individuals to be placed within a more richly populated ontological universe.

Limits, including ontological limits, are important to Arendt's understanding of plurality and the role it plays. While she is ambiguous about the types and extents of limitations of an ideal political community,[62] she is more specific when discussing the desirable and necessary limitations in the social world in which we live.

> [H]uman dignity needs a new guarantee which can be found only in a new political principle, in a new law on earth, whose validity this time must comprehend the whole of humanity while its power must remain strictly limited, rooted in and controlled by newly defined territorial entities.[63]

Arendt argues that, like dignity, human freedom usually exists within the territorially specific place of the republic.[64] The constituting of a republic is the basic act of political freedom and is the goal of revolution. A community, argues Arendt, needs a republic in order to achieve the security necessary for it to be free, for individuals to act in a proper political way, within the context of trust, openness, promising and forgiveness that are characteristic of a proper political situation. The plurality of individuals and the pluralism of communities are thus imperfectly, but nevertheless importantly, reflected in the states of the world as providing at least the potential for politics and, therefore, freedom.[65]

In addition to territorial limits being important to freedom, Arendt emphasized their role in restraining totalitarianism. Their acceptance robs such movements of their dynamic of permanent revolution and the overthrow of the means by which communities could resist loneliness and thus provide the basis for action against the movement.[66]

The example of territorial borders as establishing a limit on community membership relates to both Arendt's admiration of the polis as a political ideal and to the effect of the social world that limits and reduces plurality by emphasizing labor and work over political action. This move is vital to the rise of nationalism and to class—the diversity we usually think of as being important in international relations.

The pluralism of national identity is particularly important to Arendt's account of politics in the social world. However, and again important to the contributors to this book, Arendt's thought, although sometimes too quick to conflate identity with membership of a nation embodied in the sovereign state, can discuss community in more far-reaching terms. Arendt hints at this in her celebrated and controversial account of the Eichmann trial. She argues again for the fundamental importance of plurality and its links to community, but links it in this case to the nation of Jews, in many ways the paradigmatic case of a deterritorialized, transborder community. She describes the genocide against the Jews as, "an attack upon human diversity as such, that is, upon a characteristic of the 'human status' without which the very words 'mankind' or 'humanity' would be devoid of meaning."[67] It is for this reason if anything, she argues, that Eichmann deserved to die.

Arendt's approach emphasizes the vitality of community and its centrality to establishing the identity and value of the individual members. Community membership and participation is the way in which humans discover their individuality understood as being their unique "take" on the shared pattern of humanity. It is thus community that has the potential to address challenges to values. This offers, as

Schaap argues in his contribution, an Arendtian approach to issues of post-conflict justice that adds to the debate over the claims of punishment and reconciliation in situations that have become more and more important in debates in international relations.

Detaching these concerns from nations presumed to coincide with states restores a critical and transformative concern with the need to protect and respect community as the way to protect and respect individuality on the basis of real people living real lives.[68] Arendt appears uncertain about the possibilities for eradicating conflict among these different communities. But this does not reflect despair about human nature or a neorealist style structural account of the international system. Instead, Arendt's uncertainty reflects her uncertainty about all political action. She distrusts schemes aiming at defined end points and assuming or predicting certain outcomes and actions resulting from previous actions.

This lack of clear progressive intent contributes to the accusations of Arendt as a conservative.[69] Her account can seem to display faith in tradition and the time-honored practices of the community as providing a guide to current and future action. This would be to underestimate Arendt's critical power and vision. She clearly disagrees with community-based justifications of systematic exclusion, such as school segregation in the southern United States. However, she believes that the exact forms of resistance to such exclusion and the political and social forms that will enable them to be overcome cannot be predetermined or imposed. Thus removing the basis of exclusion is as far as external political authorities should go. It is up to the community to reach an acceptable operational solution via dialogue.[70]

> If she could sound like Oakeshott for a moment when arguing that the idea of starting with a blueprint and putting it into practice was preposterous, it was not because tradition determines or is always the major conditioning factor, and therefore political invention, let alone revolution is impossible, but precisely because the invention of new political institutions is needed. If they are to last, however, they must arise from a plurality of political actors debating among themselves publicly until they can reach a consensus to act together, and to continue acting together.[71]

While we once again witness potential overlap with Critical Theory, Arendt is much less certain than those who have applied Critical Theory to IR about the conditions necessary for this dialogue. At an international level, Arendt's vision remains a dialogue among communities, rather than a dialogue of individuals, because of the need to defend the freedom of the community.[72] She wants to maintain the idea and the ideal of the bounded community, so it is not individuals who need guaranteed access to a global communication community, it is the communities which they form and which represent more than the sum of the individual parts.

Communities are like repositories of the sprit not just of the living but of their antecedents and descendants because of the way they endure in time. As such the need to be true to the community places substantial limits upon political possibilities. Arendt gets round the problem of a stifling conservatism, on the basis of honoring the memory of the dead by her account of the nature of politics. In relations between communities it is fair criticism to accuse her of reifying community, but at the same time it is unfair because of the nature of the politics she discusses and the distance between it and the predominantly social and unpolitical, even antipolitical, world in which most of these issues arise.

We thus struggle to liberate Arendt's account of identity and its importance to the world from the stifling confines of the social world of modernity and globalizing capitalism. The expansion of work and labor to dominate our lives and to remove room for truly political action has also shut us off from the political aspects of our communities and the transformative potential within them, rooted in natality and plurality.

HANNAH ARENDT, INSTITUTIONS, JUSTICE AND LAW

With her emphasis on agency and the space in between, one might assume that Arendt would have little or nothing to say about institutions and the law. In fact, however, Arendt's theoretical framework has much to tell us about institutional structures, as long as we are ready to suspend our assumptions about what constitutes an institution. Moreover, although she was critical of international law and governance in some ways, this volume should not be seen as an attempt to mine Arendt's work for references to the international. Rather, the point is to demonstrate how some of Arendt's theoretical insights might be deployed to better understand emerging aspects of international and global affairs.

IR has traditionally held institutions in high regard. Indeed, if we see the discipline as older than the post–World War II era, institutions and international law are the foundations of IR as a scholarly discipline. Reacting against the nineteenth century's great power run international system, international lawyers, humanitarians, and political leaders in the Anglo-American world convened a series of conferences at the turn of the twentieth century that led to the creation of modern international law. This emphasis on international law and organizations dissipated during the World War II and Cold War periods, but was revived in Anglo-American IR in the late 1970s with the emergence of neoliberalism. With the end of the Cold War, and the turn to the United Nations in response to the Iraqi attack on Kuwait in 1990, many believed that international organizations and international law would finally achieve its hoped for promise.

International law and organizations, however, do not seem to conform well to Arendt's notions of politics. International law and organizations have focused primarily on ruling, or ways in which law and organizations can better guide the conduct of states and peoples. Both international law and international organizations have constructed an elite group of scholars, bureaucrats, and administrators who have constructed complex rules and norms. As suggested earlier, international law and organizations also tend to reify the state as the only legitimate agent in the international system, leaving the agency of individuals bound and constrained by the actions of their states.

However, Arendt does value law and collective action (an alternative way of thinking about organizations). Her work, while always wary of the solidification of structures of ruling and governance, does leave space for the role of institutions and law in the practice of politics. That space can be found in two concepts deployed by Arendt: constitutions and collective action.

As Jeremy Waldron suggests, "[For Arendt], politics needs housing, and that building such housing can be equated with the framing of a constitution."[73] Constitutions are, for Arendt, central to the creation of viable political communities. Constitutions are not simply pieces of paper, but are the living embodiment of the norms and values of a political community. Their goal is to create the polis, the space in which true political engagement can take place. Arendt emphasized that constitutions should be seen as actions, as verbs almost; a community continues to constitute itself through not only the initial drafting of its laws but through the continuous interpretation and contestation that makes up democratic politics.[74]

Does the UN Charter exist as a constitution in the way Arendt believes? While it does not function in exactly the same way as a domestic constitution, the interpretative debates that it generates suggest it plays the role that Arendt describes. Consider, for example, debates over the use of military force as they conform to the Charter's stipulations. While states tend to focus on the provisions that allow military actions in self-defense, armies of lawyers and activists have sought to limit that right in the spirit of the UN's more general presumption against the use of force to resolve disputes. This interpretative battle will continue, suggesting the importance of the constitutional structure of the Charter. Although realists will claim that the Charter and international law more generally do not matter in decisions to use force, the fact that political leaders feel the need to engage in these debates and that the most powerful state, the United States, has sought to justify its actions in the context of law, suggests that the international "constitution" does play an effective role.

More recent developments in international law, in particular the creation of an International Criminal Court, can also be better understood through an Arendtian analytic frame. Her reporting of the trail of Adolph Eichmann in 1961 gave Arendt a chance to develop her thinking on the function of courts, law, and trials. Because an Israeli court tried him, Arendt used the opportunity to dismantle Israeli assumptions about guilt and innocence in the context of both the Holocaust and their conflict with the Palestinians. She argued that David Ben Gurion, the Israeli Prime Minister at the time and a key figure in the creation of Israel, sought to use the trial as an opportunity to teach Israeli citizens the importance of Zionism. But, in so doing, Arendt suggests that many of the most important questions about institutional and individual guilt were elided.

Arendt concludes her exploration of the Eichmann trial by asking why the Israelis did not see the need for an international criminal court to try Eichmann. Although she disputes legal arguments that support an international criminal trial, Arendt concluded that the nature of the crime committed, genocide, implies that a tribunal representing all of humanity had to try Eichmann: "Insofar as the victims were Jews, it was right and proper that a Jewish court should sit in judgment; but insofar as the crime was a crime against humanity, it needed an international tribunal to do it justice."[75]

Yet, for Arendt, such a tribunal does not represent a political community, but humanity more generally defined, as opposed to her suggestions in *On Revolution* that the U.S. Supreme Court plays a role parallel to the US Senate of providing a moderating influence on excessive democratic politics.[76] Arendt's understanding of law and its relation to the political process at the national or international level leaves something to be desired. Without exploring in more depth the function of a court, an exploration that scholars are beginning to undertake in IR, Arendt leaves us without a clear sense of how the law relates to political action.

A second place in which institutions matter for Arendt is in her discussion of collective action. She explores in a number of different contexts the question of power, arguing that it only exists in moments of collective action. For those who see such moments as only sponta-neous eruptions that do not outlast the action itself, Arendt would point toward the revolutionary councils that arose in the wake of the French and American revolutions. Councils, which she compares to political parties, are institutions that undertake political action qua group—institutions that embody political agency.[77]

Arendt also argues that even those who react against institutions of governance, that is, those engaged in civil disobedience, must in fact be acting as a collective. Only by understanding themselves as part of an institution, broadly defined, can those engaged in civil disobedi-ence have any power.[78] Her comparison of power and violence—the former only possible by collectives, the latter a failure of collectives to act politically—also suggests that Arendt saw a potential for collective political agency.

But, as suggested above, Arendt would most certainly not see the actions of modern nation-states as embodied in foreign policies as the type of collective, institutional action that she advocated. Rather, states tend to reify structures of governance into rigid hierarchies with elites who remove individuals from potential sites of political action. Foreign policy is not the model of collective political action that an Arenditan political theory would support. Rather, nascent forms of political action that are arising through transnational nongovernmental networks may be a potential site of institutional development that Arendt would advocate. These ideas are explored further in Lang's discussion of anti-globalization protests in Seattle.

CONCLUSIONS: HANNAH ARENDT AND INTERNATIONAL AFFAIRS

An Arendtian theory of IR does not exist and neither does this book aim to create one. She wrote very little on the subject and many of her comments are decidedly mundane, focusing on issues of current affairs rather than theoretical concerns. By considering her critique of mainstream political theory and focusing on the issues of plurality and institutions, we have tried to show the potential benefits of an engage-ment with Arendt, benefits explored more thoroughly and not always in the same way by the contributors.

These benefits are not straightforwardly acquired. In order to utilize Arendt's work in IR we need to show some imagination in both our utilization of her categories and in searching for elements of a genuine politics. Within a great corpus of writing, like Arendt's, there are snippets and insights into international politics and some of the contributors have pursued these in order to explore contemporary issues, such as human rights. Others, echoing Hansen's claim cited earlier that Arendt is about the "temper" of political life, have taken inspiration from Arendtian ideas and categories, and attempted to stretch them in order to look at political forms and institutions that were unknown to her. Others, hopefully inspired in part by the work here, will respond in still different ways to the challenge and stimulation that we have found in Arendt's writings.

We would suggest that this introduction has pointed toward some specific areas of potential further work and engagement. For thin constructivists, like Wendt, she throws down a powerful normative gauntlet, urging them to recognize more fully the need to abandon "scientific realism" because of its failure to appreciate the ephemeral intersubjectivity of politics and the neutering effect it has on constructivism's normative agenda. More directly, she offers a challenge to postmodernism and to Habermasian critical theory in IR via her distinctive methodological approach and in her handling of two key issues: plurality, and the meaning of the political in a largely social world. Even those returning to the classical Realist tradition of Morgenthau, seeking to restore the subtlety and sophistication that the textbook treatment of Realism has so often ignored in recent years, would find Arendt of interest. Not only were they friends, but also their shared imbibing of the German theoretical tradition and reaction against the Nazism that sent them both into exile hint at some intriguing lines of enquiry, especially in their response to the problems of power in a political world, a concept that both wrestled with in different ways.

More generally, Arendt's powerful critique of an excessively narrow concept of politics as "ruling," and her warning against an overly deterministic structuralism that forgets that the world is an "artifice"— a human construction that holds within itself the potential for dramatic and surprising change—are salutary reminders of the dangers of theoretical closure. Arendt's potential significance for international relations theory is not just, therefore, as another political theorist whose specific categories, concepts, and conclusions can be grafted in to the established research agendas of the subject. She causes us to ask some serious questions about the focus, methods, and purposes of theorizing international relations.

NOTES

1. See Brian Schmidt, "Together Again: International Relations and Political Theory," *The British Journal of Politics and International Relations*, 4, no. 1 (2002). Chris Brown, "International Political Theory: A British Social Science?" *The British Journal of Politics and International Relations*, 2, no. 1 (2000). Throughout, IR will refer to the discipline of International Relations.

2. The work of theorists such as Richard Ashley, R.B.J. Walker, James Der Derian, Michael Shapiro, and Molly Cochran comes to mind in this context.

3. Andrew Linklater, Neta Crawford, and Richard Shapcott might be identified here.

4. Robert Cox and Stephen Gill serve as useful examples here.

5. Michael Doyle, John Macmillan, and David Held are emblematic.

6. Chris Brown makes this case strongly, with writers such as Terry Nardin, Michael Walzer, Mervyn Frost, Charles Beitz, Thomas Pogge, and Martha Nussbaum figuring in these debates.

7. The influence of Schmitt is significant in the work on Realism by A.J.H. Murray, e.g.; see also work by Roger Spegele and Jef Huysmans.

8. Martin Wight, "Why is There No International Theory?" in Herbert Butterfield and Martin Wight (eds.), *Diplomatic Investigations: Essays in the Theory of International Politics* (London: George, Allen and Unwin, 1966).

9. A search of Social Science citation indexes and databases suggests that only a tiny number of pieces using Arendt have appeared in international relations in recent years. The most notable include Anthony F. Lang, Jr. *Agency and Ethics: The Politics of Military Intervention* (Albany: SUNY Press, 2002); John Williams, "Toleration, Territorial Borders and the English School," *Review of International Studies*, 28, no. 4 (2002); Douglas Klusmeyer and Astri Suhrke, "Comprehending 'Evil': Challenges for Law and Policy," *Ethics & International Affairs*, 16, no. 1 (2002); Paul Saurette, " 'I Mistrust all Systematizers and Avoid Them': Nietzsche, Arendt and the Crises of the Will to Order in International Relations Theory," *Millennium: Journal of International Studies*, 25, no. 1 (1996).

10. Those seeking a comprehensive introduction should consult Dana Villa (ed.), *The Cambridge Companion to Hannah Arendt* (Cambridge: Cambridge University Press, 2000).

11. Quoted in Margaret Canovan, "Hannah Arendt as a Conservative Thinker," in Larry May and Jerome Kohn (eds.), *Hannah Arendt: Twenty Years Later* (Cambridge, MA: MIT Press, 1997), 11.

12. Bhikhu Parekh, a sympathetic critic, notes, "Arendt is not a careful and systematic thinker. She never clearly sets out her categories, defines her terms, articulates her views and defends her position. She

has also an irritating habit of making unsupported and sweeping assertions, substituting innuendos [sic] for arguments, setting herself up on a high pedestal and lecturing to her readers in a high minded tone." *Hannah Arendt and the Search for a New Political Philosophy* (London: Macmillan, 1981), xi. Those who like their criticism lacking such sympathy might consult Walter Laqueur, "The Arendt Cult: Hannah Arendt as Political Commentator," *Journal of Contemporary History*, 33, no. 4 (1998).

13. Parekh, *Hannah Arendt and the Search for a New Political Philosophy*, x, 3–19.

14. Parekh, *Hannah Arendt and the Search for a New Political Philosophy*, 14–19. See also Hannah Arendt, *The Human Condition*. (Chicago: University of Chicago Press, 1958), 28–50.

15. Her account of this process is a central element of Saurette's use of Arendt in IR. Saurette, "I Distrust all Systematisers," 6–10.

16. Arendt, *Human Condition*, 274.

17. Ibid., 257–294.

18. Ibid., 285–286.

19. Ibid., 261.

20. E.g., Emanuel Adler, "Seizing the Middle Ground: Constructivism in World Politics," *European Journal of International Relations*, 3, no. 3 (1997): 323.

21. Arendt, *Human Condition*, 42–44.

22. For a discussion of the active life, or *vita activa* as Arendt refers to it, see Arendt, *Human Condition*, 7–21. For a detailed analysis of action and its inescapably political nature, see 175–247.

23. Arendt argues that work—the production of useful human artifacts which endure beyond the requirements of immediate use and which can include works of art that give us pleasure is unpolitical because it is rooted in the material world of "things," rather than an intersubjective world of action. Labor—meeting the immediate requirements of existence, such as food and shelter—is antipolitical because it reduces humans to the condition of animals and stifles and stymies the pursuit of higher things. That so much of the world's population is compelled to devote so much time to labor Arendt sees as being, in part, the result of political factors and structures that condemn them to such a life, a life where politics is impossible. Arendt, *Human Condition*, 212. For a similar assertion in relation to contemporary U.K. politics, see Bernard Crick, "Hannah Arendt and the Burden of Our Times," *Political Quarterly*, 68, no. 1 (1997): 81.

24. Arendt, *Human Condition*, 3.

25. Ibid., 181–182.

26. Ibid., 9.

27. Ibid., 188.

28. Although see Anthony F. Lang, Jr. *Agency and Ethics* for an attempt to construct a theory of state agency that draws on Arendt.

This account, however, concludes that only by recognizing that a reified state agent does not exist; rather, state agency needs to be made more fluid and open ended—in the same way that Arendt's understanding of individual agency opens up personal identity in moments of action.

29. Hedley Bull, *The Anarchical Society: A Study of Order in World Politics* (London: Macmillan, 1977), 8–9.
30. See Bull, *Anarchical Society*, 46–51 on Hobbes and Martin Wight, *International Theory: The Three Traditions,* Brian Porter and Gabriele Wight (eds.) (Leicester: University of Leicester Press, 1991).
31. Bull, *Anarchical Society*, 101–232.
32. Robert Jackson argues that studying international politics should focus on the activities of elite power-holders, possibly as few as 1,000 in number. Robert H. Jackson, *The Global Covenant: Human Conduct in a World of State* (Oxford: Oxford University Press, 2000), 134. For a similar approach drawn more directly from a rational choice background, see Bruce Bueno de Mesquita, *Principles of International Politics: People's Power, Preferences and Perceptions* (Washington, DC: Congressional Quarterly Press, 2000) in which the author constructs a theory of world politics around the idea of individual leaders protecting their positions of power.
33. The most important account of this in IR focuses upon realism, but the points stand in relation to a wider body of work. John Vasquez, *The Power of Power Politics*, 2nd edn (Cambridge: Cambridge University Press, 1998).
34. Arendt, *Human Condition*, 247.
35. Ibid., 9.
36. John Gerard Ruggie, "What Makes the World Hang Together: Neo-Utilitarianism and the Social Constructivist Challenge," *International Organization*, 52, no. 4 (1998).
37. Arendt can thus be seen to contrast with a postmodern normative theory, like Cochran's, that stresses the virtues of ontological minimalism. Molly Cochran, *Normative Theory in International Relations: A Pragmatic Critique* (Cambridge: Cambridge University Press, 1999).
38. Alexander Wendt, *Social Theory of International Relations* (Cambridge: Cambridge University Press, 1999).
39. See Ruggie's typology, e.g., "What Makes the World Hang Together," 881–882.
40. E.g., Andrew Linklater, *Beyond Realism and Marxism: Critical Theory and International Relations* (Basingstoke: Macmillan, 1990); "The Questions of the Next Stage in International Relations Theory: A Critical Theoretical Approach," *Millennium: Journal of International Studies*, 21, no. 1 (1992); "The Achievements of Critical Theory," in Steve Smith, Ken Booth, and Marysia Zalewski (eds.), *International Theory: Positivism and Beyond* (Cambridge: Cambridge University Press, 1996); *The Transformation of Political Community: Ethical*

Foundations of the Post-Westphalian Era (Cambridge: Polity Press, 1998).

41. Arendt, *Human Condition*, 4.
42. For an account of the rise of the social world and its significance in contemporary politics, see Arendt, *Human Condition*, 22–78, 248–326.
43. Philip Hansen, *Hannah Arendt: Politics, History and Citizenship* (Cambridge: Polity Press, 1993), 4.
44. Canovan, *The Political Thought of Hannah Arendt*, 16–17.
45. Arendt, *Human Condition*, 8.
46. Ibid., 175–176.
47. Ibid., 256.
48. Samuel Huntington, *The Clash of Civilizations and the Remaking of World Order* (New York: Simon and Schuster, 1996). For a more recent, and even more pertinent example of the type of work Arendt's plurality exposes, see Huntington, "The Hispanic Challenge," *Foreign Policy*, 141 (March/April 2004): 30–45, in which he argues that the influx of Hispanics into the United States is challenging its core, Western identity.
49. Arendt, *Human Condition*, 176.
50. For a general account of this, see Arendt, *Human Condition*, 248–326.
51. Hannah Arendt, "The Concept of History," in Hannah Arendt, *Between Past and Future* (New York: Penguin, 1977). For a general discussion of her account of "History and the Decline of Politics," see Hansen, *Hannah Arendt: Politics, History and Citizenship*, 14–49.
52. Arendt, *Human Condition*, 234.
55. For an account of Arendt's view of the nature of political communities, see Parekh, *Hannah Arendt and the Search for New Political Philosophy*, 131–172.
54. Hansen, *Hannah Arendt: Politics, History and Citizenship*, 65–66.
55. This is a very crude summary of an intellectual project that has engaged Linklater for 20 years or more. The major texts are listed above, with *The Transformation of Political Community* standing as the current pinnacle of a major body of work.
56. Beate Jahn, "One Step Forward, Two Steps Back: Critical Theory as the Latest Manifestation of Liberal Individualism," *Millennium: Journal of International Studies*, 27, no. 3 (1998).
57. Hansen, *Hannah Arendt: Politics, History and Citizenship*, 54–57.
58. Hannah Arendt, "On Humanity in Dark Times: Thoughts about Lessing," in Hannah Arendt (ed.), *Men in Dark Times* (London: Jonathan Cape, 1970), 4.
59. Hannah Arendt, *Origins of Totalitarianism, New Edition with Added Prefaces* (New York: Harcourt Brace Jovanovich, 1973), 477.
60. Arendt, *Human Condition*, 55.
61. Cochran, *Normative Theory*.

62. E.g., Arendt, *Human Condition*, 190–191.

63. Arendt, *Origins of Totalitarianism*, ix.

64. Hannah Arendt, *On Revolution* (London: Faber and Faber, 1963), 279.

65. Arendt develops these ideas in the final section of *On Revolution*.

66. Arendt, *Origins of Totalitarianism*, 389, 391.

67. Hannah Arendt, *Eichmann in Jerusalem: A Report on the Banality of Evil* (London: Faber and Faber, 1963), 247.

68. E.g., John Williams, "The Ethics of Borders and the Borders of Ethics: International Society and Rights and Duties of Special Beneficence," *Global Society*, 13, no. 4 (1999).

69. For a general discussion of this issue see Canovan, "Hannah Arendt as a Conservative Thinker," in May and Kohn (eds.), *Hannah Arendt: Twenty Years Later*, 11–32.

70. Bohman, "The Moral Costs of Political Pluralism," 53–80.

71. Crick, "Hannah Arendt and the Burden of Our Times," 82–83.

72. Hansen, *Hannah Arendt: Politics, History and Citizenship*, 57.

73. Jeremy Waldron, "Arendt's Constitutional Politics," in Villa (ed.), *The Cambridge Companion to Hannah Arendt*, 203.

74. Hannah Arendt, *On Revolution* (New York: Penguin Books, 1963), 141–178.

75. Arendt, *Eichmann in Jerusalem*, 269.

76. Arendt, *On Revolution*, 231.

77. See Lang, in this volume for an exploration of the relationship between councils and governance at the international level.

78. Hannah Arendt (ed.), "Civil Disobedience," in *Crises of the Republic* (San Diego: Harcourt, Brace, Jovanovich, 1972), 49–102.

CHAPTER 2

HANNAH ARENDT: A BIOGRAPHICAL AND POLITICAL INTRODUCTION

Patricia Owens

> That even in the darkest of times we have the right to expect some illumination, and that such illumination may well come less from theories and concepts than from the uncertain, flickering, and often weak light some men and women, in their lives and works, will kindle under almost all circumstances and shed over the time span that was given them on earth—this conviction is the inarticulate background against which these profiles were drawn.
>
> Arendt, *Men in Dark Times*

There is much, perhaps too much, information about the life of Hannah Arendt (1906–1975), the German–American political theorist, teacher, and writer. As probably the only woman in the traditional philosophy "canon," a leading member of the fashionable postwar New York circle of intellectuals and Jewish exiles, author of the hugely controversial report *Eichmann in Jerusalem*, and former lover of the philosopher and disgraced Nazi-sympathizer, Martin Heidegger (itself the subject of a less than stellar novel[1]), Arendt's life does appear to fascinate. She was also not averse to relating the lives of those she admired. Her published work includes a biography of Rahel Varnhagen, Jewish salon hostess of the early 1800s in Berlin, and a collection of essays written over 15 years on figures such as Rosa Luxemburg, Isak Dinesen, Walter Benjamin, and Bertolt Brecht. "The definitive biography, English style," she believed, "is among the most admirable genres of historiography. Lengthy, thoroughly documented, heavily annotated, and generously splashed with quotations."[2] From the volumes of correspondence she left with her husband, Heinrich Blucher, Heidegger, friends and mentors, as well as excerpts from her mother's *Unser Kind*, the diary she kept of Hannah's early years, information on Arendt's life, loves, and hates is readily available and has itself been the subject of a definitive account.[3] Commentaries on the private life and personal opinions of Hannah Arendt have spilled almost as much ink as her professional, public work.

As if to add fuel to the fire, Walter Laqueur wrote a caustic essay in 1998 entitled "The Arendt Cult: Hannah Arendt as Political Commentator."[4] The ever-growing number of monographs and dissertations written on Arendt and the amount of Internet sites dedicated to things "Arendtian" were noted. He comments that there has been a Hannah Arendt stamp and streets named after her in Germany. There are Arendt prizes. Lufthansa even flies a Hannah Arendt airplane. With a critical commentary from Laqueur, we are ushered through personal letters addressed to Arendt's husband and friends on her views on all manner of events and often scathing opinions of various persons.

From her call for the establishment of a Jewish army to her alleged "paranoid" fear in the 1950s of World War III, Laqueur seems troubled by not only Arendt's fame but also, in his words, the seeming "discrepancy between Arendt as a political philosopher and the poverty of her judgment" about current events.[5] The accuracy and relevance of Arendt's personal tastes and judgments on the events of her day—ad hoc opinions on the news or preference to travel in Europe over Israel—is, of course, a matter of opinion. That she distrusted President John F. Kennedy and thought the social services in the United States were in ill repair are strangely included among Laqueur's long list of "misjudgements." It is significant, we are told, that Arendt never learned to drive. She thus had to rely on "imagination . . . to compensate for a lack of knowledge about reality."[6]

This claim is startling. On the one hand, Arendt's early critique of the Vietnam War was perceptive, as was her prediction of the effect of public relations machinery on the political.[7] Moreover, Arendt's work has been influential in political movements perhaps even Laqueur would not deem "misjudged." In 1960s Berkeley, as Martin Jay recounts, "the Free Speech Movement was deeply influenced by her work during its formative period."[8] On the other hand, Arendt's writing has also been notoriously difficult to categorize or marshal in direct support of a particular public policy. But this was in line with her thinking; she was not concerned with offering a programmatic theory that might be "applied."[9] Famously when asked by Hans Morgenthau whether her position was "liberal" or "conservative" she responded as though the question itself were truly silly; she "couldn't care less" because "the real questions of this century will [not] get any kind of illumination by this sort of thing."

What Laqueur's essay reveals is less something important about Arendt's life and work or even her everyday opinions, what we might consider the discrepancy between political philosophy as a trade and the ability to advise presidents. Rather it inadvertently brings into focus something of the bad taste that remains after surveying much of the literature on Arendt's life and its presumed relationship to her political theory. As Arendt herself suggested, "The connection of an artist's life with his work has always raised embarrassing problems, and our eagerness to see recorded, displayed, and discussed in public what once were strictly private affairs and nobody's business is probably less legitimate than our curiosity is ready to admit."[10] The impropriety is the suspicion that Hannah Arendt's status as a first-class thinker arises in part from her dramatic biography and celebrity status as a woman "philosopher."[11]

To be sure, Arendt has hardly been a feminist heroine. Unlike her identity as a Jew, she believed being a woman, politically speaking, was irrelevant. In a speech on accepting the Lessing Prize of the Free City of Hamburg in 1959 she acknowledged that for "many years . . . the only adequate reply to the question, Who are you? to be: A Jew. That answer alone took into account the reality of persecution."[12] That same year, in contrast, she became the first woman to become a full professor at Princeton University, but "she threatened to refuse the invitation because the university stressed the 'first woman' aspect in their report to the *New York Times*."[13] In 1933 she suggested that, "whenever the women's movement crosses a political front it does so only as a unified, undifferentiated whole, which never succeeds in articulating concrete goals (other than humanitarian ones)."[14] With such blanket statements, her dismissal of feminist scholarship,[15] and strict separation of public from private, it is not difficult to see why feminists have criticized Arendt. Famously, the poet Adrienne Rich believed that she personified "the tragedy of a female mind nourished on male ideologies."[16]

But Laqueur points to the association between Arendt's eminence and her gender more crudely by suggesting that the "Arendt Cult," especially in the academy, may above-all be explained by "the attraction she has exuded for women."[17] Some feminists have indeed taken a different route to Adrienne Rich. The seeming "contingency" and "instability" that forms the basis of Arendtian democratic citizenship, at least in feminist "post-modern" readings, denies the existence of preexisting (read homogenizing) identities of gender, class, or race in political action.[18] However, Laqueur more subtly invokes Arendt's gender, describing her as "a highly emotional person" who was not "willing to shut up."[19] Putting aside this problematic reading of Arendt's influence, if there were even some truth to the suspicion that we read Arendt because she was a famous woman it would be a tragedy.[20] Though she is as yet an underutilized resource in the discipline of IR, Arendt's writings are more enduring than any voyeuristic fad or gendered fascination with her affairs. The legacy of her writing and the times in which she wrote offers much illumination. It is this conviction that inspires this short biographical sketch.

Born October 14, 1906, in Hanover, Germany, Hannah was the only child of secular, middle-class Jews, Paul and Martha (Cohn) Arendt. Her father died when she was seven thus her mother principally raised her after moving to Königsberg. At the age of 16, by which time she had "read almost everything," Arendt began studying classics and Christian theology at the University of Berlin. Within two years she was at Marburg University, arriving in 1924, where she embarked on her infamous relationship with Martin Heidegger, the young dynamic faculty member who was already gaining a dedicated following for his original brand of *Existenzphilosophie*.

This controversial relationship has been the subject of a voluminous and often-bitter literature since it was revealed as not a brief fling between professor and student but an intense 4-year affair.[21] The major source of the controversy, of course, was Heidegger's open sympathy for the rising Nazi regime and Arendt's alleged exoneration of him years later. During his inaugural address when elected Rector of the University of Freiburg in 1933, Heidegger hailed Nazi storm troopers in the audience and welcomed the restoration of Germany's spiritual health under Hitler. He proceeded to ban Jewish professors from the University, including his former teacher Edmund Husserl, which Arendt believed might have directly contributed to the aged philosopher's death. The portrayal of Arendt as an emotional dupe to Heidegger has been rightly condemned as "tabloid scholarship."[22] What is galling to many, however, is that she resumed a friendship with Heidegger after the war and, in 1971, wrote a defense of her former mentor on the occasion of his eightieth birthday.

In 1925, Arendt moved to the University of Heidelberg to study with Karl Jaspers, under whose supervision she wrote her doctoral thesis on the concept of love in the thought of St. Augustine.[23] She remained close friends with Karl Jaspers and his wife Gertrude; their long correspondence reveals not only the influence of Jaspers' existentialism on her thinking but also her continued reverence and effort to distribute his philosophy internationally.[24] The monograph produced from the Ph.D. has been little used by interpreters of Arendt's thought. However, central to her account of political action in *The Human Condition* was her development of Augustine's idea of "natality," that inherent to human beings is the notion of new beginnings. Natality, which Arendt likens to a "miracle," becomes the ontological root of her unique understanding of political "action."[25] Repeatedly, and in contrast to the traditional philosophical obsession with death, we find in Arendt's account the new beginning and promise of political freedom inherent in *birth*—humans as "a being whose essence is beginning."[26]

As Arendt completed her Ph.D. in 1929, she met her first husband Günther Stern whom she would marry a year later. Throughout this period Arendt became increasingly involved in Jewish and Zionist politics, as it became ever more evident that the tide of anti-Semitism was about to overwhelm life in Germany. But she also continued to write, producing her biography of Varnhagen.[27] Arendt's scathing critique of what she saw as Rahel's incessant introspection and apolitical life, her "worldlessness," presaged critical themes Arendt would develop in later work. Political action, she believed, was a specifically *worldly* and world-making activity, requiring the existence of others. Excessive introspection and concern for the private self—also typical of modern liberal democracies in Arendt's view—produced individuals too assimilated to the pursuit of wealth and consumption to be responsive to radical republican citizenship. This theme emerges in *On Revolution*, where Arendt, like Thomas Jefferson, believed that "the danger was that all power had been given to the people in their private capacity and that there was no space established for them in their capacity of being citizens."[28]

"In telling Rahel's story," suggests Seyla Benhabib, "Hannah Arendt was bearing testimony to a political and spiritual transformation that she herself was undergoing. There is thus a mirror effect in the narrative. The one narrated about becomes the mirror in which the narrator also portrays herself."[29] Arendt was dealing with the inescapable fact of Jewish identity increasingly imposed by the German regime. She started work for the German Zionist Organization in 1933 to make public growing crimes against the Jews. The Gestapo arrested her when she was found gathering material to research anti-Semitic propaganda in the Prussian State Library. Released eight days later by a sympathetic policeman, a "charming fellow" she thought, Arendt fled the country without documents, leaving Germany for Paris. Hannah Arendt had become a stateless Jew. But she was perhaps more actively political during this period than at any other time during her life. Work undertaken by Arendt in this period included directing Youth Aliyah, an organization that rescued Jewish children and physically and psychologically prepared them for the exodus to Palestine.

In 1936, Arendt met Heinrich Blücher, a German political refugee (a communist and former member of Rosa Luxemburg's Spartacus League), who would become her second husband. She divorced Stern in 1939 and married Blücher on January 16, 1940. They were physically separated and interned a few months later. But after escaping detention as an "enemy alien" in Gurs, both Arendt and Blücher were reunited, fleeing to the United States in 1941. Before leaving Paris, Arendt developed a friendship with Walter Benjamin, who entrusted her with the manuscripts of his writing. After his suicide, she would eventually deliver these papers to members of the Frankfurt School who had already decamped to New York. However, Arendt suspected Theodor Adorno of suppressing and refusing to publish those parts of Benjamin's work deemed "not sufficiently dialectical."[30] Perhaps with this danger of intellectual gatekeeping in mind Arendt later edited and wrote an introduction for a collection of Benjamin's work, *Illuminations*, published in 1968.[31]

From 1941, Arendt continued as a writer and editor in New York through the remainder of the war and the early postwar years. She contributed to magazines such as *Jewish Frontier* and the German language newspaper *Aufbau* (Reconstruction), arguing for the creation of a Jewish army and the establishment of a dual-state in Palestine for both Arabs and Jews. She was an editor at Schocken Books between 1946 and 1951 and directed research for the Commission on European Jewish Cultural Reconstruction, the effort to locate and redistribute Jewish cultural artifacts after the Holocaust.

Arendt began work on what would be her first major book in 1944, a masterful study of the link between twentieth century Fascism and nineteenth century nationalism, imperialism, and racism. *The Origins of Totalitarianism*, which was published in 1951, the year she became a U.S. citizen, made Arendt an intellectual celebrity. Though the work was later criticized for drawing too simplistic a parallel between Nazi Germany and the U.S.S.R.—thus making Arendt falsely appear as an apologist for American Cold War hysteria—the book would endure as a major treatise on this "novel" form of government. Arendt's own

"Jewish experience" and her reading of how European Jewry seemed ill prepared for the rise of anti-Semitism fundamentally oriented her later thinking about politics.[32] Making use of material unpublished at the time, Margaret Canovan has persuasively argued that almost all of Arendt's subsequent work finds its origins in this concern with understanding totalitarian ideology and government.[33] "Understanding . . ." she wrote, "is an unending activity by which, in constant change and variation, we come to terms with and reconcile ourselves to reality, that is, try to be at home in the world."[34]

The account of "statelessness" in *Origins*, for example, can be read through her own personal experience and her observation that human rights or rather the "right to have rights"[35] could only be understood *politically*. "The concept of human rights," she argued, "can again be meaningful only if they are redefined as a right to the human condition itself, which depends upon belonging to some human community, the right never to be dependent upon some inborn human dignity which de facto, aside from its guarantee by fellow-men . . . does not exist."[36] The only thing that could guarantee human rights and a "home in the world," Arendt was suggesting, were contingent political circumstances, a definite and historically grounded public sphere.

It was to these themes—the possibility of constituting meaningful political spheres in the modern age—that Arendt would dedicate the majority of her later writing in the United States. In 1958 her major work of political philosophy, *The Human Condition*, was published (as was *Rahel Varnhagen*.) *The Human Condition* was a somewhat misleading title given its contents and her intentions. Arendt's U.S. English-language publishers suggested *The Human Condition* because the more accurate European title, *The Vita Activa*, was presumed to be less catchy. Arendt's actual preference was *Amor Mundi*, love of the world. The purpose was to contrast her approach with the disdain that she thought philosophers had traditionally treated the public world of human affairs. The European title was also more accurate because *The Human Condition* did not deal with the other side of the *vita activa*, the *vita contemplativa*. Eventually, of course, Elisabeth Young-Bruehl would choose *For Love of the World* as the subtitle to Arendt's biography.

It was in *The Human Condition* that Arendt explicated her "unusual" reading of the activities of labor, work, and action. "The distinction between labor and work which I propose is unusual," she wrote. However, "The phenomenal evidence in its favor is too striking to be ignored."[37] Arendt's account provided a kind phenomenological differentiation between three fundamentals. Typical of Arendt this is not "phenomenological" in the traditional philosophical sense, that objects/phenomena can be analyzed or reduced to their essence and experienced through consciousness without the aid of prior theoretical commitments. Arendt's teacher Heidegger, for example, was concerned with describing "things in themselves" without theoretical preconceptions. Arendt *politicized* Heidegger's perspective and viewed the activities of labor, work, and action as conditioning, but not wholly determining, the human world. The human condition is not human nature; it "never conditions us absolutely."[38] When we act in the public world we "constantly create" our own "self-made conditions."[39]

In 1961 Arendt published *Between Past and Future*, a series of essays on history, philosophy, and politics, and travelled to Jerusalem to cover for *The New Yorker* magazine the trial of Adolf Eichmann, the Nazi bureaucrat charged with directing the transportation of Jews to the death camps. The essays from *The New Yorker* were expanded and published in 1963 as *Eichmann in Jerusalem, A Report on the Banality of Evil*. This would undoubtedly become her most controversial book and, according to Arendt, was "the object of an organized campaign."[40] As a result of the storm she lost many friends and her ties with the organized Jewish community in the United States were effectively severed. For she appeared to complicate the absolute innocence of the Jews, pointing out that the Jewish Councils—the leaders not the people themselves—often cooperated with the Nazis by providing lists of names.

The primary source of indignation for Zionist and wider Jewish circles, however, was Arendt's depiction of Eichmann as not radically evil but "banal"; "one cannot extract any diabolical or demonic profundity from Eichmann."[41] He was an "ordinary," unremarkable functionary, she believed, not the sadistic monster many seemed to want him to be. "He *merely*, to put the matter colloquially, *never realized what he was doing* . . . That such remoteness from reality and such thoughtlessness can wreak more havoc than all the evil instincts taken together which, perhaps, are inherent to man—that was, in fact, the lesson one could learn in Jerusalem."[42] The question of "thinking" and the importance of political "judgement," attributes Eichmann obviously lacked, were themes Arendt later pursued in the posthumously published *The Life of the Mind*.[43] Her ultimate goal was that we might more effectively "think what we are doing"[44] in the modern age of totalitarianism and political terror.

In 1963, and thus somewhat overshadowed by the Eichmann affair, *On Revolution* appeared in print. Arendt's historical narrative interlaced the difference between two classic revolutions, in eighteenth century France and America, a painstaking contrast between "freedom" and "necessity." Revolution, for Arendt, was "That new experience which revealed man's capacity for novelty."[45] That is, to not only break the shackle of the past but also the hindrance of a predictable future. The American Revolution, in particular, was presented as a philosophical and political break with traditional values.[46] The Declaration of Independence seemed a quintessentially modern (some have interpreted Arendt to mean "post"-modern[47]) attempt to derive a new concept of power—the transcendence of the Christian political tradition of founding authoritative principles in the other-worldly.[48] Though Arendt's "ideal-type"[49] account of this period was undoubtedly a partial story, largely ignoring the violent exclusion of women, Native Americans and slaves, it is in re-reading the U.S. founding that she perceived at least a partial answer to a problem that she had identified in her earlier work concerning politics in modernity: How in the absence of authoritative principles to impose could public freedom both thrive *and* be rendered more stable?[50]

Though she was often snotty about the mass cultural conformity of the United States, Hannah Arendt was an American citizen and she took seriously that fact. Responding to the Cold War McCarthy investigations into "un-American activity" she wrote,

> America, this republic, the democracy in which we live, is a living thing that cannot be contemplated and categorized, like the image of a thing which I can make; it cannot be fabricated . . . If you try to "make America more American" or a model of democracy according to a preconceived idea, you can only destroy it. Your methods, finally, are the justified methods of the police, and only of the police.[51]

Arendt praised the "American" civic-republican culture reactivated by civil rights and anti-Vietnam War demonstrators. Pointing specifically to the American-English origin of the term—yielding "only with great difficulty to translation"[52]—she claimed "that civil disobedients are nothing but the latest form of voluntary association, and thus they are quite in tune with the oldest traditions of the country."[53]

In a series of political essays from the 1960s, *Crises of the Republic*, which were published in 1972, Arendt criticized the Vietnam War offering a long response to the publication of the *Pentagon Papers*. There is no real indication, however, that she planned to address global politics in any greater depth. The chapters in this volume suggest Arendt's writing can be marshaled to support a variety of critical theoretical positions, however in many ways her political theory complements classical realism. Indeed, this may partly explain her relative silence on matters traditionally associated with IR. Her sharp differentiation between politics and violence, for example, seems on the surface to be quite in keeping with the classic realist understanding of the difference between the domestic and the international realm. "Violence," she argued, "is traditionally the *ultima ratio* in relationships between nations and the most disgraceful of domestic actions."[54] Where peace and order is supposed to reign inside the state potential war is the norm in the system of states.[55]

Arendt was a friend of both classical realists Raymond Aron and Hans Morgenthau and she praised another realist hero, Machiavelli, for his appreciation of the "splendor of the public realm."[56] However, her reading of Machiavelli's glorification of violence challenges straightforward IR realist appropriations of his texts. Machiavelli's "realist" contention that politics and violence were two sides of the same coin actually expressed, Arendt argued, *not* his "so-called realistic insight into human nature" but nothing more than "his futile hope that he could find some quality in certain men to match the qualities we associate with the divine."[57] In other words, the "Machiavellian" justification of violence derived from his effort to found a new body politic in the absence of traditional morality, the very same question Arendt was grappling with. It came from Machiavelli's search for a "new absolute" (which ultimately became violence) upon which to ground politics.

Like Machiavelli, however, Arendt viewed political action as an end itself and even considered international "politics" favorably compared to political life in liberal bureaucratic states. "Only foreign affairs," she wrote, "because the relationships between nations still harbour hostilities and sympathies which cannot be reduced to economic factors, seem to be left as the purely political domain."[58] For IR scholars slightly bored with the ins and outs of "domestic" politics in the West this insight may resonate. But the discipline itself does not escape criticism. "And even here the prevailing tendency is to consider international power problems and rivalries as ultimately springing from economic factors and interests."[59] Typically, Arendt does not expand on what she means.

Readings of a "realist" Arendt are overly simplistic, of course. In *Origins of Totalitarianism*, she offers an account of imperialism that is largely Marxist in orientation. Though the subject of imperial rule—past and present—is virtually ignored in the discipline of IR it is clear that she understood the relationship between domestic political developments and global expansion. As discussed elsewhere in this volume, she understood that the bourgeoisie's political emancipation was directly linked to imperialism. "The bourgeoisie," Arendt wrote, "turned to politics . . . for it did not want to give up the capitalist system whose inherent law is constant economic growth, it had to impose this law . . . and proclaim expansion to be an ultimate political goal of foreign policy."[60]

Because *Origins* and *The Human Condition* established Arendt as one of the major thinkers of her generation they afforded her a sequence of illustrious fellowships and professorships. She taught at Princeton, the University of California, Berkeley (1955), University of Chicago (1963–67), Columbia, Wesleyan, and finally the New School for Social Research (1967–75). She "never really wanted to be a professor," however, and managed to preserve six months of every year for writing. Heinrich Blücher, her husband, died in 1970. That year Arendt delivered her lectures on Kant at the New School, which were also published posthumously and contain the beginnings of her thoughts on political "judgement."[61] In 1975, she received the Sonning Prize for Contributions to European Civilization, which no American and no woman had previously received. She had truly come to figure "in contemporary humanist discourse as [one of its] charismatic legitmators."[62]

Hannah Arendt was delivering the Gifford Lectures based on chapters of *The Life of the Mind* in Aberdeen, Scotland when she suffered her first heart attack. Later, she collapsed and died of a second attack in her New York City apartment on December 4, 1975. Found in her typewriter was a blank page with the single heading of "Judging," the third and final part of *The Life of the Mind*, which was never completed. Two volumes, *Thinking* and *Willing*, were edited and published in 1978 by her great friend, pen-pal and literary executor, Mary McCarthy. She is buried next to Heinrich in the cemetery of Bard College, New York.

NOTES

1. C. Clement, *Martin and Hannah* (Amherst, NY: Prometheus Books, 2001).
2. Arendt, "Rosa Luxemburg: 1871–1919," in H. Arendt, *Men in Dark Times* (New York: Harcourt, Brace & World, 1968), 33.
3. E. Young-Bruehl, *Hannah Arendt: For the Love of the World* (New Haven, CT: Yale University Press, 1982).
4. W. Laqueur, "The Arendt Cult: Hannah Arendt as Political Commentator," *Journal of Contemporary History*, 33, no. 4 (1998): 483–496.

5. Laqueur, "The Arendt Cult," 485.

6. Ibid., 491.

7. "The goal was now the image itself, as is manifest in the very language of the problem-solvers, with their 'scenarios' and 'audiences,' borrowed from the theater." H. Arendt, "Lying in Politics," *Crises of the Republic* (New York: Harcourt Brace Jovanovich, 1969), 17–18.

8. M. Jay, "The Political Existentialism of Hannah Arendt," in M. Jay, *Permanent Exiles: Essays on the Intellectual Migration from Germany to America* (New York: Columbia University Press, 1985), 238.

9. H. Arendt, "On Hannah Arendt," in M. Hill (ed.), *Hannah Arendt: The Recovery of the Public World* (New York: St. Martin's Press, 1979), 309.

10. Arendt, "Isak Dinesen: 1885–1963," *Men in Dark Times*, 98.

11. Arendt is often regarded as a philosopher but she refused to accept the label due to the disdain with which she thought they had traditionally treated the public world of human affairs since Plato. Bidding philosophy her "final farewell" in a television interview in 1964 she said her profession was "political theory." Young-Bruehl, *Hannah Arendt*, 327.

12. Arendt, "On Humanity in Dark Times: Thoughts about Lessing," in *Men in Dark Times*, 17.

13. Young-Bruehl, *Hannah Arendt*, 272.

14. H. Arendt, "On the Emancipation of Women," in H. Arendt, *Essays in Understanding: 1930–1954* (New York: Harcourt Brace and Company, 1994), 68.

15. To a friend who had been disappointed on meeting Simone de Beauvoir, author of the ground-breaking feminist text *The Second Sex*, Arendt said, "The trouble with you, William, is that you don't realize that she's not very bright. Instead of arguing with her you should flirt with her." Arendt in C. Brightman (ed.), *Between Friends: The Correspondence of Hannah Arendt and Mary McCarthy, 1949–1975* (London: Secker and Warburg, 1995), xiii.

16. Quoted in M. G. Dietz, "Feminist Receptions of Hannah Arendt," in B. Honig (ed.), *Feminist Interpretations of Hannah Arendt* (Pennsylvania, PA: Pennsylvania State University Press, 1995), 24.

17. Laqueur, "The Arendt Cult," 484.

18. B. Honig, "Arendt's Account of Action and Authority," in B. Harig, *Political Theory and the Displacement of Politics* (Ithaca, NY: Cornell University Press, 1993), 76–125.

19. Laqueur, "The Arendt Cult," 491, 489.

20. This is not to suggest that insights cannot be drawn from making a link between Arendt's public and private life. Julia Kristeva has most recently taken a gendered psychoanalytical route to interweave Arendt's personal life and work with the theme of "female genius," J. Kristeva, *Hannah Arendt*, trans. Ross Guberman (New York: Columbia University Press, 2001). Also see H. F. Pitkin, *The Attack of the Blob: Hannah Arendt's Concept of the Social* (Chicago: University of

Chicago Press, 1998). For a compelling critique of this psychoanalytical trend, see S. Benhabib, "The Personal is not the Political," *Boston Review* (October/November, 1999).

21. E. Ettinger *Hannah Arendt/Martin Heidegger* (New Haven, CT: Yale University Press, 1995).
22. L. Disch quoted in W. H. Honan, "Book on Philosopher's Life Stirs Scholarly Debate Over Her Legacy," *The New York Times* (November 5, 1995). Also see R. Wolin, *Heidegger's Children: Hannah Arendt, Karl Löwith, Hans Jonas, and Herbert Marcuse* (Princeton, NJ: Princeton University Press, 2001). For a more sober assessment of the intellectual relationship between Arendt and Heidegger, see D. Villa, *Arendt and Heidegger: The Fate of the Political* (Princeton, NJ: Princeton University Press, 1996).
23. H. Arendt, *Love and Saint Augustine*, ed. Joanna Vecchiarelli Scott and Judith Chelius Stark (Chicago, IL: University of Chicago Press, 1995).
24. L. Kohler and H. Saner (eds.), *Hannah Arendt-Karl Jaspers Correspondence, 1926–1969*, trans. R. and R. Kimber (New York: Harcourt Brace Jovanovich, 1992).
25. H. Arendt, *The Human Condition* (Chicago, IL: University of Chicago Press, 1958), 247.
26. Arendt, "Understanding and Politics," *Essays in Understanding*, 321. Arendt's concept of natality influenced Jean Bethke Elshtain's critique of the relationship between war and masculine discourse in international theory. See J. B. Elshtain, "War and Political Discourse: From Machiavelli to Arendt," *Meditations on Modern Political Thought: Masculine/Feminine Themes from Luther to Arendt* (London: Praeger, 1986), 103–113.
27. The book was not published until 1958. See H. Arendt, *Rahel Varnhagen: The Life of a Jewess*, ed. Liliane Weissberg, trans. R. and C. Winston (Baltimore, MD: Johns Hopkins University Press, 1997).
28. H. Arendt, *On Revolution* (New York: Viking Press [1963] 1970), 253.
29. S. Benhabib, "The Pariah and Her Shadow: On the Invisibility of Women in Hannah Arendt's Political Philosophy," *Political Theory*, 23, no. 1 (1995): 11.
30. Young-Bruehl, *Hannah Arendt*, 167.
31. See W. Benjamin, *Illuminations*, ed. and intro. Hannah Arendt, trans. Harry Kohn (London: Jonathan Cape, 1970).
32. Richard Bernstein has also situated Arendt's writing and her own "Jewish-ness" historically on a range of issues. R. Bernstein, *Hannah Arendt and the Jewish Question* (Cambridge, MA: MIT Press, 1996).
33. M. Canovan, *Hannah Arendt: A Reinterpretation of Her Political Thought* (Cambridge: Cambridge University Press, 1992).
34. Arendt, "Understanding and Politics," 307–308.
35. H. Arendt, *Origins of Totalitarianism* (New York: Meridian Books [1951] 1958), 296.
36. H. Arendt, *The Burden of Our Time* (London: Secker and Warburg, 1951), 439. This was the first English edition of *Origins*.

37. Arendt, *The Human Condition*, 94.
38. Ibid., 11.
39. Ibid., 9.
40. H. Arendt, *Eichmann in Jerusalem: A Report on the Banality of Evil* (New York: Viking Press, 1964), 282.
41. Ibid., 288.
42. Ibid., 287–288.
43. H. Arendt, *The Life of the Mind* (New York: Harcourt Brace Jovanovich, 1978).
44. Arendt, *Human Condition*, 5.
45. Arendt, *On Revolution*, 34.
46. Arendt overstates the radical break with traditional values. "America," as Williams writes, "was born and bred of the British Empire . . . [which] produced another culture [in the United States] based on the proposition that expansion was the key to freedom, prosperity, and social peace." W. A. Williams, *Empire as a Way of Life* (Oxford: Oxford University Press, 1980), 17, 23.
47. See F. M. Dolan, *Allegories of America: Narratives, Metaphysics, Politics* (Ithaca, NY: Cornell Univerity Press, 1994) and Michael Hardt and Antonio Negri, *Empire* (Cambridge, MA: Harvard University Press, 2001).
48. Arendt, *On Revolution*, 186.
49. Arendt likened her reading here to a Weberian ideal-type. Arendt, "On Hannah Arendt," 328–333.
50. This was in contrast to the Reign of Terror that arose after the French Revolution. See Arendt, *On Revolution*, 217–285.
51. Arendt, "The Ex-Communists," in *Essays in Understanding*, 400.
52. Arendt, "Civil Disobedience," in *Crises of the Republic*, 98.
53. Ibid., 96.
54. H. Arendt, "Tradition and the Modern Age," *Between Past and Future: Six Exercises in Political Thought* (New York: Meridian, 1963), 22.
55. Arendt's division between politics and violence appears in much of her work but is most explicitly stated in "On Violence," in *Crises of the Republic*, 151. See other essays in this volume.
56. Arendt, *On Revolution*, 29.
57. Ibid., 39.
58. Arendt, "What is Freedom?" *Between Past and Future*, 155.
59. Ibid., 155.
60. Arendt, *The Origins of Totalitarianism*, 126.
61. H. Arendt, *Lectures on Kant's Political Philosophy*, ed. and with an interpretive essay by Ronald Beiner (Chicago, IL: University of Chicago Press, 1982).
62. M. Jay, "Name-Dropping or Dropping Name? Modes of Legitimation in the Humanities," in M. Jay, *Force Fields: Between Intellectual History and Cultural Critique* (New York: Routledge, 1993), 168.

CHAPTER 3

HANNAH ARENDT, VIOLENCE, AND THE INESCAPABLE FACT OF HUMANITY

Patricia Owens

On the other hand, humanity, which for the eighteenth century, in Kantian terminology, was no more than a regulative idea, has today become an inescapable fact. This new situation, in which "humanity" has in effect assumed the role formerly ascribed to nature or history, would mean in this context that the right to have rights, or the right of every individual to belong to humanity, should be guaranteed by humanity itself. It is by no means clear that this is possible . . . For it is quite conceivable, and even within the realm of practical political possibilities, that one fine day a highly organized and mechanized humanity will conclude quite democratically—namely by majority decision—that for humanity as a whole it would be better to liquidate certain parts thereof.

Arendt, *The Origins of Totalitarianism*

By the end of 1990s, academic and policy-making circles widely projected the new Western mode of combat for the globalized twenty-first century to be wars principally justified as "humanitarian." Yet immediately after the 9/11 attacks, for good or ill, this presumed legacy of the so-called human rights decade seemed perilous. Could anyone imagine another Somalia, Bosnia, or Kosovo where the integrity of the Western homeland itself was under threat? "Humanitarian intervention" gave way to "War on Terror" as the rationale for force. But the legacy of the "new military humanism"[1] of

the 1990s has not dissipated as rapidly as many thought. The United
States sought vigorously to defend both the decisions to go to war
and the conduct of its armed forces in Afghanistan (2001–2002) and
Iraq (2003–2004) in a language profoundly shaped by liberal
discourses of "humanitarianism".[2] Several have pointed to the Kosovo
operation—an exemplar of "humanitarian war"[3]—as proof of
the United States' benign post-9/11 intentions and/or to reinforce
the global separation between civilized and uncivilized use of force by
states.[4]

We should accordingly not be surprised in the future if Western
military campaigns continue to be legitimated in "humanitarian" as
well as "anti-terrorist" terms. Robert Keohane has suggested, for
example, that "the distinction between self-defense and humanitarian
intervention may become less clear. Future military action in failed
states, or attempts to bolster states that are in danger of failing, may
be more likely to be described *both* as self-defense and as humanitarian
or *public-spirited*."[5] The United States, in particular, has largely
succeeded in the ideological task of mapping the normative discourse
of "humanitarianism" onto its national security (also deemed "civili-
sational") interests and identity.

But what does it mean for violence to be described (and defended)
as "public-spirited?" Jürgen Habermas, perhaps the most influential
"public sphere" theorist in political and international theory, justified
NATO's violent confrontation over Kosovo in an effort to extend the
virtues of "post-national" citizenship rights to those suffering human
rights abuses abroad.[6] Where liberal international theory has
traditionally been presented as the most closely associated with the
ideology and practice of such military practices,[7] Habermas's "deliberative" theory has recently provided much theoretical sustenance.
Of course, explanations for "humanitarian war" are varied, and
include beliefs in the emergence of new international society "norms"
about organized violence, U.S. militarism, and hegemony. Yet also
important for some has been the so-called normative interest in
transforming "exclusionary political community," the notion of
global public spheres at the vanguard of "progressive" transnational
change.[8]

NATO's 1999 actions over Kosovo, for example, were deemed
avant-garde not least because they were underpinned, in part, by
appeals to the conscience of a flowering transnational public sphere.
With Kosovo, Habermas remarked (once again) that, "The transformation of the law of nations into a law of world citizens is thus on the
agenda."[9] On this reading NATO was supporting the extension of

cosmopolitan commitments to defend human rights across borders. Habermas again:

> the critique of [NATO's] ideology finds no basis for its suspicions . . . [U]niversalistic justifications do not always mask the particularity of concealed interests. What a "hermeneutics of suspicion" claims to find behind the attack on Yugoslavia is rather meagre.[10]

This chapter draws on a neglected source in international theory, the political writings of Hannah Arendt, to suggest that Habermas and his followers are mistaken.[11] We ought to be suspicious of efforts to legitimate wars in the name of "humanity." Arendt's discussion of the relationship between organized violence and the political and coercive nature of appeals to "reason" provide a critical vantage point on the assumptions of "humanitarian" interventionists, past and probably future. Often criticisms of Western wartime invocations of "humanity"— and the "professional idealists"[12] that support such claims—follow the earlier warnings of Carl Schmitt. In his well-known words,

> When a state fights its political enemy in the name of humanity, it is not a war for the sake of humanity, but a war wherein a particular state seeks to usurp a universal concept against its military opponent. At the expense of its opponent, it tries to identify itself with humanity in the same way as one can misuse peace, justice, progress and civilization in order to claim these as one's own and to deny the same to the enemy . . . humanity is an especially useful ideological instrument of imperialist expansion.[13]

Though sympathetic to this critique, the intention of the chapter is to move to the foreground Arendt's insights. However, a preliminary comment on Arendt and Habermas is in order.

The stakes of the Arendt–Habermas dispute are potentially great for how we conceive politics and democracy in modernity. Their differences however, have received a great deal of attention in political theory and do not require much further elaboration here.[14] Arendt exercised a profound influence on Habermas's understanding of emancipation through human interaction and he has read his own theoretical categories, not always accurately, onto Arendt's.[15] Not only did she directly influence Habermas, but also contemporary deliberative thinkers have seized on her "narrative model of action" and account of political judgment to read "with Arendt against Arendt." For example, an integral part of Seyla Benhabib's project of reviving a feminist Critical Theory has been a "Habermasian" reading of Arendt.[16]

However, because Arendt's work revives an *agonistic* conception of public space, less dependent on assumptions of rationality and more open to the performative dimensions of public life, a straightforward deliberative reading of her is problematic. "Agonistic" in this context refers to the incessant competition and contestability of political concepts and identities manifest in "the passionate drive to show one's self" in public.[17] Agonistic (often also "post-modern") thinkers are attracted to Arendt because, as Dana Villa describes, the "meaning and authoritativeness . . . of political institutions in her writing are determined by the clash of conflicting interpretations. So conceived, the public sphere is, above all, an institutionally articulated site of perpetual debate and contestation."[18] In Bonnie Honig's formulation, the arena "of Arendt's performative action is the radically contingent public realm where anything might happen, where the consequences of action are boundless, unpredictable, unintended, and often unknown to the actors themselves."[19] This is quite removed from the world of deliberative rationality; a useful step away from a Habermasian conception of language as merely a function of making cognitive statements about truth or identity toward investigating the force contained in the *performative* act of articulation.

The differences between Arendt and Habermas, however, go beyond the deliberative/agonistic dichotomy common to so much of political theory. For this debate, though important in the arcane of this literature, may obscure what is a far more significant conceptual and practical problem of how we consider the relationship between publics and violence.[20] In *The Structural Transformation of the Public Sphere*, Habermas famously offered an account of the bourgeois "public sphere's" rise, transformation, and decline as a historical-sociological prelude to his theory of communicative action.[21] Following Kant, Habermas observed the emergence of a critically reasoning public in eighteenth-century European cities as the conduit of "deliberative rationality." That is, unrestricted, "undistorted" conversation could be the means to political legitimation. Clearly this model of a debating and coffee drinking public depended upon a distinctive configuration of liberal social and economic interests and could not, even according to Habermas, feasibly (or desirably) be transposed to late-modern society. However, the *ideal* given form at that time—that in informal institutional settings authority could be legitimized by the public use of intersubjective reason—shapes the deliberative model of public space. A public realm grounded by a common commitment to the force of the better argument, to deliberative rationality, and faith in publicity was heralded as *the* mode of coming to terms with, if not settling, political disputes.[22]

This "public sphere" observed by Habermas was primarily a "category of bourgeois society"; its primary function was to bring into being the bourgeoisie's consciousness of itself *as* a "society." Importantly, however, neither imperialism nor nationalism were explicitly linked to public sphere structure in Habermas's initial account. In particular, the relationship between the imperial international system and the political awakening of the bourgeoisie is rather dramatically under-emphasized. In *The Origins of Totalitarianism*, in contrast, Hannah Arendt explicitly suggests that the bourgeoisie's political emancipation was *directly* linked to imperialism; indeed it was the "first stage" of the bourgeoisie's political rule. "The bourgeoisie," she wrote, "turned to politics . . . for it did not want to give up the capitalist system whose inherent law is constant economic growth, it had to impose this law . . . and proclaim expansion to be an ultimate political goal of foreign policy."[23]

Provoked by Arendt's observation so conspicuously absent in Habermas's account, the goal of this chapter is to investigate how recent deliberative theories of emerging *global* and *transnational* publics similarly overlook more contemporary relations of global power and subordination—manifest in recent "humanitarian wars"— that are constituted in and through the invocation of "publics." Deliberative theorists of "humanitarian war," following Habermas, locate violence outside of the political (as barbaric and irrational). Arendt, in contrast, positions violence as constitutively outside; the historical and political context of each (violence and the public) is mutually related and codependent. One does not have to agree with Arendt's own sharp distinctions between public and private, or even between politics and violence, to recognize that how she formulated those distinctions is important and offers a critical perspective on so-called humanitarian war. The concepts that Arendt explicitly points to, which Habermas and his followers largely rationalize away or ignore when considering the "structural transformation" of global publics, are precisely those useful for understanding the potential and actual violence of powerful states marshalling the "inescapable fact of humanity."

PUBLICS AND VIOLENCE, REASON AND FORCE

Since Habermas's deliberative theory has to date been the received reading of the "public sphere" in international theory it is important to show how the categories established by him have been appropriated. Although bourgeois and singular in origin, this recent literature on the "public" has begun to recognize the existence of a plurality of spheres and issue areas. According to Mike Hill and Warren Montag, "there is also a sphere of all spheres. The public sphere thus conceived is the totality formed by the communicative interaction of all groups, even nominally dominant and subaltern."[24] Indeed, responding to the numerous criticisms of *The Structural Transformation*, Habermas revised his influential notion of a single authoritative bourgeois public realm conceiving a globalized "postnational" world of numerous debating publics less encumbered by the constraints of material inequality and nationalism.[25] For if the conflict between national identity and the ideal universalism of an "egalitarian legal community" is integral to both the concept and historical emergence of the nation-state, deliberative democrats could now celebrate newfangled forms of communication and human rights discourses that appear to destabilize particularistic identities.[26]

The context for any contribution from deliberative public sphere theory to our understanding of "humanitarian" justifications for war has, of course, been "globalization" and new "cosmopolitan" discourses of human rights.[27] With the emergence of new supra-territorial constituencies, extensive multilateralism, and transformations in the organization of "legitimate" violence at the end of the Cold War we seemed to be witnessing a radical reordering of the global political and economic architecture. John Guidry et al., following Habermas, accordingly suggest that an emerging "transnational public sphere offers a place where forms of organization and tactics for collective action can be transmitted across the globe. . . . More generally, the spread of human rights ideologies and movements exemplifies the power and consequences of this public sphere's global reach."[28] The dissonance between the notion of state sovereignty and existing power arrangements under globalization seemed to demand a revision of our notions of rights and governance, conceptions of the "public," and justifications for the use of force.

The conflict between order and justice, between state sovereignty and human rights, would thus seem to be the tension—the normative cutting edge—that animates much of the global public and "humanitarian intervention" literatures. James Bohman and Matthias Lutz-Bachmann suggest, for example, "If there is any room for coercion in international law, it is in the enforcement of human rights precisely against states that use their sovereignty to abuse human rights for particular political, religious, or nationalist goals."[29] Though there is already more room for violence in international law than these authors would allow,[30] it is worth interrogating the space opened for violence by these deliberative invocations of human rights ideologies. It is also worthwhile because the globalization literature, in which work on global or international publics is usually situated, has itself tended to be overly economist and "cultural" in emphasis, ignoring the centrality of military force in the "globalizing" process.

The literature on the potentialities for global or international publics remains embryonic. However, recent efforts to provide a more comprehensive international public sphere theory along deliberative lines have emerged.[31] Because Habermas's "communication-based" model of interaction, according to John Dryzek, can operate with the "fluid boundaries" indicative of the global arena, deliberative theory is the most "appropriate for we can now look for democracy in the character of political interaction that generates public opinion."[32] Following Habermas's distinction between "instrumental" and "communicative" rationality, Mark Lynch conceives the structure of global politics as comprising both traditional forms of "strategic interaction" (instrumental action resembling the market) and a public sphere of "communicative action" (resembling the forum) based on deliberation, dialogue, and persuasion.[33] The international public sphere, a feature of social structure with both material and normative dimensions, is where state action is "justified, interpreted, and contested" ideally in accordance with "the demands of rational argumentation."[34] Nicholas J. Wheeler has built upon similar arguments to justify the "norm" of "humanitarian intervention" within the international "society of states."[35]

Deliberative theorists claim they do not necessarily seek to discover behavior that is devoid of power and interest but to reveal the conditions where "public justification oriented to shared norms, goals or identity"[36] pushed behavior toward a different course of action. For example, according to Wheeler an important reason for Argentina's support for NATO during U.N. debates about the legitimacy of the Kosovo campaign was "its growing commitment to democratic values at home [which] was being reflected in a commitment to defend human rights internationally."[37] On this reading, states can be held accountable for their actions by revealing the potential (not assumed) gap between "humanitarian" discourse and political action. Dialogue, deliberation, and persuasion in public spheres are conceived as much a structural feature of international politics as its presumed opposite, domination, imposition, and the use of force.[38]

This opposition between "reason" and "force" as articulated in deliberative theory requires further examination because its consequences, especially when extended to the international sphere, are wide and problematic. Mike Hill and Warren Montag are (almost)

right to suggest that "Absolutely central to the notion of the public
sphere in all its versions is the opposition between reason and force."
In their words, "the public sphere can remain the site of rational communication and deliberation as long as it is the site of communication
alone and not action, as long as its participants are content to let
reason decide . . . and never resort to the use of force or even the
threat of force."[39] The authors are almost right because Arendt, as
discussed later, would replace "reason" with "power" as the opposite
of violence. Moreover, the presumed antagonism between "speech
and action" is certainly wrongheaded, speech itself being a kind of
"communicative" (Habermas) or "performative" (Arendt) action.[40]
Indeed, strictly speaking, force and violence are not the same. "*Force*,"
in Arendt's words, "which we often use in daily speech as a synonym
for violence . . . should be reserved in terminological language, for
the 'forces of nature' or the 'forces of circumstances' . . . to indicate
the energy released by physical or social movements."[41]

Nonetheless, mirroring this traditional opposition in deliberative
theory between force and the councils of reason, theories of international or global publics are dependent upon a structural and ideological
separation of the world. "Some international structures," Lynch
argues, "more resemble the market, with its strategic bargaining
behaviour, while others more resemble the forum, with communicative action and persuasion."[42] Citing Habermas, Wheeler similarly
makes the distinction "between power that is based on relations of
domination and force, and power that is legitimate because it is
predicated on shared norms."[43] (He does this without considering
whether the "norms" themselves may actually be domination and
force.) This argument is also common in constructivist writing in
international theory. If states cannot come up with sufficient or "plausible" legitimating reasons for their behavior they will necessarily be
constrained.[44] Liberal discourse is apparently especially prone to the
shaming or "accountability politics" crucial to deliberative accounts.[45]

International "public" space is accordingly presented as discursive
in a rational-communicative form usually epitomized by the "peaceful" or "humane" liberal regimes. Mary Kaldor's recent work on
changing patterns of "legitimate" violence epitomizes the implicit
opposition between the civilized, liberal West and a world of (at best)
continuing noncooperation or "barbarism" (at worst).[46] The most
crucial feature in any effort to theorize cosmopolitan democracy, she
argues, is "whether the capacity for regulating violence can be
reinstated in some new way on a transnational basis and whether barbarism can be checked by an alert and active cosmopolitan citizenry."[47]

Consider a related assumption in the "humane warfare" literature that was renewed during and after the Kosovo war. In contrast to the "humane" West, suggests Christopher Coker, "Elsewhere in the world war is becoming more inhumane, not less . . . War is becoming more dirty . . . Whatever we wish to call it . . . it has a logic [that] runs counter to what the West is trying to do—to make war less cruel."[48]

Deliberative notions of an imminent global public depend on a seemingly progressive teleology of historical development that presents the West as already civilized and democratic. There is one international realm characterized by Habermasian communicative discourse, an extension of either Lockean or Kantian logics of cooper-ation.[49] This is the "peaceful" or "humane" realm where normative/deliberative discourses and attempts at justification constrain (usually liberal) state behavior. The traditional Hobbesian realm of strategic interaction is its necessary and constitutive opposite, where the poten-tial for "barbaric" war still predominates.[50] In other words, the crucial distinction animating deliberative theorists is not only (or even) between the traditional norm of state sovereignty as against the defense of human rights—as so often presented in the literature—but also more problematically a world of two spheres with differing modes of "inter-action."

Not only is this global separation implicated in the production of violence in numerous and problematic ways, for example in making it easier to justify military intervention as a kind of colonial civilizing mission,[51] but it also serves to obscure the hierarchical relations and interpenetration that exists between these only seemingly separate "spheres." Prior to the Bosnia and Kosovo military interventions, for example, IMF-led efforts to "reform" the international financial architecture since the 1970s, including the imposition of severe austerity measures to liberalize the Yugoslav economy, contributed directly to the breakdown of domestic order in the federal state, which was exploited by opportunistic politicians. The result, of course, was the refugee and humanitarian crises in which the West then inter-vened.[52] The language of deliberative theory, in which humanitarian intervention is defined as a civilizing mission, obscures such analyses of the historical role of the West in violent social breakdown.

More importantly, by drawing on Habermas as *the* theorist of the public, numerous assumptions about global politics are uncritically accepted. The assumed intrinsic and violent hierarchy between global spheres rearticulates assumptions from Habermas's earlier idealization of the bourgeois public. Under the mask of liberal humanitarianism, these assumptions, which privilege certain modes of being public and certain speakers, justify the imposition of Western-derived hegemonic notions of what deliberative communication can and will provide. However, not only is there an implicit structural violence in the deliberative rationality assumed by discourse ethics, there is an explicit effort to rationalize violence in the form of "humanitarian" war. Violence is inherent to the modern territorial state and any apparent transcendence of state structures toward new forms of publics must attend to how violence and expansion are therefore newly marshalled. Yet the often hidden violence of public spheres as well as imperial military interventions should point international theorists to the practical political problems of accepting Habermas's work as foundational.

The repercussions and consequences of the Habermasian approach, even when considering the possibility of "postnational" and multiple publics, are therefore potentially huge. The idealized bourgeois publics in the European cities served to enhance the power of one class and one gender and one civilization over another. New global public sphere discourses similarly serve to rationalize violence. The remainder of this chapter will suggest that Hannah Arendt, in contrast, may offer a model of theorizing not the ideal public transposed to "the global," as Habermas and his followers have attempted. Rather she offers an account of how the search for extrapolitical groundings for public spheres, including those based on deliberative rationality, would almost necessarily be violent. Arendt helps us by not simply attending to the creative dimensions of the political beyond a narrow focus on rights. She usefully conceives the public explicitly in contradistinction to all of the things that deliberative theorists assume away. Arendt, in short, is significantly more cognizant of the difficult relationship between organized violence and the political.

POWER, VIOLENCE, JUSTIFICATION
AND LEGITIMACY

Violence is the evil twin of Arendtian politics. As John McGowan has effectively shown, "Arendt's definition of the political . . . often seems constructed primarily through negations. Arendt consistently links with violence what she wishes to exclude from politics."[53] This exclusion is most evident in *The Human Condition*. "Only sheer violence is mute," she wrote, "and for this reason alone can never be great. . . . To be political, to live in the *polis*, meant that everything was decided through words and persuasion and not through force and violence."[54] In her most explicit essay on the subject, "On Violence," Arendt depicts the activity as the almost inevitable response of political minorities unable to create a realm for action in the modern bureaucratized polity: "the greater the bureaucratization of public life the greater the attraction of violence."[55] In *On Revolution,* Arendt's purpose in contrasting the French and American precedents was to shatter the grip of French Revolutionary categories, to suggest that revolution, the foundation of a republic, need not be bloody. In doing so, she challenged the conventional wisdom that "whatever brother-hood all human beings may be capable of has grown out of fratricide."[56] Yet, in an effort to show that even goodness habitually incites direct, sometimes violent, action at the expense of speech, her discussion of Herman Melville's novella *Billy Budd* depicts the young sailor stammering impotently in his innocence able only to answer evil with a violent (and lethal) blow.[57]

Why this radical exclusion of and thereby intimate connection between violence and the political throughout Arendt's work? To be political, in her writing, to speak and to act in public was to be most free; freedom is the raison d'être of the political realm where citizens most fully disclose and actualize who they are.[58] Because humans reveal their distinctiveness through speech and action, it is partly through encountering the diversity of speakers and actors in public, a space in theory at least open to all, that we discover the fullest extent of both individuality and human plurality. In Arendt's words,

Action, the only condition that goes on directly between men without the intermediary of things or matter, corresponds to the human condi-tion of plurality, to the fact that men, not Man, live on the earth and inhabit the world. While all aspects of the human condition are some-how related to politics, this plurality is specifically *the* condition . . . of all political life.[59]

Within a "common space of appearances" political action is consti-tuted as a realm of human *inter*-action in a public space, where diverse citizens act through speech and suasion. There is something ethereal at the core of this political action "since there are no tangible objects into which it could solidify; the process of acting and speaking can leave behind no such results and end products. For all its intangibility, however, this in-between is no less real than the world of things we visibly have in common."[60] Political meaning could only arise through human *inter*-action—the promise of politics was that humans "form a world *between them.*"[61]

Arendt, however, cannot be assimilated to the view that the exten-sion of public deliberation necessarily guarantees a healthy public realm. As Margaret Canovan has shown, Arendt did not believe in "anything remotely resembling universal concurrence in objective truth" or that political disputes could be resolved *by purely rational means*.[62] Collisions between authentic moral experiences were unavoidable in the public realm. In Arendt's words,

> If morality is more than the sum total of *mores*, of customs and standards of behavior solidified through tradition and valid on the grounds of agreements, both of which can change with time, it has, at least politically, no more support than the good will to counter the enormous risks of action by readiness to forgive and be forgiven, to make promises and to keep them.[63]

Only those faculties arising from within the political sphere itself—the ability to forgive and to make promises—could constrain the boundlessness and risk of action, or "provide stability in the ocean of future uncertainty where the unpredictable may break in."[64] Never balking from the irreducible relativity of human opinion, Arendt demonstrated how the search for extrapolitical groundings for the public realm would be almost habitually violent.[65]

Consider Max Weber's mechanistic "work"-like characterization of politics as the competition for control over the legitimate use of violence; to be a truly political being is to have one's hand on the "wheel of history," not to *be* violent but to use violence when necessary.[66] This conception of politics is described as consonant with "work" given Arendt's tripartite distinction between the activities of labor, work, and action. Arendt conceived "work" in terms of the activity of "making" the "world," the "human artifice" of objects and the built environment surrounding humanity.[67] This is a durable realm; a space of artificial, manmade objects—laws, institutions, and cultural settings—that make the earth our home. (The "public" is also partly constituted as a human artifact in this sense, denoting "the world itself, in so far as it is common to all of us."[68]) Importantly, however, work is not only the creation of a lasting world. It is also a realm of violence, of humans acting upon and radically altering objects, where human force manipulates and fabricates earth-given nature for the end of creating a home. It is the realm in which the means are justified exclusively by reference to the ends. Albeit necessary, these are the activities of force and control.

Where violence is the essence of Weberian power, Arendt, in contrast, depicted violence and power as opposites. What distinguished violence, for Arendt, was its "instrumental character."[69] Violence is organized and controlled by political entities and, indeed, is constitutive of entities such as the state. "Power" in contrast "is never the property of an individual; it belongs to a group and remains in existence only so long as the group keeps together."[70] Or in other words, violence, which always relies on implements or "things," differs from power, which arises *in-between* people, the "realm of appearances," not "things" to be shaped. One individual may possess the implements of violence and they are functional insofar as they can command others to obey. Power, in contrast, is "never the property of an individual; it belongs to a group and remains in existence so long as the group keeps together."[71]

Derived from the "active support and continuing participation of all matters of public interest"[72] power appears among—in-between—people in the public realm. This model is in some accordance with Michel Foucault's understanding of power as "a complex strategical situation in a particular society."[73] In Foucault's words, "there is no binary and all-encompassing opposition between rulers and ruled at the root of power relations, and serving as a general matrix—no such duality extending from the top down and reacting on more and more limited groups to the very depths of the social body."[74] Similarly, for Arendt, power must not be equated with the dichotomous interaction between rulers and the "consenting" ruled.[75] Rather, it "corresponds to the human ability not just to act but to act in concert."[76] It is a collective act based on speech. Power, in other words, "is the only human attribute which applies solely to the worldly in-between space by which men are mutually related."[77]

Arendt most forcefully drew this distinction between power and violence in a discussion of the difference between "justifications" and "legitimacy" and we may use this distinction to critique deliberative readings of "humanitarian" war. In Arendt's words,

> Power springs up whenever people get together to act in concert, but it derives its legitimacy from the initial getting together rather than from any action that then may follow. Legitimacy, when challenged, bases itself on an appeal to the past, while justification relates to an end that lies in the future. Violence can be justifiable, but it will never be legitimate.[78]

Violence is always instrumental and can only be *justified*—in extreme circumstances—on a means–ends basis. "Its justification loses its plausibility the further its intended end recedes into the future."[79] "Power," in contrast, "needs no justification, being inherent in the very existence of political communities."[80]

From an Arendtian perspective deliberative theorists have accordingly only justified (to themselves) but not *legitimated* "humanitarian" war. This form of violence is honorable, deliberative theorists are led to suggest, if those intervening agree through fair procedures that the violent means justify the ends.[81] Similar assumptions about the function of U.N. debate over Kosovo formed the basis of attempts to endorse that war. "NATO's action," according to Wheeler, "was for the most part greeted with either approval or acquiescence by the society of states."[82] The assumed procedural rationality of UN debate, despite the lack of Security Council approval, bestowed "legitimacy" on this illegal violence. Moreover, war on this occasion was considered "legitimate" because "whilst the bombing accelerated Serb ethnic cleansing and led to thousands of Kosovars being killed, this has to be set against the fact that NATO's use of force made possible KFOR and a measure of political autonomy."[83] For Marc Lynch, "The intervention's putative legitimacy came from the net positive effect of the intervention—whatever the procedural violations, whatever the mixed motivations, the outcome vindicated the intervention."[84]

In making these claims the distinct notions of "justification" and "legitimacy" are conflated. Through a means–ends calculation interventionary violence is "legitimated" in terms of the presumed "humanitarian" outcome of the case. This is only a *justification* for violence, however, based on a selective and premature reading of Kosovo's future highly sympathetic to NATO and KFOR (and while NATO stood by as Kosovo-Serbs and Roma were ethnically cleansed after the bombing). Former Kosovo Liberation Army (KLA) leaders who continue to employ "terror" tactics against both Kosovo and Serb-Albanians have been empowered, subverting elections, assassinating opponents, and demanding protection money from civilians. As Arendt suggested, "The practice of violence, like all action, changes the world, but the most probable change is to a more violent world."[85]

For action over Kosovo to be *legitimate* in Arendtian terms it is the "initial getting together" of states that we must adjudicate. In this regard also, the standards of procedural rationality are found wanting. As well as the abstentions and threatened vetoes by the usual suspects at the United Nations (Russia and China), the notion that the wider "international community" meaningfully called for war against Belgrade is inaccurate unless we are to exclude representatives of most of humanity. In any case, properly speaking violence itself can never be legitimate; it can only be instrumentally deployed in-line with Arendt's rejection of all means–ends categories applied to politics: "the means are always the decisive factor."[86]

In just war terminology, the "means" of violence, or *jus in bello*, ought to be proportional to the ends, the evil incurred in conducting war cannot be greater than the evil it was designed to relieve, and those deemed "innocent," usually non-combatants, should be spared (or at least not deliberately targeted). Arendt's distinction between justification and legitimacy, based on her understanding of power and violence, also speaks to the tension in the just war tradition between means and ends. In Michael Walzer's words, this tension can be summarized as the "dilemma of winning and fighting well: the military form of the means–end problem, the central issue in political ethics."[87] Even if we accept for the sake of argument that NATO's actions were sufficiently embedded in humanitarian concerns, the use of aerial bombardments and the development of *combatant* immunity by flying above 15,000 feet drastically undermined the ends. Zero battle deaths for NATO left hundreds more civilians dead. The only politically legitimate method of air power (or so NATO leaders calculated) was less than effective, despite the sophisticated weaponry, for protecting civilians.[88] In other words, the terms of the democratic legitimation of the intervention for liberal publics in the West (no NATO casualties) constrained the justness, the justification, of its methods.

Arendt might have pointed out in this context that "inhumanity and destructive effectiveness increase in proportion to the distance separating the opponents."[89] But perhaps we do not *need* to offer moral sanction or "legitimacy" to liberal state violence to justify even a violent response to human rights atrocities. In contrast to deliberative theorists, witness Molly Cochran's refusal to legitimize military intervention within her "pragmatic" theoretical framework. In Cochran's words, "pragmatic critique cannot sanction violence and its own form of absoluteness: once a life has been taken, it cannot be given back. . . . There are no assurances regarding outcomes that the ends will in fact justify the means or that violence will secure better ways of coping or a workable solution."[90] Violence itself is not ruled out here. However, mirroring Arendt's formulation, "Pragmatic critique can recognize this as the required *instrumental*, rather than ethical, decision."[91]

Arendt did not offer a framework for how such decisions were to be made. It was a principled dimension of her political philosophy that such endeavors were destructive of the very political freedom such blueprints sought, at least in theory, to render. Habermas's exclusive focus on public reason, his desire to "re-rationalize" the public realm, conceives public life merely in terms of its formally deliberative dimensions. Such an imposition, however, invariably ignores the very different existential grounds of being Arendt envisioned in the *vita activa*; politics is such that no theory can adequately be "applied" without destroying the very essence of political life. Thus, in contrast to any Habermasian-inspired sense of instrumentally applying thought to action there is no ideal unity between thinking and doing in Arendt's work. To think and to act are not the same: "all our categories of thought and standards for judgment seem to explode in our hands the instant we try to apply them."[92]

If public spheres provide the place in which we have the right to political freedom, where our opinions are "significant" and actions "effective"[93] then even without a logical or (Habermasian) rational "banister" on which to lean we are not lost. "Even though we have lost yardsticks by which to measure, and rules under which to subsume the particular," wrote Arendt, "a being whose essence is beginning may have enough of origin within himself to understand without preconceived categories and to judge without the customary rules which is morality."[94] This anti-foundationalism, Arendt's doubt concerning the existence of universal (including rational) principles to impose on the public realm, is manifest in her humanist position. Without absolute standards found beyond humanity we are not help-less inasmuch as "standards and judgments are human themselves."[95] Arendt's work can be conceived as an effort to fashion a public realm not through violence, even if justified by rational deliberation, but "under the condition of human plurality,"[96] that is, one which embraces unpredictability, futility, and contingency. If the creative power of the public realm was the essence of politics it was also the only "guarantee on earth"[97] for human dignity, of human rights, and the only foothold against violence.

CONCLUSION

Recent military campaigns that have been justified in the language of "freedom" and human rights are important for supporters and critics alike; they represent the virtues and horrors of what a potentially global public might be capable of achieving. While more recent liter-ature has been cognizant of the way nationalism would need to be overcome for a global public based on "constitutional patriotism" to emerge, international theorists have not adequately addressed how understanding "post" sovereign relations in the global North requires locating it in more contemporary histories of Western expansion and engagement.[98] Although Habermas and his followers are certainly critical of the level of democracy in the West and do not consciously seek to replicate in the global arena the ills of contemporary liberal society, one material effect of their agenda is the violent externalization of the project of liberal democracy under the label "humanitarian intervention." With the ethical credentials of liberal regimes already assumed in most of this literature the hierarchical politics behind "communicative discourse" is largely concealed. Just as Habermas's earlier bourgeois idealization of public debate, with its dependence on industrial and imperial society, served to enhance forms of domination, new public sphere discourses similarly rationalize (justify but not legitimate) violence. More research on this relationship is required. Arendt's work could be central to this endeavor, especially in evaluating the possibilities of a more meaningful defense of human rights in multiple publics that is not, like her era and ours, based on "prejudice, hypocrisy, and cowardice in the face of the cruel majesty of a new world."[99]

Hannah Arendt sought to confront the enduring problems of humans as political animals and provides a compelling elucidation of the "public" dimension of human life. Unlike Nietzsche, who viewed the modern democratic individual as but a herd animal subject to slave morality, and Weber, who saw humanity stranded in an "iron-cage" of rationality, Arendt held out more hope for the promise of democratic politics where publics still existed as places of instability, incessant debate, and re-founding, of boundless action that was always nonviolent. A democratic theorist of the public, Arendt was not straightforwardly a theorist of human rights, "humanitarianism," or war. With the exception of a few passages in *The Origins of Totalitarianism*, she hardly referred to "human rights" as such, favoring instead the categories of "action," "opinions," "freedom," and "plurality" to refer to the politics in which rights would make sense. It was in this vein that she hoped to supply us with political categories that have been concealed, but not totally destroyed, by the modern age.

Taking seriously Arendt's work should lead scholars to be less sanguine about the apparent progressiveness of human rights ideologies and associated military interventions than is often the case.[100] She held a deeply ambivalent view of the concept of humanity and by extension justifications for political action that invoked humanitarianism. In an essay originally published in 1945 on the question of collective responsibility for Nazism, and at a time when many

Germans felt shame at the very thought of being German, Arendt
acknowledged, rather, a sense of shame at being human. She wrote,

> Our fathers' enchantment with humanity . . . did not even conceive of
> the terror of the idea of humanity. . . . For the idea of humanity, when
> purged of all sentimentality, has the very serious consequence that in
> one form or another men must assume responsibility for all crimes
> committed by men and that all nations share the onus of evil commit-
> ted by all others. . . . To follow a non-imperialistic policy and maintain
> a non-racist faith becomes daily more difficult because it becomes daily
> clearer how great a burden mankind is for man.[101]

Arendt's point concerning human rights was not to philosophize
about their moral standing, the enforcement of an international rights
regime, or the establishment of legal frameworks to which weak and
powerful states were to comply. It was, she argued,

> Not the loss of specific rights, then, but the loss of a community willing
> and able to guarantee any rights whatsoever, has been the calamity
> which has befallen ever-increasing numbers of people. Man, it turns
> out, can lose all so-called Rights of Man without losing his essential
> quality as man, his human dignity. Only the loss of the polity itself
> expels him from humanity.[102]

History had taught Arendt that for all the legalistic and moral talk
of the inalienable "Rights of Man" it was precisely at the moment
when these human rights were needed most that they were usually
nowhere to be found. When individuals lost the political community
supposed to protect them they became *precisely* nothing but
"human." And this was the problem. Arendt is still right; in our current era the category of "human being in general"[103] cannot yet carry
the burden of responsibility for the protection of rights.

NOTES

For comments on earlier drafts, the author would like to thank Ken Booth,
Helen Kinsella, Nick Wheeler, and two anonymous reviewers.

1. Noam Chomsky, *The New Military Humanism: Lessons From Kosovo*
   (Monroe, ME: Common Courage Press, 1999).
2. Patricia Owens, "Accidents Don't Just Happen: The Liberal Politics of
   High-Tech 'Humanitarian' War," *Millennium: Journal of
   International Studies*, 32, no. 4 (2003): 595–616.
3. Adam Roberts, "NATO's 'Humanitarian War' Over Kosovo,"
   Survival, 41, no. 3 (1999): 102–123.

4. Seyla Benhabib, "Unholy War," *Constellations*, 9, no. 1 (2002): 34–45.
5. Robert O. Keohane, "The Globalization of Informal Violence, Theories of World Politics, and 'The Liberalism of Fear,' " in Craig Calhoun, Paul Price, and Ashley Timmer (eds.), *Understanding September 11* (New York: The New Press, 2002), 87. Emphasis added.
6. Jürgen Habermas, "Bestiality and Humanity: A War on the Border between Law and Morality," in William Joseph Buckley (ed.), *Kosovo: Contending Voices on Balkan Interventions* (Michigan: Eerdmans Publishing, 2000), 306–316. On the 1998–1999 Kosovo crises, see Julie A. Mertus, *Kosovo: How Myths and Truths Started a War* (Berkeley, CA: University of California Press, 1999) and Timothy Judah, *Kosovo: War and Revenge* (New Haven: Yale University Press, 2000).
7. Michael Doyle, "International Intervention," *Ways of War and Peace: Realism, Liberalism, and Socialism* (New York: W.W. Norton and Company, 1997), 389–420.
8. "If all attempts at reason have failed, and the force is employed by internally democratic states who could justify their actions before a critical international public, then military intervention could potentially become a progressive force." Mark Lynch, "Critical Theory: Dialogue, Legitimacy, and Normative Justifications for War," in Jennifer Sterling-Folker (ed.), *Making Sense of IR Theory* (Boulder, CO: Lynne Rienner, 2005).
9. Habermas, "Bestiality and Humanity," 307. Habermas made similar claims in the wake of the 1990–1991 Gulf War. See *Between Facts and Norms: Contributions to a Discourse Theory of Law and Democracy*, trans. William Rehg (Cambridge: Polity Press [1992] 1996), 514.
10. Habermas, "Bestiality and Humanity," 312.
11. Not all international theorists who draw on Habermas support *more* "humanitarian interventions," although this may be the outcome. For example, Neta Crawford develops a modified Habermasian discourse ethical model to decide when it may be appropriate to intervene to "promote or protect human rights values." Neta Crawford, *Argument and Change in World Politics: Ethics, Decolonization and Humanitarian Intervention* (Cambridge: Cambridge University Press, 2002), 425. This interpretation is different to one offered earlier where Crawford is depicted as more supportive of humanitarian intervention in principle than may actually be the case. Patricia Owens, "Review Article: Theorising Military Intervention," *International Affairs*, 180, no. 2 (2004): 355–365.
12. The phrase is taken from Arendt's description of those who called for but failed to establish an effective bill of human rights in the interwar period. She notes, "The groups they formed, the declarations they issued, showed an uncanny similarity in language and composition to that of societies for the prevention of cruelty to animals." See Arendt,

The Origins of Totalitarianism (New York: Meridian Books [1951]
    1958), 292.

13. Carl Schmitt, *The Concept of the Political* (Chicago, IL: University of
    Chicago Press, 1996), 54.

14. See Margaret Canovan, "A Case of Distorted Communication: A
    Note on Habermas and Arendt," *Political Theory*, 11, no. 1 (1983):
    105–116.

15. For Habermas's discussion of Arendt and communicative power, see
    "Hannah Arendt: On the Concept of Power," *Philosophical-Political
    Profiles*, trans. Frederick G. Lawrence (London: Heinemann [1976]
    1983), 171–187 and *Between Facts and Norms*, 146–150.

16. Selya Benhabib, *The Reluctant Modernism of Hannah Arendt* (London:
    Sage, 1996). Benhabib wants to abandon Arendt's potentially irrespon-
    sible and "masculinist" Greek agonism. At best, she argues, if peers are
    ever to compete for excellence on the public stage (Benhabib's not
    Arendt's reading of agonism), this would imply a kind of moral and
    political homogeneity which simply does not exist in late-modern
    society. Moreover, when the "theatre" of politics is restricted to the
    public stage, this rigidifies the problematic distinction between public
    and private that feminists have been at pains to lay to rest for decades.
    Though Arendt's neglect of gender issues is more difficult to refute, it
    is not the case that she wanted to simply reinstitute some Greek-
    inspired model of the *polis*. This reading has been rebutted most effec-
    tively by R. Tsao, "Arendt against Athens: Rereading *The Human
    Condition*," *Political Theory*, 30, no. 1 (2002): 97–123.

17. Hannah Arendt, *The Human Condition* (Chicago, IL: University of
    Chicago Press, 1958), 194.

18. Dana Villa, *Politics, Philosophy, Terror: Essays on the Thought of
    Hannah Arendt* (Princeton, NJ: Princeton University Press, 1999),
    116.

19. Bonnie Honig, *Political Theory and the Displacement of Politics*
    (Ithaca, NY: Cornell University Press, 1993), 93.

20. It is also possible that the deliberative-agonistic dichotomy is over-
    stated in commentary on Arendt's work when we no longer conflate
    the ethos or principle animating a political act with the performance of
    the act itself. For example, the presumed distinction between an ago-
    nistic *politics* and a deliberative *ethos* may not be so divergent in the
    case of Arendt's reading of the American Revolution, with the actors
    enthused by the "interconnected principle of mutual promise and
    common deliberation." As Bonnie Honig suggests, when reading
    Thomas Jefferson's famous words "We hold these truths to be self-
    evident," Arendt emphasized the authority of the agreement of "we
    hold," rather than the "self-evident" nature of the truth. The signifi-
    cant revolutionary act was the "necessarily relative" agreement of the
    Founders. That the authority of the Declaration was contained within

itself, that it derived its own legitimacy, meant it met the dual yardstick of neither being autocratically enforced nor needing to appeal to grounds outside. Her stress on action, what appears in the world, meant she understood that when "men begin to act, their action *displays* the principle that animates it." Thus deliberation *and* performativity were coexistent, if only for a fleeting moment among a small group of men, at the U.S. founding. Hannah Arendt, *On Revolution* (New York: Viking Press [1963] 1970), 215, 92–94, 194, 124.

21. See Jürgen Habermas, *The Structural Transformation of the Public Sphere* (Cambridge, MA: MIT Press [1962] 1991) and *Theory of Communicative Action*, trans. Thomas A. McCarthy (Boston, MA: Beacon Press, 1984).

22. See Craig Calhoun (ed.), *Habermas and the Public Sphere* (Cambridge, MA: MIT Press, 1992).

23. Arendt, *Origins of Totalitarianism*, 126.

24. Mike Hill and Warren Montag, "What Was, What Is, the Public Sphere? Post–Cold War Reflections," in Mike Hill and Warren Montag (eds.), *Masses, Classes, and the Public Sphere* (London: Verso, 2000), 3. Also see Martin Kohler, "From the National to the Cosmopolitan Public Sphere," in Daniele Archibugi, David Held, and Martin Köhler (eds.), *Re-imagining Political Community: Studies in Cosmopolitan Democracy* (Cambridge: Polity Press, 1998), 58–71; Craig Calhoun, "Imagining Solidarity: Cosmopolitanism, Constitutional Patriotism, and the Public Sphere," *Public Culture*, 14, no. 1 (2002): 147–171; H. Brunkhorst, "Globalising Democracy Without a State: Weak Public, Strong Public, Global Constitutionalism," *Millennium: Journal of International Studies*, 31, no. 3 (2002): 675–690; N. H. Samhat and R. Payne, "Regimes, Public Spheres and Global Democracy," *Global Society*, 17, no. 3 (2003): 273–295.

25. Jürgen Habermas, *The Post-National Constellation: Political Essays* (Cambridge: Polity Press, 2001). For one of the earliest and most influential critiques of Habermas, see Nancy Fraser, "Rethinking the Public Sphere: A Contribution to the Critique of Actually Existing Democracy," in Bruce Robbins (ed.), *The Phantom Public Sphere* (Minneapolis, MN: University of Minnesota Press, 1993), 1–32.

26. See Andrew Linklater, *The Transformation of Political Community: Ethical Foundations of the Post-Westphalian Era* (Cambridge: Polity Press, 1998) and Selya Benhabib, *The Claims of Culture: Equality and Diversity in the Global Era* (Princeton, NJ: Princeton University Press, 2002).

27. See e.g., Mary Kaldor, "A Decade of Humanitarian Intervention: The Role of Global Civil Society," in Helmut Anheier, Marlies Glasius, and Mary Kaldor (eds.), *Global Civil Society 2001* (Oxford: Oxford University Press, 2001), 109–143; U. Beck, "The Cosmopolitan Perspective: Sociology in the Second Age of Modernity," in

Steven Vertovec and Robin Cohen (eds.), *Conceiving Cosmopolitanism: Theory, Context, and Practice* (Oxford: Oxford University Press, 2002), 61–85.

28. John A. Guidry, Michel D. Kennedy, and Mayar N. Zald, "Globalization and Social Movements," in Guidry, Kennedy, and Zald (eds.), *Globalizations and Social Movements: Culture, Power, and the Transnational Public Sphere* (Ann Arbor, MI: University of Michigan Press, 2000), 7.

29. James Bohman and Mathias Lutz-Bachmann, "Introduction," in Bohman and Lutz-Bachmann (eds.), *Perpetual Peace: Essays on Kant's Cosmopolitan Ideal* (Cambridge, MA: MIT Press, 1997), 18.

30. Martii Koskenniemi, *The Gentle Civilizer of Nations: The Rise and Fall of International Law, 1870–1960* (Cambridge: Cambridge University Press, 2001).

31. For a good critique, see Molly Cochran, "A Democratic Critique of Cosmopolitan Democracy: Pragmatism from the Bottom-Up," *European Journal of International Relations*, 18, no. 4 (2002): 517–548.

32. John Dryzek, *Deliberative Democracy and Beyond: Liberals, Critics, Contestations* (Oxford: Oxford University Press, 2000), 129.

33. Mark Lynch, *State Interests and Public Spheres: The International Politics of Jordan's Identity* (New York: Columbia University Press, 1999), 3. This distinction is made by Habermas in numerous places, but for an early statement see *Toward a Rational Society: Student Protest, Science and Politics* (London: Heinemann [1969] 1971).

34. Lynch, *State Interests and Public Spheres*, 36, 41.

35. Nicholas Wheeler, *Saving Strangers: Humanitarian Intervention in International Society* (Oxford: Oxford University Press, 2000). The work of English School theorist Hedley Bull has been used to suggest the overlap between international public spheres and the notion of a "society of states." "Bull's emphasis on shared norms, expectations, and institutions," according to Lynch, "involves communicative action and the public sphere dimension of structure." Lynch, *State Interests and Public Spheres*, 34.

36. Lynch, *State Interests and Public Spheres*, 40.

37. Wheeler, *Saving Strangers*, 280.

38. "World politics already depends as much on the process and content of arguments as on coercion and relations of military power." Crawford, *Argument and Change*, 420.

39. Hill and Montag, "What Was, What Is, the Public Sphere?" 6.

40. Arendt, *The Human Condition*, 26.

41. Hannah Arendt, "On Violence," in Hannah Arendt (ed.), *Crises of the Republic* (New York: Harcourt Brace Jovanovich, 1972), 143–144.

42. Lynch, *State Interests and Public Spheres*, 35.

43. Wheeler, *Saving Strangers*, 2.

44. See Martha Finnemore, *The Purpose of Intervention: Changing Beliefs about the Use of Force* (Ithaca, NY: Cornell University Press, 2003).
45. Margaret E. Keck and Kathryn Sikkink, *Activists Beyond Borders: Advocacy Networks in International Politics* (Ithaca, NY: Cornell University Press, 1998), 206.
46. Mary Kaldor, "Reconceptualizing Organized Violence," in Archibugi, Held, and Köhler (eds.), *Re-imagining Political Community*, 91–110. Cf. according to Arendt, "violence is neither beastly nor irrational." Arendt, "On Violence," 160.
47. Kaldor, "Reconceptualizing Organized Violence," 109.
48. Christopher Coker, *Humane Warfare* (London: Routledge, 2001), 22–23. Also see Michael Ignatieff, *Virtual Wars: Kosovo and Beyond* (London: Chatto and Windus, 2000); Colin McInnes, *Spectator Sport Warfare: The West and Contemporary Conflict* (Boulder, CO: Lynne Reinner, 2002).
49. On Lockean international order, see Alexander Wendt, *Social Theory of International Politics* (Cambridge: Cambridge University Press, 1999).
50. For a similar argument about the democratic peace literature, see Tarek Barkawi and Mark Laffey, "The International Relations of Democracy, Liberalism, and War," in Barkawi and Laffey (eds.), *Democracy, Liberalism, and War: Rethinking the Democratic Peace Debate* (Boulder, CO: Lynne Rienner, 2001), 1–23.
51. Anne Orford, *Reading Humanitarian Intervention: Human Rights and the Use of Force in International Law* (Cambridge: Cambridge University Press, 2003).
52. Susan Woodward, *Balkan Tragedy: Chaos and Dissolution after the Cold War* (Washington, DC: Brookings Institution, 1995), 47–81.
53. John McGowan, "Must Politics Be Violent? Arendt's Utopian Vision," in Craig Calhoun and John McGowan (eds.), *Hannah Arendt and the Meaning of Politics* (Minneapolis, MN: University of Minnesota Press, 1998), 270. Arendt's reflections on violence have not received a great deal of attention relative to other dimensions of her thought. One other more detailed treatment can be found in Iris M. Young, "Power, Violence, and Legitimacy: A Reading of Hannah Arendt in an Age of Police Brutality and Humanitarian Intervention," in Martha Minnow (ed.), *Breaking the Cycle of Hatred: Memory, Law, and Repair* (Princeton, NJ: Princeton University Press, 2002), 260–287. While broadly critical of NATO's actions over Kosovo, Young accepts that the organization was principally motivated by humanitarianism during the campaign.
54. Arendt, *The Human Condition*, 26.
55. Arendt, "On Violence," 178.
56. Arendt, *On Revolution*, 20.
57. Ibid., 79.
58. Arendt, *The Human Condition*, 79–135.

59. Ibid., 7.
60. Ibid., 183.
61. Arendt, *On Revolution*, 174. Emphasis added.
62. Canovan, "A Case of Distorted Communication," 109. Emphasis added.
63. Arendt, *The Human Condition*, 245.
64. Arendt, *On Revolution*, 175.
65. Arendt, "What is Authority," in Hannah Arendt (ed.), *Between Past and Future* (New York: Viking Press, 1968 [1954]), 91–142. See also Villa, *Politics, Philosophy, Terror*, 114, 116.
66. Max Weber, *From Max Weber: Essays in Sociology*, trans. edited, and intro. H. H. Gerth and C. Wright Mills (Oxford: Oxford University Press, 1946), 115.
67. Arendt, *The Human Condition*, 136–174. Recent theoretical efforts to found, to literally bring into being, a global public sphere through the discourse and practice of "humanitarian violence" can also be understood as part of this "politics-as-making" tradition. Patricia Owens, "Hannah Arendt and the 'Politics-as-Making' Tradition: A Critique of Deliberative Global Public Sphere Theory." Unpublished manuscript.
68. Arendt, *The Human Condition*, 52.
69. Arendt, "On Violence," 145.
70. Ibid., 143.
71. Ibid.
72. Arendt, "Civil Disobedience," in *Crises of the Republic*, 85.
73. Michel Foucault, *The History of Sexuality* (London: Penguin, 1978), 93.
74. Ibid., 94.
75. Arendt, "On Violence," 135.
76. Ibid., 143, 155.
77. Arendt, *On Revolution*, 175.
78. Arendt, "On Violence," 151.
79. Ibid.
80. Ibid.
81. Crawford, *Argument and Change*, 425–435.
82. Wheeler, *Saving Strangers*, 242.
83. Ibid., 283–284.
84. Lynch, "Critical Theory."
85. Arendt, "On Violence," 177.
86. Hannah Arendt, "Hermann Broch, 1886–1951," *Men in Dark Times* (New York: Harcourt, Brace and World, 1968), 148.
87. Michael Walzer, *Just and Unjust Wars: A Moral Argument with Historical Illustrations*, 2nd edn (New York: Basic Books, 1992), xxx–xxxi.
88. Human Rights Watch report approximately 500 civilian deaths as a direct result of the campaign, not including the deaths caused by the

acceleration of the refugee crises due to the bombing. See "Civilian Deaths in the NATO Air Campaign," February 2000. See http://www.hrw.org/ reports/2000/nato/ [downloaded August 14, 2001].

89. Arendt, "On Violence," 152.

90. Molly Cochran, *Normative Theory in International Relations: A Pragmatic Approach* (Cambridge: Cambridge University Press, 1999), 252.

91. Ibid., 252.

92. H. Arendt, "Mankind and Terror," in Jerome Kohn (ed.), *Essays in Understanding, 1930–1954* (New York: Harcourt, Brace and Company, 1994), 302.

93. Arendt, *The Origins of Totalitarianism*, 296.

94. Arendt, "Understanding and Politics," in *Essays in Understanding*, 321.

95. M. Canovan, *Hannah Arendt: A Reinterpretation of Her Political Thought* (Cambridge: Cambridge University Press, 1992), 174.

96. Arendt, *On Revolution*, 39.

97. Arendt, *Origins of Totalitarianism*, ix.

98. For the beginnings of such an account, see Tarek Barkawi and Mark Laffey, "Retrieving the Imperial: *Empire* and International Relations," *Millennium: Journal of International Studies*, 131, no. 1 (2002): 109–127.

99. Arendt, *Origins of Totalitarianism*, 269.

100. For a highly problematic effort to marshal Arendt's ideas to defend NATO's Kosovo intervention, see Jeffrey C. Isaac, "Hannah Arendt on Human Rights and the Limits of Exposure, or Why Noam Chomsky is Wrong about the Meaning of Kosovo," *Social Research*, 69, no. 2 (2002): 263–295. Isaac misses much of the force of Chomsky's critique of NATO's invocation of human rights discourses, ignoring the centrality of human rights issues to Chomsky's other scholarship, as well as almost entirely neglecting to address the structure of global power in which human rights claims are made. For a more persuasive discussion of Arendt and the theme of human rights, see Jeffrey C. Isaac, "A New Guarantee on Earth: Hannah Arendt on Human Dignity and the Politics of Human Rights," *American Political Science Review*, 90, no. 1 (1996): 61–73.

101. Arendt, "Organized Guilt and Universal Responsibility," in *Essays in Understanding*, 131.

102. Arendt, *Origins of Totalitarianism*, 297.

103. Ibid., 302.

CHAPTER 4

FORGIVENESS, RECONCILIATION, AND TRANSITIONAL JUSTICE

Andrew Schaap

> In so far as morality is more than the sum of *mores* . . . it has, at least politically, no more to support itself than the good will to counter the enormous risks of action by readiness to forgive and be forgiven, to make promises and keep them. These moral precepts are the only ones that are not applied to action from the outside, from some supposedly higher faculty or from experiences outside action's own reach. They arise, on the contrary, directly out of the will to live together with others in the mode of acting and speaking.
>
> Arendt, *The Human Condition*

Arendt's turn to forgiveness to redeem politics, in *The Human Condition*, is riveting. In her account of the human activities of labor, work, and action, Arendt argues that work redeems human existence from the futile cycles of labor by fabricating a durable world in terms of which historical consciousness is possible. Public action and speech, in turn, redeem human life from the meaninglessness generated by the instrumentality of work by producing the stories in terms of which we make sense of the world. Yet, even politics—the highest of human activities—requires redemption. Because in politics we always act among a plurality of free agents, we lack control over the consequences of our actions. Thus, political action not only invests the physical world with meaning by producing a web of human relationships; it also renders fragile the intersubjective world it constitutes.

Given the condition of non-sovereign freedom, there is an inherent tendency in action "to force open all limitations and cut across all boundaries."[1] Due to this transgressive quality, action threatens, even while it conditions the possibility of, community. Yet, unlike labor and work, there is no higher faculty to appeal to in order to redeem politics from the uncertain and irrevocable consequences of action. Against the antipolitical desire to master action by organizing public life in terms of rule *from above*, then, Arendt turns to the activities of promising and forgiving to redeem politics *from the inside*. On this account, readiness to forgive is an inherently, political attitude. Moreover, Arendt insists that, in the absence of a mutual willingness to forgive, politics would not be possible in the first place. For "without being forgiven, released from the consequences of what we have done, our capacity to act would, as it were, be confined to one single deed from which we could never recover; we would remain the victims of its consequences forever."[2]

Arendt's suggestive but brief remarks about the centrality of forgiveness in politics have fascinated and puzzled her readers since they were first published in 1958. However, at the end of the twentieth century there was renewed and often urgent interest in this aspect of Arendt's work as citizens within many polities struggled to come to terms with political violence that had been fueled by the Cold War. In the wake of grave state wrongs and/or protracted civil war, it seemed that forgiveness had to be possible in politics if there was to be any hope of former enemies recognizing each other as comembers of the same political association. Consequently, in the 1990s, "forgiveness" and "reconciliation" became central terms of political discourse in many polities throughout the world.[3] Indeed, reconciliation was often promoted by the international community as a public good that ought to be balanced against that of justice within transitional societies.[4] Following these developments (and, in particular, the advent of the Truth and Reconciliation Commission (TRC) in South Africa) there has been a growing interest among IR scholars, legal theorists, theologians, philosophers, and political scientists in both political forgiveness[5] and transitional justice.[6] Attempts to reckon with a painful past are often associated with a transition to democracy during which a range of official responses is available to a new regime. These include amnesty and criminal trials, reparation and restitution, purges, official investigations and constitution making. Such measures are usually referred to as forms of transitional justice since they are associated with a period of rapid political change during which the demand for retributive justice must be balanced against the imperative to consolidate a democratic regime.[7] Yet institutional reform and legal remedies alone are usually felt to be insufficient to address the legacy of political violence. For, in such circumstances, ordinary citizens need to find good grounds to live together in the first place if they are to affirm the legitimacy of shared institutions.

In this context, reconciliation is often promoted as a form of nation building in polities divided by past wrongs such as South Africa, Chile, Northern Island, and Australia. As Priscilla Hayner observes, reconciliation "implies building or rebuilding relationships today that are not haunted by the conflicts and hatreds of yesterday."[8] In the reconciled polity, she argues, the wrongs of the past could be discussed openly and without bitterness in public. Relationships between former antagonists would be based on responding to present challenges rather than identifying each other in relation to past events. Moreover, there would be some common agreement on fundamental historical facts concerning what wrongs were perpetrated.

In this chapter, I develop an Arendtian account of political forgiveness against the background of recent discussion about reconciliation and transitional justice within the study of international relations.[9] I begin by reviewing the philosophical literature on the nature of personal forgiveness. I argue that forgiveness involves not only relinquishing a just claim against one who has wronged us but also setting aside resentment against one's enemy. While it may not be possible to cease resenting the other as an act of will, it is possible to *want* to forgive and to seek grounds for setting aside resentment. I then consider what might constitute *political* grounds for forgiveness. Against the liberal and realist traditions of IR theory, I argue that neither necessity nor reason are adequate grounds for political forgiveness. For if a willingness to forgive depends on the dictates of necessity it is reduced to compromise whereas if it is conditional on having moral reasons it becomes redundant. Following Arendt, I argue that appropriate grounds for forgiveness in politics are, rather, the natality of the other and frailty of the world. Political forgiveness, on this account, does not refer to the closing moment of reconciliation in which wrongdoers are restored to community with those they have wronged. Rather, readiness to forgive makes possible a politics in which members of a divided polity contest each other's understandings of the violence of the past and its significance for their political association.[10] Drawing on this account of the political grounds for forgiveness, I consider the relation between amnesty and political forgiveness in the workings of the Truth and

Reconciliation Commission in South Africa. In the final section, I offer some speculations about the place of forgiveness in sustaining what John Williams (in this volume) refers to as the "international space in-between."[11]

SETTING ASIDE RESENTMENT

Forgiveness involves not only renouncing one's just claims against an other but setting aside a resentful view of her as "the one who wronged me."[12] Ceasing to identify the other with the consequences of her actions establishes the possibility of friendship in the wake of wrongdoing. While we do not cease to judge the other's actions as wrong, we open ourselves to an understanding of her that is more encompassing than her singular relation to us as our transgressor. Yet resentment is not set aside easily. Nor, perhaps, should it be. As Jeffrie Murphy observes, we quite properly feel resentful in response to being wronged.[13] What we resent is not only the material harm inflicted on us but also the insulting message the harmful act carries with it. In wronging us the other reveals her contempt for us by failing to treat us as her moral equal. As response to this demeaning experience, resentment involves a defiant assertion of one's value and entitlement to respectful treatment. Resentment is oriented to the recovery and confirmation of one's moral status, which is called into question by a wrong.[14]

If we are often right to resent our transgressor, then, there may be circumstances in which we are wrong to forgive her. A forgiving disposition is commendable so long as it keeps resentment within proper bounds, checks it against the excesses that arise from human weakness and vanity.[15] Yet to forgive too readily may be to acquiesce in wrongdoing. Forgiveness risks lapsing into "condonation" when we do not protest but simply overlook a wrong in order to maintain a relationship with the other.[16] Being too ready to forgo resentment may betray low self-esteem and so constitute a failure "to take oneself, one's projects and one's entitlements seriously enough."[17] Or it might reflect a moral indifference to the other as someone who is "not worth my time." In this context, Murphy insists that genuine forgiveness is not simply ceasing to resent but "forswearing resentment on moral grounds." He also argues that forgiveness should be "compatible with self-respect, respect for others as moral agents, and respect for the rules of morality or the moral order."[18] As such, forgiveness is only appropriate if the wrongdoer demonstrates genuine remorse. For, in doing so, he withdraws his endorsement of the insulting message the wrong communicated and re-affirms his commitment to the shared norm he violated.

Yet, as Jean Hampton argues, to insist too strongly on having moral reasons to forgive is to overlook the gift-like nature of forgiveness.[19] While retribution, remorse, reparation, and restitution may make us more inclined to forgive they cannot be necessary conditions for forgiveness. For to demand reasons why one ought to forgive is, in fact, to assume an unforgiving disposition.[20] Forgiveness becomes redundant when we reserve it only for those who have earned it from us. For then it is simply the acknowledgment that we are no longer the victims, that we are no longer justified in resenting our transgressor.[21] In its gift-like aspect, by contrast, forgiveness is an offer of trust in advance. While our transgressor does not deserve our forgiveness, we venture it nonetheless for the sake of a potential relationship. By offering forgiveness we invite our transgressor into society with us and, thus, make ourselves vulnerable to being wronged again. But, in doing so, we present our wrongdoer with an opportunity to recognize the wrongfulness of his actions and assume responsibility for them. In this way, forgiveness forgoes guarantees, the certainty of reasons, "in favor of a boldly, venturesomely aspiring and active pursuit of Value."[22]

The possibility of setting aside resentment, of comprehending the other as more than one's transgressor, must be allowed if there is to be a place for hope and trust in the politics of a divided society. However, those who have been the victims of an unjust regime might quite rightly be suspicious of the quietism implicit in making a political virtue out of forgiveness. As Frantz Fanon points out, the ideological benefit of promoting the Christian message of forgiveness in the colonial context is that it assists in "calming down the natives."[23] Those who continue to benefit from unjust social arrangements are likely to counsel the oppressed to "forgive and accept" when, in fact, they are morally entitled to "resent and resist."[24] Resentment may, therefore, have an important role to play in politics in animating protest that draws attention to the rights and respect due to members of an oppressed social group. As such, it is often politically appropriate to resent those implicated in past wrongs by virtue of their position as beneficiaries of an unjust regime or as members of a group whose values are sovereign.[25] Indeed, such just resentment often animates demands for recognition. Central to a politics of recognition is the defiant self-assertion of an oppressed group, the reclamation of historical agency by remembering the past from the perspective of the defeated.

Important as this task may be, however, it risks entrenching resentment. For such a history may fixate on grievances and emphasize "events that reinforce [a group's] sense of injustice and bruised pride."[26] While the demand for recognition often entails only the claim that a social group receives its due, when nurtured by a moralistic and unforgiving disposition, the fact of historical oppression may be taken as "proof of ultimate merit."[27] The establishment of friendly civic relations in a polity divided by past wrongs depends upon the possibility of setting aside the hard feelings occasioned by painful memories without forgetting or condoning what went before. The memory of offence may preclude the possibility of giving up resentment or hatred of our former enemy as a simple act of will. Yet, as David Novitz recognizes, it is possible to choose whether to fuel resentment through stubborn partiality or to seek grounds for forgiveness by entertaining the perspective of our transgressor. The task of relinquishing resentment, on this account, begins from a "willingness and ability to see things differently and to depart from our own settled perspective."[28] Wanting to forgive might, in this way, sustain a reconciliatory politics between former enemies in the absence of a moral consensus on the significance of past wrongs.

Cheshire Calhoun provides an insightful account of how one can be true to the past without making forgiveness conditional on the wrongdoer's repudiation of her acts. Grounds for the "aspirational forgiveness" that Calhoun advocates are revealed to us through telling a story that makes biographical, but not necessarily moral, sense of how the other could wrong us. Such a story is not intended to show the other as one worthy of forgiveness by separating the sin from the sinner. Rather, it situates the wrongs perpetrated against us in the biographical context in which the other makes sense of her own actions. This leads to a kind of understanding that confirms our perception of the past and the injury perpetrated against us. But it does not demand that the one who wronged us be different from what she is before we are willing to entertain society with her. We find grounds for overcoming resentment by making our transgressors' actions intelligible "by forgivingly understanding how they have made sense of their lives."[29] Importantly, in the context of political reconciliation, this means engaging with the collective meanings and narratives in terms of which our former enemy might previously have made sense of the violence of the past.[30]

THE INADEQUACY OF NECESSITY AND REASON AS GROUNDS FOR FORGIVENESS IN POLITICS

The value of forgiveness in our intimate relations with others is clear. In relations of love we are both most vulnerable and most likely to trespass moral bounds. Moral injury is so common that without the mutual capacity for forgiveness we could not sustain any friendship for long. Yet, although trespass is also frequent in politics, the appropriateness of forgiveness in public life is less obvious. As Arendt observes, although promising has long been recognized as indispensable to political life, forgiveness has "always been deemed unrealistic and inadmissible in the public realm."[31] Realists, who construe politics in terms of strategy and domination, are likely either to consider a forgiving disposition to be softheaded and bound to bring an actor to grief or to suspect that it cloaks some particular interest he is actually pursuing. Liberals, anxious to devise just institutions to contain politics, are bound to worry that the partiality of forgiveness will compromise justice or that it will lead to intrusive demands being made of citizens. Whereas realists would subordinate forgiveness to the dictates of necessity, liberals would constrain forgiveness within the bounds of reason. For the realist, forgiveness should be compatible with a "responsibility to the future" that involves weighing "objective interests that come into play."[32] In politics, according to Max Weber, an "ethic of absolute ends" must be tempered by this "ethic of responsibility." An ethic of ultimate ends is concerned only with the goodness of action. As such, it tends to encourage actors either to withdraw from worldly involvement or to commit one last evil to end all evils. By contrast, an ethic of responsibility demands a sensitivity to the consequences of our actions and a willingness to do what is necessary, which may mean employing morally dubious means, in order to secure the best outcomes in political affairs. Forgiveness is unpolitical when animated only by an ethic of absolute ends because it fails to recognize nonmoral constraints imposed on action by circumstances. To follow the command to love one's enemy and turn the other cheek when wronged without regard for circumstances and consequences is therefore likely to lead to disaster in politics.

On the other hand, the political realist may be willing to forgo a just claim for retribution when this appears necessary for the survival of the political association. As Peter Digeser points out, when conceived in terms of an ethic of responsibility, political forgiveness suggests a "take-it-on-the-chin" attitude on the part of the victims. Acknowledgment of the tragic choices political actors must sometimes confront in politics suggests that those who become victims of political wrongs ought to "simply accept that this is how the world works (sometimes we must do evil and sometimes we must suffer it) and get on as best we can."[33]

This kind of willingness to overlook wrongdoing for the sake of social harmony might be appropriate in certain political circumstances. For instance, when amnesty is granted to perpetrators in order to secure a peaceful transition to democracy. However, following Kolnai, forgiveness is reduced to condonation when justified in these terms. Whereas forgiveness condemns the wrong but seeks to overcome the resentment it occasions, condonation waives moral judgment entirely. Furthermore, taking necessity as the ground of political action ultimately leads to cynicism in relation to the possibility of forgiveness in politics. For the realist is likely to suspect, with Nietzsche, that the weak wield the offer of forgiveness (which presupposes the guilt of those it is offered to) as a rhetorical weapon by which to gain political influence.[34] Moreover, in the absence of freedom, forgiveness loses its normative significance as an invitation to society with the other. When those wronged forgive out of necessity (the recognition that they lack the power to pursue their claims to just retribution) forgiveness is not freely given but bargained away.[35]

By contrast, liberals, who are concerned to establish and preserve the rule of law, demand moral reasons for forgiveness in politics. If politics is the public means through which the private freedoms of individuals are secured, then forgiveness is appropriate in the public sphere only if it does not compromise those rights or exceed those duties of citizenship appropriate to a constitutional democracy. We should forgive only if this is compatible with the dictates of justice and we need only forgive to the extent that this makes possible the minimal level of civility necessary to maintain peaceful civic relations. Forgiveness sits uncomfortably with a liberal politics that "shies away from demanding purity of heart from its citizens."[36] Thus Digeser argues that it is a mistake, in the context of a modern state that must accommodate moral plurality, to conceive political forgiveness in terms of overcoming resentment.[37] Rather, he advocates a form of political forgiveness in terms of which citizens might publicly affirm their commitment to civic association with their former enemies while continuing to resent them in private.

Moreover, Digeser is concerned about the potential for short-circuiting justice that a willingness to forgive might lead to. There is a paradoxical relation between forgiveness and justice, which revolves around the problem of whether forgiveness is "other" than justice. If forgiveness involves forgoing one's just claim against another this seems to implicate forgiveness in injustice.[38] Yet, if we should only forgive the other as justice demands, then forgiveness becomes redundant. Jacques Derrida has recently expressed this paradox by arguing that forgiveness is impossible; for we only have no need of forgiveness when an offence is forgivable but only when we are confronted with the unforgivable.[39] If forgiveness is to be worth its name, Derrida insists, it must be unconditional: we must forgive what cannot be forgiven. There is thus a tension inscribed in the concept of forgiveness between "the idea which is also a demand for the *unconditional*, gracious, infinite, and economic forgiveness granted *to the guilty as guilty*" and "a conditional forgiveness proportionate to the recognition of the fault, to repentance, to the transformation of the sinner who then explicitly asks forgiveness."[40]

In contrast to Derrida's insistence on a pure forgiveness, Digeser argues against a gift-like conception of political forgiveness in order that it might be compatible with the dictates of justice and the demands of democratic citizenship. While in our private life we might bestow forgiveness as a gift on an undeserving wrongdoer, in public life forgiveness cannot be a mysterious act of grace but *must be conditional* on reasons that are consistent with the demands of democratic citizenship. In his view, political forgiveness ought not be an alternative but a supplement to procedural justice. Political forgiveness ought to be offered in recognition of the imperfection of basically just institutions and, as such, ought to pick up where "justice reaches its limits."[41] We ought to forgive state wrongs only when these are the outcome of basically just institutions, which realize justice imperfectly due to the complexity of the moral world.

Yet, taking moral reason as the only legitimate ground for forgiveness in politics appears to preclude the possibility of forgiveness as a legitimate response to injustice in precisely those circumstances in which it is most needed. Due to his concern that forgiveness might lead to the short-circuiting of justice, Digeser insists that political forgiveness should not be performed unless victims and transgressors agree on a history of what has happened, which is publicly verifiable and includes a common understanding of "who did what to whom" and "who owes what to whom."[42] However, making political forgiveness conditional on a shared account of past wrongs is to set a very hard condition for reconciliation indeed.[43] Political forgiveness would be a simple matter in a polity whose members could broadly agree on the significance of past wrongs. For such a polity would no longer be divided but would have largely accomplished what political forgiveness must help to bring about. Contrary to Digeser, forgiveness is most often invoked as a source of hope in politics when the possibility of consensus about the past seems remote.

Neither reason nor necessity will do, then, as political grounds for forgiveness. Conceiving forgiveness in relation to a courageous facing up to political necessity implicates it in the condonation of wrongdoing. Yet, forgiveness seems to become redundant in political life when subordinated to the dictates of moral reason. By contrast, Hannah Arendt's ethic of worldliness accords forgiveness a central role in politics because it takes the fragility of the web of human relationships and the freedom of the other to begin anew as grounds for forgiveness.

POLITICAL GROUNDS FOR FORGIVENESS

Following Arendt, political grounds for forgiveness stem from a recognition of the predicament of non-sovereign freedom. Like promising, forgiveness is an inherently political faculty because it presupposes plurality. We learn the need to forgive and be forgiven from our experience of living together with others. Moreover, we depend on others to forgive us. No one can forgive himself because a forgiveness enacted in isolation from others could "signify no more than a role played before one's self."[44] On this account, grounds for forgiveness in politics are the frailty of the world and the natality of the other. Forgiveness is an appropriate response to frailty since it saves the world from ruin by bringing to an end a process of reaction that would otherwise endure indefinitely in the web of human relationships. As response to natality, forgiveness releases the other from the consequences of her action. By no longer holding her to account for "what" she is, forgiveness frees the other to engage in the play of the world. In its world-delimiting moment, as response to the frailty of the world, forgiveness brings a process of interaction to an end. In its world-rupturing moment, as response to the natality of the other, it affirms the possibility of a new beginning.

Arendt writes that forgiving "serves to undo the deeds of the past, whose 'sins' hang like Damocles' sword over every new generation."[45] But, of course, they cannot be undone in any literal sense. The accomplishment of forgiveness, rather, is to refuse the past the power to determine the possibilities of the present. Arendt's notion of a process of interaction that endures in the web of human relationships captures the sense in which a past event may persist in memory as a "present threat" to a particular category of people within a polity. This threat is a semantic one in the sense that the event continues to exert a claim, in the present, of the subordinate social status of those wronged. As Pamela Hieronymi argues, the memory of an offence that goes publicly unrecognized *as wrong* "makes a claim. It says, in effect, that you can be treated in this way, and that such treatment is acceptable."[46] It is in this context that we ought to understand Arendt's point that the achievement of forgiveness, as with punishment, is that it "put[s] an end to something that without interference could go on endlessly."[47] Punishment and forgiveness undo the deed in the sense that they undo its meaning or, as Hieronymi puts it, they allow us to "leave the original meaning of the event in the past."[48]

In the case of willed evil and crime, punishment rather than forgiveness is appropriate in order to undo the meaning of the wrong. Punishment undoes the meaning of a wrong by negating the "evidence of superiority implicit in the wrongdoer's original act."[49] Through the symbolic defeat of the wrongdoer at the hands of the victim, punishment annuls the significance of the original act as evidence of the wrongdoer's superiority. It annuls the insulting message of the wrong that perpetrator and victim are not equal in value. Punishment leaves the meaning of the act in the past in the sense that *then* the wrong confirmed the subordinate social status of those it was perpetrated against, whereas *now* it is recognized as an illegitimate act of oppression. Similarly, apology is intended to undo the meaning of a wrong by withdrawing endorsement of the insulting message the act communicated.

Likewise, a political undertaking to forgive is a struggle to settle the meaning of the wrongful act in the past for the sake of our life in common. As Albert Memmi demonstrates in his portrait of the colonizer who can only choose between evil or uneasiness,[50] we become implicated in certain stories enacted in the world (such as the story of colonization), in which we may not want to be involved but which we are dragged into nonetheless according to our social position.[51] As response to the frailty of the world, forgiveness undoes the meaning of a wrong by bringing to an end the story that implicates the other in an original transgression. Trust is ventured in this moment since it involves a suspension of judgment or what Jean Bethke Elshtain calls "knowing forgetting." As she writes, this does not mean that "one falls into radical present-mindedness and the delusion that the past counts for nothing; rather, one assesses and judges just what the past does count for in the present—how much it should frame, shape, and even determine present events."[52] What is suspended is not judgment of the wrongfulness of the act, but the judgment that this confirms the other as one's enemy in the present.[53] Trust is ventured for the sake of establishing a new relation based on mutual recognition of each other as co-builders of a common world.

Respect for the other as co-builder of a common world, which is the basis for political forgiveness, differs from that Kantian form of respect that applies to individuals as autonomous beings who share the universal capacity for reason. Instead, it applies to individuals as political beings who share a particular world as their common end.[54] As such it presupposes an interdependence based not only on our shared need for security but also on the presence and acting of others for a sense of the reality and worth of things. Through engaging in an incessant discourse about this world, we invest it with meaning. The disclosure of a world thus also entails the constitution of a "we." Although social reality opens up to each of us in different ways, the fact of its being perceived in common is felt. The "we" that emerges from this common sense of the world is fragile because it depends on our speaking and acting in public for it to be brought into being.[55]

Although our sense of morality depends upon recognizing a universal quality in the other such as dignity or sacredness on the basis of which we accord rights to all, in order to be politically relevant this quality can not be attributed to human nature but must be articulated and actualized through our belonging within particular associations. As Arendt writes, "philosophy may conceive of the earth as the home-land of mankind and of one unwritten law, eternal and valid for all. Politics deals with men, nationals of many countries and heirs to many pasts."[56] To forgive the other for the sake of the fragile world one (potentially) holds in common with her is, therefore, to forgive her in her neighborly relation to us rather than on the basis of our shared moral status as rational beings or creatures of God.

This entails a kind of political humility, an attitude of care and moderation. We forgive because we may also need to be forgiven. For only a person who believes he has no need of forgiveness could wish to live in an unforgiving world. In being politically disposed to forgive, then, one discounts the historical fact of oppression as evidence of moral superiority or collective innocence. The possibility of forgiveness depends in this way on an "awareness that there is a virtual reciprocity in what the oppressors did to the oppressed," that those wronged were on the side of good as a matter of historical fact not as a matter of principle, that is, "not because they are the good people."[57] As response to frailty, forgiveness involves an awareness of evil as "banal" or, better, *mundane* in the sense that it is *of the world*. This is to recognize, as Bert van Roermund writes, "that what the oppressors did to the oppressed belongs to the evil humans do to each other, and not to a mythic evil that intrudes on the world of humans from outside. In reconciliation, evil becomes 'ordinary' in the profound sense of 'among us.' "[58]

As response to the natality of the other, forgiveness undoes the meaning of the wrong by ceasing to recognize the other only in terms of his past actions or those of his fellow group members. We undo the meaning of the deed as evidence of the identity of the other. As Arendt puts it, to forgive in this sense is to insist on seeing the individual as "more than whatever he did or achieved."[59] Forgiveness, in this context, is world rupturing because it resists the categories by which we habitually make sense of the world, inviting the other to disclose that difference which exceeds his identity. This moment is hopeful since it is predicated on the potential inherent in the other to begin anew. To forgive for the sake of who the other is, is to release him from the consequences of his actions so that he can remain a free agent. We forgive the other "what" he is (our transgressor) for the sake of "who" he might reveal himself to be through action.

The release that forgiveness offers is indispensable in politics to mitigate despair at the moral irresponsibility and haphazardness that arises from the predicament of non-sovereign freedom. Care for the world must balance but not overwhelm that agonistic striving through which the difference of individuals and the common-ness of the world are disclosed. When care overwhelms the agent it gives rise to depressive guilt, a surfeit of which leads to withdrawal from the world for fear of being implicated in political injustice.[60] It is in this context that the possibility of forgiveness allows us to remain free agents, willing participants in the play of the world. As response to the other that is "unconditioned by the act that provoked it," forgiveness testifies to our shared potentiality to act anew.[61] Forgiveness reveals the natality of the forgiver since, in contrast to retaliation, it is not a predictable reaction. Rather it is a response that is both unexpected and unpredictable. As such, it entails an invitation to the other to engage in politics with us.

An ethic of worldliness thus furnishes political grounds for forgiveness, which are not reducible either to those of the realist or the liberal. Forgiving for the sake of a fragile world has an affinity with an ethic of responsibility in that it is distinct from a more absolute form of forgiveness based on love (such as the unconditional forgiveness advocated by Derrida). In undertaking to forgive for the sake of the world we share in common, we must consider the significance and consequences of our act for our life in common. We cannot forgive with the blindness of love.[62] However, it differs fundamentally from the realist's ethic of responsibility because it is not predicated on a consequentialist morality. For the struggle to settle the meaning of the wrong in the past is not the same as forgetting or "overcoming" the past. Rather, it seeks to establish a provisional closure, one that acknowledges the persistent claims of the past in the present—and, therefore, the impossibility of any final reconciliation—but which resists the power of the past to determine the possibilities of the present.

Moreover, a forgiveness based on respect for the other as co-builder of a common world does not presuppose a shared moral vocabulary or form of life but rather a willingness to entertain the other's point of view. As such it is compatible with citizenship in a diverse society. But in contrast to the chastened form of citizenship advocated by the liberal, who would reduce forgiveness to toleration, an ethic of worldliness invites those who wronged us to engage with us in a contentious debate about the significance of past events for our life in common. In forgiving we affirm our potentiality to act anew, to establish new relationships. But since this is an inherently free act, its terms cannot be dictated in advance by the demands of justice. The way of political forgiveness does not necessarily follow the logic of right that the political liberal insists on. Rather, the willingness to forgive invites the other to politics. Instead of presupposing community between wrongdoers and wronged, the possibility that a "we" might emerge from public interaction is invoked as a matter of faith. This common aspiration delimits a future horizon in terms of which former enemies might come to a shared understanding of what went before. In this way, as Bert van Roermund writes in a slightly different context, readiness to forgive makes available a past to look forward to.[63]

AMNESTY, AMNESIA, AND ANAMNESIS

If the moral achievement of retributive justice is, as Arendt insists, that it holds the individual to account for his actions and refuses to accept excuses such as "just following orders," this can also be its political failure.[64] For, as Pablo de Grieff points out, imputing criminal guilt to particular individuals tends to exonerate those implicated in past wrongs as tacit supporters or beneficiaries of an unjust regime.[65] Of course, amnesty is even more likely to obscure political responsibility for past wrongs. Punishment, at least, symbolizes a collective condemnation of past wrongs. Amnesty, by contrast, suggests collective forgetting, a failure to take past wrongs seriously at all.

What was fascinating about the way in which transitional justice was pursued in postapartheid South Africa, however, was that amnesty was linked to reckoning with the past rather than simply wiping the slate clean. As van Roermund succinctly puts it, amnesty was associated with "anamnesis rather than amnesia." The deal of granting amnesty in return for full disclosure of the truth was supposed to provide a way of burying rather than obliterating the past, "a way of covering that uncovers the meaning of what has happened."[66] Consequently, a subtle relationship seemed to emerge between the provision of amnesty to perpetrators and the possibility of political forgiveness between ordinary citizens. This suggests that, in certain circumstances, a willingness to forgive might sustain a policy of amnesty and, conversely, amnesty might contribute to the possibility of political forgiveness. So long as state crimes go unpunished what a wrongdoer gets away with is a "claim of relative superiority."[67] Failure to prosecute a perpetrator in this way amounts to acquiescence in the message his crime communicated about the inferior social status of the victims. To add insult to injury, when amnesty is associated with forgiveness rather than acknowledged as strategic compromise, it seems that this failure is passed off as a moral achievement. Yet, during a transition to democracy or at the conclusion of a civil war, punishment of state criminals may not be politically feasible due to the kinds of reasons emphasized by realists. For example, military leaders may threaten to overthrow a civilian government that attempts to punish the leaders of the former regime. The relentless pursuit of justice might be self-defeating in such circumstances since it could well return a polity divided by past wrongs to authoritarian rule or civil war. An ethic of responsibility would demand that justice be sacrificed in order to safeguard the establishment of democratic institutions.

While Archbishop Desmond Tutu sometimes defends the provision of amnesty in South Africa on such grounds, he often also makes a stronger claim that it represents "another kind of justice."[68] In contrast to a focus on retribution, restorative justice is centered on repairing relationships. Such a model of justice is suggested in the Interim Constitution of South Africa, which states that "there is a need for understanding, but not for vengeance, a need for reparation, but not for retaliation, a need for *ubuntu* but not for victimization."[69] Tutu implies that amnesty might sometimes be justified as a collective act of forgiveness, according to which waiving punishment does not simply sacrifice justice for politically expedient reasons but upholds justice according to the ideal of restoration. Indeed, he often insists that restorative justice is preferable to retribution, which is akin to revenge.

However, as David Crocker discusses, retribution and revenge are not the same.[70] Fundamentally, this is because retribution mediates the just demand to punish the wrongdoer with the intervention of an impartial third party in the form of legal institutions. Although in practice revenge and retribution may go together, we commonly understand that retribution becomes unjust the more it shades into revenge. Indeed, it was to the extent that the postwar Nuremberg trials were perceived to amount to "victor's justice" (according to which the conquerors exact tribute from the defeated) that they were regarded with cynicism. By contrast, the legitimacy of Nuremberg and more recent attempts to prosecute state criminals in an international court of law depends on the extent to which these are judged to have been impartial (rather than "political," in the realist sense of the word). Retribution is not reducible to revenge, then. Indeed, it is morally preferable to amnesty as a demonstration of a new regime's commitment to upholding the rule of law.

Moreover, Christopher Bennett argues that just retribution is as fundamental to the restorative ideal of reconciliation as is forgiveness.[71] Bennett, himself an advocate of restorative justice,[72] insists that genuine reconciliation requires the repudiation of past wrongs and this should be expressed publicly and institutionally through punishment. Like apology, atonement and reparation, a willingness to accept just punishment demonstrates that a perpetrator is remorseful, which establishes the possibility of his forgiveness and return to the moral community. Amnesty, then, cannot be *justified* as a collective act of forgiveness in terms of the restorative ideal of justice because it fails to hold the wrongdoer to account for his actions. Consequently, Bennett insists, there is no "third way" between the justice of retribution and the injustice of amnesty. Rather, we are left with a stark choice between the moral reasoning of the liberal (that being true to the past requires retribution) and the political willingness of the realist (to forget past wrongs in order to ensure the survival of the political association). Though the compromise of the realist may sometimes be called for, we should recognize this for the sacrifice of justice that it is rather than pass it off as another kind of justice.

But reducing the question of amnesty to these terms seems to miss something important about what was aspired to in South Africa. This may not have amounted to another kind of justice, but it did appear to involve more than just *Realpolitik*. When Babalwa Mhlawuli appeared before the TRC and said "We want to forgive, but whom should we forgive?" she did not demand reasons why she ought to forgive but sought grounds on which it was possible to forgive. This attitude of wanting to forgive, according to van Roermund "anticipates and eradicates the point where doing justice could become obstructive for civil peace. It steers away from the pitfalls of *fiat justitia, perat mundus*" (Let justice be done though the world may perish). In South Africa, it seems, it was not the acknowledgment of wrongdoing by perpetrators that established the possibility of forgiveness. Rather, it was the readiness to forgive, a willingness on the part of those wronged "to defer the right to just retribution, that made possible the revelation of truth."[73]

In South Africa, amnesty was not conditional on a perpetrator showing remorse but, rather, on his making a full disclosure of the truth and demonstrating that his wrong was associated with a political objective. This meant that the amnesty commission had to judge applicants both as individuals who committed isolated crimes and as members of a class who were pursuing political objectives. As Scott Veitch writes, judges were called on "to make an overt judgement about the 'political objective' of the offence, and in so doing . . . necessarily engage a collective meaning for both the offence and applicant's role in its commission" *and* somehow understand this to "fit the 'full disclosure' unique to the applicant."[74] It was this effort to make political sense of the perpetrator's actions, one that necessarily deprioritized the logic of right, which linked it with a wider struggle for political forgiveness. For in associating individual acts with political objectives, the amnesty process implicated all those on behalf of whom perpetrators claimed to act.

In this context, the truth the TRC sought to disclose was not the truth of the event but the "truth of memory."[75] The connection between political objective and full disclosure drew the amnesty applicants and the law into a political reassessment of the past, one which demanded a confrontation between actors' self-understandings then and now. Being true to the past, in this sense, required both making political sense of how wrongs came to be perpetrated as well as the moral judgment that these acts were wrong. By making political sense of past wrongs those social meanings that structured the perpetrator's actions and that make his choice of evil comprehensible come to the fore. To be sure, granting amnesty based on such an understanding could not amount to a collective act of forgiveness. Yet, the amnesty process appeared to be sustained (in part, at least) by wanting to forgive. Similarly, the truth telling associated with amnesty made way for a wider process of political forgiveness by engaging the collective meanings perpetrators shared with ordinary citizens.

The South African experience suggests that, in order to conceive reconciliation politically, we need to reverse the order of our moral thinking. In certain circumstances, it may be that forgiveness "makes politics itself possible."[76] Rather than achieving closure by restoring social harmony, readiness to forgive creates a space for truth telling and the assumption of political responsibility. As such, it opens the possibility of an interpretative struggle over the significance of past wrongs and the terms of political association. Political forgiveness is not so much oriented to restoring wrongdoers to a moral community but to disclosing the commonness of a world that is constituted by diverse and possibly incommensurable perspectives. As such, a disposition to forgive, indeed, describes an attitude with which we might come to politics, one that might enable us to work out and sustain a good we hold in common. However, it is not conditional on a prior moral consensus and recognition of common political authority. Rather, political forgiveness opens the way to their realization.

FORGIVENESS AND THE INTERNATIONAL SPACE IN-BETWEEN

Throughout this chapter I have considered political forgiveness, reconciliation, and transitional justice in terms of the context to which they are usually applied: the bounded community of a sovereign state. However, as my introductory remarks intimate, the politics of reconciliation are most often enacted against the background of international involvement both in contributing to political violence and mediating a society's attempt to reckon with past wrongs. Moreover, in certain contexts, reconciliation might be one option alongside secession.

In what sense, then, might a readiness to forgive help to sustain the *international* space in-between? John Williams rightly points out that Arendt is a "theorist of the bounded community" and her reflections on forgiveness appear to be predicated on a commitment to such a community; "the will to live together with others in the mode of acting and speaking."[77] Yet it not evident that this commitment to community must be defined in terms of the modern nation-state. Indeed, as Lang and several other contributors to this volume demonstrate, Arendt's work provides a valuable resource for considering the possibility of international political action. This is due in no small part to her attempt to think about political action in relation to the condition of non-sovereign freedom.

While, for Arendt, laws and institutions may delimit a space for politics in order that we might actualize our freedom by appearing before each other in public, these institutions cannot sustain politics in themselves but depend on the spontaneous action of individuals. Consequently, the in-between of the political, for Arendt, is clearly not the domain of the nation-state but rather the self-organization of people acting in concert (e.g., revolutionary councils, the kibbutz, the town-hall meeting). On this account, there is no reason to suppose that political actors should respect state-instituted boundaries when these serve to constrain opportunities for collective action and self-determination rather than to delimit a horizon within which action is meaningful and human freedom can be actualized.

While Arendt does not comment directly on the possibility of forgiveness across and between political communities, her reflections on promising (that other moral precept that is inherent to politics) are enlightening in respect to this. For they show how promising helps to delimit a space for politics between communities, a point which is clearly demonstrated by the importance of the promise "Never Again" in the context of a reconciliatory politics. Promising delimits a space for politics by institutionalizing shared expectations in law. As such, law need not be conceived in terms of the imperative of a sovereign entity. Indeed, for the Romans, the law needed no such basis but was the outcome of conflict. Law was predicated on an alliance, which not only established peace but also constituted a new unity between two different entities that had been thrown together by war. Thus, a war was concluded to the satisfaction of the Romans not merely with the defeat of an enemy but "only when the former enemies became 'friends' and allies (*socii*) of Rome."[78] The Romans thus recognized in alliances and covenants a powerful institution for the "creation of politics at the point where it was reaching its limits."[79] For alliances allowed the extension of politics beyond "relationships between citizens of one and the same City (as the Greek conception of politics was limited) to include relations 'between foreign and dissimilar nations.' " On this account, as Jacques Taminaux puts it, law is the "institution of a relationship between conflictual sides of a pluralistic interaction."[80]

Just as promising might help to *delimit* a space for politics across and between political communities this suggests that a readiness to forgive might help to *sustain* such an international space in-between. Importantly, however, whereas a state such as Germany may make reconciliation a goal of foreign policy and has the authority to offer such things as reparation, restitution, and apology in pursuit of this end,[81] no state can possess a corresponding authority to forgive on behalf of its citizens (whether dead or alive). Nevertheless, the readiness of individuals to extend forgiveness across and between territorial borders may be crucial in sustaining an international space in-between members of communities that have perpetrated political violence against each other as, for instance, in the former Yugoslavia.

Finally, what role might the international community play in promoting reconciliation in transitional societies? And to what extent, might the role of third parties play in encouraging or discouraging the readiness to forgive among ordinary citizens divided by past wrongs? David Crocker argues persuasively that "international civil societies (and international regimes) can promote transitional justice by providing domestic groups and democratically elected governments with such things as material resources, relevant tools, international legitimacy and moral support."[82] Moreover, groups within international civil society can promote a culture of universal human rights within a transitional society by appealing to internationally recognized norms and conventions. Similarly, Juan Mendez has stressed the positive role that international tribunals and the International Criminal Court (ICC) can potentially play in promoting reconciliation "in its truest form" by preventing amnesty from being passed off as forgiveness.[83] Yet, similarly "too much or the wrong kind of international response to a country's past rights violations can do more harm than good for democratization and transitional justice."[84] Efforts by third parties to bring perpetrators to justice can erode the democratic legitimacy of a society's efforts to reckon with past wrongs. Consequently, as Brad Roth argues, the insistence by international actors on the prosecution of human rights violators may actually serve to curtail the space for politics that a readiness to forgive helps to sustain, if such an attempt fails to "take account of the moral ambiguities that attend unmediated civil and inter-communal conflict."[85]

NOTES

1. Hannah Arendt, *The Human Condition* (Chicago, IL.: University of Chicago Press, 1958), 190.
2. Ibid., 237.
3. See Andrew Rigby, *Justice and Reconciliation: After the Violence* (Boulder: Lynne Rienner Publishers, 2001).
4. See David Crocker, "Transitional Justice and International Civil Society: Toward a Normative Framework," *Constellations*, 5, no. 4: 492–517.
5. See Christopher Bennet, "Is amnesty a collective act of forgiveness?" *Contemporary Political Theory*, 2, no. 1 (2003): 67–76; Jacques Derrida,

On Cosmopolitanism and Forgiveness (London and New York: Routledge, 2001); Peter Digeser, *Political Forgiveness* (Ithaca: Cornell University Press, 2001); Jean Bethke Elshtain, "Politics and Forgiveness," in N. Biggar (ed.), *Burying the Past: Making Peace and Doing Justice after Civil Conflict* (Washington, DC: Georgetown University Press, 2001); Trudy Govier, *Forgiveness and Revenge* (London: Routledge, 2001); Claire Moon, "Prelapsarian State: Forgiveness and Reconciliation in Transitional Justice," *International Journal for the Semiotics of Law*, 3 (2004); Donald Shriver, *An Ethic for Enemies: Forgiveness in Politics* (New York: Oxford University Press, 1995); and Erenesto Verdeja, "Derrida and the Impossibility of Forgiveness," *Contemporary Political Theory*, 3 (2004): 23–47.

6. See Priscilla Hayner, *Unspeakable Truths: Confronting State Terror and Atrocity* (New York and London: Routledge, 2002); Samuel Huntington, *The Third Wave: Democratisation in the Twentieth Century* (Norman, OK: University of Oklahoma Press, 1991); Neil J. Kritz (ed.), *Transitional Justice: How Emerging Democracies Reckon with Former Regimes. Volume I: General Consideration* (Washington, DC: United States Institute of Peace Press, 1995); Martha Minnow, *Between Vengeance and Forgiveness: Facing History after Genocide and Mass Violence* (Boston, MA: Beacon Press, 1998); and Ruti Teitel, *Transitional Justice* (Oxford and New York: Oxford University Press, 2000).

7. Efforts to reckon with state wrongs, though, have not been confined to new democracies, which must tread lightly in their justice-seeking measures for fear of a military coup or return to civil war. In many mature democracies, the memory of offence continues to be a source of grievance for a section of the population and presents a legitimation crises for the state.

8. Hayner, *Unspeakable Truths*, 161.

9. This has been most prominent in *Ethics & International Affairs*. See David Crocker "Reckoning with Past Wrongs: A Normative Framework," *Ethics & International Affairs*, 13 (1999): 43–64; Susan Dwyer, "Reconciliation for Realists," *Ethics & International Affairs*, 13 (1999): 81–98; Lyn Graybill, "South Africa's Truth and Reconciliation Commission: Ethical and Theological Perspectives," *Ethics & International Affairs*, 12 (1998): 43–62; David Little, "A Different Kind of Justice: Dealing with Human Rights Violations in Transitional Societies," *Ethics & International Affairs*, 13 (1999): 65–80; Margaret Popkin and Nehal Bhuta, "Latin American Amnesties in Comparative Perspective: Can the Past be Buried?" *Ethics & International Affairs*, 13 (1999): 99–116; Juan Mendez, "National Reconciliation, Transitional Justice and the International Court of Justice," *Ethics & International Affairs*, 15, no. 1 (2001): 25–44; and Brad R. Roth "Peaceful Transition and Retrospective Justice: Some Reservations (A Response to Juan Mendez)," *Ethics & International Affairs*, 15, no. 1 (2001): 45–50.

10. In this account I am primarily concerned with the possibility of politics between "ordinary citizens" who remain divided by the memory of past wrongs rather than that between perpetrators of human rights violations and their victims.

11. Some of the material included in this chapter was previously published in "Political Grounds for Forgiveness," *Contemporary Political Theory*, 2 (2003): 77–87.

12. Jean Hampton, "Forgiveness, Resentment and Hatred," in J. Murphy and J. Hampton (eds.), *Forgiveness and Mercy* (Cambridge: Cambridge University Press, 1988), 38.

13. Jeffrie Murphy "Forgiveness and Resentment," in J. Murphy and J. Hampton (eds.), *Forgiveness and Mercy* (Cambridge: Cambridge University Press, 1988), 14–34.

14. As Pamela Hieronymi puts it, "Resentment affirms what the act denies—its wrongness and the victim's worth. And so, in a way, resentment is a fight response. It fights the meaning of the past event, affirming its wrongness and the moral significance of the victim and the wrongdoer"; "Articulating an Uncompromising Forgiveness," *Philosophy and Phenomenological Research*, 62, no. 3 (2001): 547.

15. Murphy, "Forgiveness and Resentment," 15.

16. Aurel Kolnai, "Forgiveness," in Aurel Kolnai (ed.), *Ethics, Value and Reality* (London: The Athlone Press, 1977), 215–216.

17. David Novitz, "Forgiveness and Self-Respect," *Philosophy and Phenomenological Research*, 58, no. 2 (1998): 306–307.

18. Murphy, "Forgiveness and Resentment," 24.

19. Hampton, "Forgiveness, Resentment and Hatred," 36–37.

20. Joanna North, "Wrongdoing and Forgiveness," *Philosophy*, 62 (1987): 505.

21. Kolnai, "Forgiveness," 217.

22. Ibid., 233.

23. Franz Fanon, *The Wretched of the Earth* (London: MacGibbon and Kee, 1965), 53.

24. Murphy, "Forgiveness and Resentment," 11.

25. Albert Memmi, *The Colonizer and the Colonized* (London: Earthscan Publications, 1990), 78–79.

26. Novitz, "Forgiveness and Self-Respect," 305.

27. Graham Little, *The Public Emotions: From Mourning to Hope* (Sydney: ABC Books, 2001), 142.

28. "Forgiveness and Self-Respect," 309.

29. Cheshire Calhoun, "Changing One's Heart," *Ethics* 103 (1992): 96.

30. Indeed, in her account of "reconciliation for realists", Susan Dwyer suggests that the "core notion is that of bringing apparently incompatible descriptions into narrative equilibrium." I have some reservations about what I take to be Dwyer's undue optimism about the possibility of "narrative incorporation". However, I am generally sympathetic to the account of reconciliation she argues in favor of, which, I think, is

not only compatible with but supports the political conception of forgiveness developed here; Dwyer, "Reconciliation for Realists," 88–89.

31. Arendt, *The Human Condition*, 243.

32. Max Weber, "Politics as a Vocation," in *From Max Weber*, trans. H.H. Gerth and W. Mills (London: Routledge & Kegan Paul, 1948), 116.

33. Digeser rejects this view; see *Political Forgiveness*, 177.

34. See Digeser, *Political Forgiveness*, 21–23. Since politics is construed as a means through which actors pursue goals, talk of forgiveness can only obfuscate the material interests that are really at stake in political conflict. By keeping one eye fixed on the past, concern with forgiveness and guilt distracts attention from the future with which the political actor is properly concerned. For the realist, the past has only marginal political importance in relation to the immediate clash of interests and might as well be forgotten in order to concentrate our attention more thoroughly on shaping the future; Weber, *From Max Weber*, 198.

35. Bert van Roermund, "Never Again," Paper presented at the colloquium on *Law, Time and Reconciliation*, Centre for Law and Society, University of Edinburgh, May 15–16, 2002.

36. Digeser, *Political Forgiveness*, 17f.

37. For, although it may be laudable to strive to overcome resentment toward others in our private lives, we stretch the bonds of ordinary human sentiment too far in seeking to extend such generosity to those with whom we lack sustained emotional contact and whose values seem alien to our own. Moreover, it may be too intrusive, given the difficulty of properly discerning how people feel in the public sphere, for political forgiveness to require a change of heart in the person wronged.

38. Kant, for instance, was "suspicious of philanthropy, mercy and forgiveness in their efforts to limit justice." While "fellow feeling is a duty" for Kant, he insists that it "should not be allowed to dilute the demands of morality and justice" (Booth 2001: 783).

39. Jacques Derrida, *On Cosmopolitanism and Forgiveness* (London and New York: Routledge, 2001). Derrida departs fundamentally from Arendt in understanding forgiveness as entirely extraneous to politics; see p. 59f. However, while real enough, this departure is based in part on a misunderstanding since Arendt does not equate politics with a juridical order as Derrida implies but similarly seeks to articulate forgiveness in relation to the ideal of non-sovereign freedom.

40. Derrida, *On Cosmopolitanism and Forgiveness*, 34–35—emphases in the original. I think Derrida overstates this paradox by identifying unconditional forgiveness with the unforgivable rather than simply the undeservingness of those who need forgiveness. But the paradox remains real nonetheless. For critical discussions of Derrida's essay see Claire Moon, "Prelapsarian State" and Ernesto Verdeja "Derrida and the Impossibility of Forgiveness."

41. Digeser, *Political Forgiveness*, 43–55; 186–191.
42. Ibid., 55–59.
43. As Brad Roth observes, "Reconciliation cannot always presuppose or await a shared moral understanding; frequently enough, it requires an agreement to disagree, even about fundamental principles," Roth, "Peaceful Transition and Retrospective Justice: Some Reservations," 46.
44. Arendt, *The Human Condition*, 237.
45. Ibid., 237.
46. Hieronymi, "Articulating an Uncompromising Forgiveness," 546.
47. Arendt, *The Human Condition*, 241.
48. Hieronymi, "Articulating and Uncompromising Forgiveness," 550.
49. Jean Hampton, "The Retributive Idea" in Murphy and Hampton (eds.), *Forgiveness and Mercy*, 129; see also Herbert Morris, *On Guilt and Innocence: Essays in Legal Philosophy and Moral Psychology* (Berkeley, CA.: University of California Press, 1976), 126–127.
50. Memmi, *The Colonizer and the Colonized*, 109. In refusing colonialism, the colonizer lives the contradiction of renouncing its values while benefiting from its privileges. Yet in accepting colonialism, he accepts himself as a "non-legitimate privileged person . . . a usurper" and thus accepts the "blame implied by that role"; Memmi, *The Colonizer and the Colonized*, 118, 117. In seeking to legitimate his position he is driven to demonstrate his superiority further and so only depends upon his guilt.
51. For an analysis of Arendt's (and Jasper's) work on collective responsibility and its significance for political reconciliation see Andrew Schaap, "Guilty Subjects and Political Responsibility: Jaspers, Arendt and the Resonance of the 'German question' in Politics of Reconciliation," *Political Studies*, 49, no. 4 (2001): 749–766. For a more recent articulation of an Arendtian account of political responsibility in contrast to that suggested by Giorgio Agamben see my "Assuming Responsibility in the Hope of Reconciliation," *borderlands e-journal* 3, 1 (2004), http://www.borderlandsejournal.adelaide.edu.au/issues/vol3no1.html.
52. Elshtain, "Politics and Forgiveness," 43.
53. I am indebted to Zenon Bankowski for pointing out how forgiving sometimes involves suspending judgment. I think this is what Arendt is getting at when she looks for nontheological terms for forgiveness as dismissing or releasing the other. Similarly, she prefers trespassing, missing, failing and going astray to "sinning" and changing one's mind, returning, retracing one's steps to "repenting"; Arendt, *The Human Condition*, 240, n. 78.
54. See Hannah Arendt, *Lectures on Kant's Political Philosophy*, ed. and with an interpretive essay by Ronald Beiner (Chicago, IL.: University of Chicago Press, 1982), 22–27.
55. See especially Arendt, *The Human Condition*, 50–57.

56. Hannah Arendt, *Men in Dark Times* (New York and London: Harcourt Brace and Co., 1968), 81.
57. Bert van Roermund, "Rubbing Off and Rubbing On: The Grammar of Reconciliation," in E. Christodoulidis and S. Veitch (eds.), *Lethe's Law: Justice, Law and Ethics in Reconciliation* (Oxford & Portland, OR.: Hart Publishing, 2001), 182–183.
58. Van Roermund, "Rubbing Off and Rubbing On," 183.
59. Arendt, *Men in Dark Times*, 248.
60. See Graham Little, *The Public Emotions* (Sydney: ABC Books, 1999), 194–196.
61. Arendt, *The Human Condition*, 241.
62. In their introduction to Derrida's essay, Simon Critchley and Richard Kearney write that Derridean politics involves the "negotiation between the unconditional and the conditional, between the absolute and the relative, between the universal and the particular"; Derrida, *On Cosmopolitanism and Forgiveness*, xi. Indeed, Derrida (p. 45, emphasis in original) writes that it is "between these two poles [the conditional and the unconditional], *irreconcilable but indissociable*, that decisions and responsibilities are to be taken." Insofar as Derrida does conceive political forgiveness in these terms, he comes close to the Arendtian conception of forgiveness defended here. However, as Ernesto Verdeja points out, Derrida privileges the unconditional and disparages the conditional throughout his essay, in opposing a forgiveness based on pure love to one conceived in relation to the fallen realm of politics; Verdeja, "Derrida and the Impossibility of Forgiveness," 27–28. Following Arendt, by contrast, the demand to forgive derives from a love that transcends the political realm not from a juridical order on which politics is predicated. Rather, politics and political forgiveness, are undertaken in what Gillian Rose calls the "broken middle" between law and love, without privileging one over the other but constantly negotiating their competing demands according to the circumstances of action; see Zenon Bankowski, "Remorse and Reconciliation," paper presented at the colloquium on *Law, Time and Reconciliation*, Centre for Law and Society, University of Edinburgh, May 15–16, 2002.
63. Van Roermund, "Never Again."
64. Hannah Arendt, *Eichmann in Jerusalem: A Report on the Banality of Evil* (New York: Penguin Books, 1977), 5f.
65. Pablo de Grief, "Trial and Punishment: Pardon and Oblivion," *Philosophy and Social Criticism*, 22, no. 3 (1996): 105.
66. Van Roermund, "Rubbing Off and Rubbing On," 178.
67. Hampton, "The Retributive Idea," 134.
68. Desmond Tutu, *No Future Without Forgiveness* (New York: Doubleday, 1999).
69. Cited in Johnny de Lange, "The Historical Context, Legal Origins and Philosophical Foundations of the South African Truth and

Reconciliation Commission," in C. Villa-Vicencio and W. Verwoerd (eds.), *Looking Back Reaching Forward: Reflections on the Truth and Reconciliation Commission of South Africa* (London: Zed Books, 2000), 21. The indigenous concept of *ubuntu* (according to which people should be friendly, hospitable, magnanimous, compassionate, open, and non-envious) was often referred to in South Africa to lend further legitimacy to the Christian ideal of reconciliation.

70. Crocker distinguishes retribution from revenge on six grounds: (1) retribution addresses a wrong whereas we may seek revenge on our enemy in response to a slight or unintended injury; (2) retribution is constrained, proportionate to the wrong perpetrated, whereas revenge tends to be insatiable, limited neither by prudence nor a sense of just desert; (3) retribution is impersonal and impartial, imposed by a third party, whereas revenge is sought directly by an interested party who is aggrieved by the wrong; (4) retribution takes no satisfaction in seeing the other brought low (beyond the pleasure of seeing justice done) whereas revenge is "sweet"; (5) retribution is principled—it is committed to upholding a general rule or norm rather than being a response only to this particular injury; (6) retribution rejects collective guilt—it can only be dealt to individuals who are directly responsible for their own actions (or inactions). By contrast, a vengeful attitude tends to impute blame collectively and we may exact revenge on an enemy by harming his (innocent) fellow group members; David Crocker, "Retribution and Reconciliation," Institute for Philosophy and Public Policy, University of Maryland, Winter–Spring Report 2000, Available http://www.puaf.umd.edu/IPPP/Winter-Spring00/ (accessed June 30, 2004).

71. Christopher Bennett "Is amnesty a collective act of forgiveness?" *Contemporary Political Theory*, 2, no. 1 (2003): 67–76.

72. Christopher Bennett "The Varieties of Retributive Experience," *The Philosophical Quarterly*, 52, no. 207 (2002): 145–163.

73. Van Roermund, "Rubbing Off and Rubbing On," 179–183.

74. Scott Veitch, "The Legal Politics of Amnesty," in Christodoulidis and Veitch (eds.), *Lethe's Law*, 39.

75. Veitch, "The Legal Politics of Amnesty," 40.

76. Elshtain, "Politics and Forgiveness," 53.

77. Arendt, *The Human Condition*, 246.

78. Hannah Arendt, *On Revolution* (New York: Penguin Books, 1990), 188.

79. Jacques Taminaux, "Athens and Rome," in Dana Villa (ed.), *The Cambridge Companion to Hannah Arendt* (Cambridge: Cambridge University Press, 2000), 176.

80. Arendt cited in Taminaux, "Athens and Rome," 177. Indeed, the *res publica* was itself the outcome of war between the patricians and plebeians, "whose internal strife was concluded through the famous laws of the Twelve Tables" (OR: 188). Moreover, the foundation

myth of Rome was based on Virgil's reversal of the Homeric epic of the sacking of Troy according to which the "end of the war is not victory and departure for one side, extermination and slavery and utter destruction for the others, but 'both nations, unconquered, join treaty forever under equal laws' [Virgil] and settle down together" (OR: 209).

81. See L. G. Feldman, "The Principle and Practice of 'Reconciliation' in German Foreign Policy: Relations with France, Israel, Poland and the Czech Republic," *International Affairs*, 75, no. 2 (1999): 333–356.
82. Crocker, "Transitional Justice and International Civil Society," 512.
83. Mendez, "National Reconciliation, Transitional Justice, and the International Criminal Court," 44.
84. Crocker, "Transitional Justice and International Civil Society," 513.
85. Roth, "Peaceful Transition and Retrospective Justice: Some Reservations," 48.

CHAPTER 5

HANNAH ARENDT AND "THE RIGHT TO HAVE RIGHTS"

Bridget Cotter

The importance of the issue of human rights has increased greatly in international relations since the end of the Cold War, and refugees have often been at the center of debate, concern, and action. The response to perceived refugee crises is indicative of important elements of these wider debates about human rights and their place in an international system that remains based around the sovereign state. Indeed, in places such as Bosnia and Kosovo the creation of large numbers of refugees through the forced expulsion of populations has proved a catalyst for and focus of diplomatic and military action by coalitions of states. However, while willing to express their condemnation for policies that create refugees, the political debate in many states, including those Western states ostensibly most closely linked to the ideal of human rights, has highlighted contradictions, conflicts, and tensions.

Hannah Arendt's writings on refugees and statelessness have often been neglected by Arendt scholars and are largely unknown to the world of contemporary literature on refugees. As with most subjects that she addressed, her main value and usefulness as a theorist lies in her ability to expose with adeptness and clarity the contradictions and tensions within and among the principles and practices of Western modernity. She was less focused on proposing solutions. Instead, she tended to issue warnings against neglect and to encourage vigilance of protective political institutions. Such vigilance was a key characteristic of the active citizenship that Arendt so admired. Today, when the question of refugees and asylum are hot topics on all Western political agendas, political analysts are expected to come up with precise solutions. However, despite Arendt's failure to do so, her work is still relevant in helping us to understand the experience of the refugees and the challenges they pose to modern democratic states. As a former refugee herself, Arendt was able to evoke with painful clarity a picture of the peculiar existential and physical sufferings of the refugee. As a political theorist, her analysis exposes the contradictions and tensions within the liberal democratic project that are thrown into stark relief by the existence of refugees.

For Arendt, refugees were the "most symptomatic group in contemporary politics."[1] While totalitarian regimes have done the most to produce the uprootedness and misery of the refugee, in Arendt's opinion, the existence of refugees also exposes several conflicts and contradictions of the European liberal democratic nation-state. The primary conflict is between the liberal democratic commitment to universal individual rights, on the one hand, and the claim of the liberal democratic state to national sovereignty, on the other. National sovereignty has negative consequences for the rights of man, and, for a number of reasons, the situation of refugees is symbolic of these consequences. Thus, Arendt's work on refugees and statelessness identifies both philosophical and practical problems that lie at the heart of liberal democratic theory and practice. It is through the experience of those who lack rights, whose social and legal status is marginal or nonexistent, that we can see the contradictions and failures of current thought and practice.

We can begin with some definitions. For Arendt, a refugee is someone who has been expelled from his country and who has thereby been deprived of citizen's rights. While most clear-cut in the case of those ordered from their state by their government, it is also necessary to include those who have been "constructively expelled" by the pursuit of policies or the creation of a political climate that makes it impossible to enjoy the normal rights of citizenship and that engenders a fear of persecution. For Arendt, there was no useful distinction between refugees and stateless persons because, while refugees may not be de jure stateless, they were de facto stateless.[2]

Arendt also points to two defining and conflicting features of the rights of man. First, they were established during the American and French Revolutions, which means that, while an idea of natural universal rights is much older, they were only practically realized in the context of two struggles that were *national* in character. Second, and in spite of this, they were declared and are still seen as natural, inalienable, and universal. And yet all over the world, they can only be enforced within states that agree to enforce them, and usually only for citizen-members. The rights of citizens are exclusive and conditional since they only apply to those who legally belong to a nation-state. If the rights of man truly existed, says Arendt, they would be available to everyone *without conditions* by virtue of membership in the human race.[3]

A third definitional issue concerns "national sovereignty." For Arendt, this refers to two separate principles, although she does not always clearly distinguish between them. First, it is "state sovereignty" which is located in the global state system, with its origins in the Treaty of Westphalia, in which each state has absolute jurisdiction within its own borders and only within them. Second, "national sovereignty" also refers to "people's sovereignty," which consists in the democratic right of a citizenry to self-determination. These may appear to be the same in the normal running of the liberal democratic state. However, they are separable since a state can be sovereign but not democratic. In addition, there are several important ways in which people's sovereignty is thwarted by state sovereignty, for example, in issues related to national security. For Arendt, both have negative consequences for the full realization of the rights of man.

State sovereignty has two such consequences, both of which are made obvious by the existence of refugees. First, the rights of man cannot be enforced outside the state. As Edmund Burke argued after the French Revolution, the rights of man are mere "abstract principles" which de facto do not exist. Burke's preference for the "Rights of Englishmen" established the exclusive rights of nationals as nationals rather than the universal rights of man as man or as citizen in general because without legal membership in a state, individuals have nothing to protect their rights.[4] Even French republicanism with its proclaimed commitment to cosmopolitanism and universal citizenship could not guarantee the universal rights of man. The French Declaration of the Rights of Men and Citizens could really only guarantee the rights of men who were citizens. So, says Arendt, the guiding principle of the nation-state is not that everyone is born with inalienable rights, but that "every individual is born with inalienable rights guaranteed by his nationality."[5]

The conflict between state sovereignty and individual rights was exposed by the post–World War I emergence of refugees in large numbers, a trend that has recurred and accelerated in the wake of almost every major conflict since. The rights of man were "defined as 'inalienable' because they were supposed to be independent of all governments; but it turned out that the moment human beings lacked their own government and had to fall back upon their minimum rights, no authority was left to protect them and no institution was willing to guarantee them."[6] The refugees from Nazism found this out when, expelled from their homelands, they were only reluctantly accepted by other states, and then only temporarily, or not accepted at all. Their terrible plight proved that rights were, indeed, alienable from the person, so that the phrase "human rights" came to represent either "hopeless idealism or . . . feeble-minded hypocrisy."[7]

In classical liberal thought, civil laws are supposed to rest on the natural laws and rights, but, in fact, the rights of man—which were seen by classical liberal theorists as natural rights—are dependent on civil law, says Arendt. While the duty to obey civil law is imposed on noncitizens, they can still be actively excluded from the rights and protections that the state affords its citizens. That the rights of man are only safe within a state is proven by the fact that to become a refugee is to become a charity case. "Neither physical safety . . . nor freedom of opinion changes their fundamental situation of rightlessness. The prolongation of their lives is due to charity and not to right, for no law exists which could force the nations to feed them; their freedom of movement, if they have it at all, gives them no right to residence which even jailed criminals enjoy as a matter of course; and their freedom of opinion is a fool's freedom, for nothing they think matters anyhow."[8]

The second negative consequence of state sovereignty stems from the state's right to restrict membership. This effectively means that states have the right to deny citizenship (and all rights that accompany it) to any individual or category of people and to turn away the refugees of other states. Regardless of whether the right to exclude is a right in state law, international law, or no law at all, and regardless of whether states choose to exercise it (as the Nazis did in the 1930s and 1940s, Idi Amin's Uganda did in the 1970s and the Serbs and Croats did in the 1990s), this state's right is implied by the principle of national sovereignty. Arendt refers to this right to restrict membership as "the sovereign right of expulsion."[9] "Theoretically, in the sphere of international law, it had always been true," Arendt states "that sovereignty is nowhere more absolute than in matters of 'emigration, naturalization, nationality, and expulsion'. . ."[10] The fact that the state has the right to exclude people from rights is at odds with the universalism and inalienability of the rights of man upon which the liberal democratic state and its laws are founded. The difficulty that refugees have in claiming their rights demonstrates this contradiction between state sovereignty and human rights.

While the "international community," since the 1950s, objects on moral grounds to the state's denial of rights to its own citizens and enshrines such objections in its guidelines and declarations, on only a handful of occasions—even since Arendt died—has it seen fit to recognize these guidelines as laws that should be enforced, by, for example, trying war criminals. The current case of Milošević is instructive in that he argues (as did many of those who objected to military intervention against Yugoslavia in Kosovo) that no state had the right to intervene in the affairs of Yugoslavia because the Kosovan conflict was a civil war, not an invasion by a foreign country. This argument continues to hold water with many.

In Europe, there is a history of putting this right of exclusion into practice, in spite of a professed commitment to individual rights. Arendt notes several examples from before World War II. Germany, for example, began a raft of denationalizing measures in 1933 with one that gave the state the right to denationalize any nationals living abroad (which later became automatic for Jews, including those forcibly transported to Poland). In this, they followed Russia's 1921 measures to denationalize defectors. In the interwar years, most European countries passed laws that would allow them to get rid of sections of the population—even if they did not use the laws.[11] Many of these were wartime measures, such as a French statute in 1915 that allowed the government to deport "naturalized citizens of enemy origin who retained their original nationality," and a Portuguese decree in 1916 that "automatically denaturalised all persons born of a German father." Others gave the state the right to cancel the "naturalization of persons who had committed anti-national acts during the war" (Belgium in 1922 and 1934) and "persons not worthy of Italian citizenship" (1926).[12] In the postwar years, Arendt states that the United States was even considering depriving of citizenship those U.S.-born Americans who were communists.[13]

After World War II, the European Convention on Human Rights (1949) and the Geneva Convention of 1951 have both attempted to enshrine protection for those refugees fleeing persecution and seeking asylum, suggesting the centrality of the plight of refugees to the human rights project. Since the end of the Cold War even greater attention and weight have been given to the principle and enforcement of human rights. Despite measures such as the International Criminal Court, and war crimes tribunals (following conflicts in Yugoslavia and Rwanda), there are, however, still countries willing to use their sovereign right to expel and persecute their citizens.

Serious human rights abuses aside, it must also be remembered that even democracies restrict and erode citizen's civil rights (which are based on the idea of human rights) on the grounds of national security. Under the rule of national sovereignty, they have a perfect right to do so. In the post-9/11 world, Western states are also increasingly exercising their right to exclude, in the name of national security, and are continuing to privilege state sovereignty and security over human rights.

All of this shows that, in practice, the rights of man are neither inalienable nor universal and that the principle of state sovereignty can be used to deny individual rights and to produce refugees. The full realization of human rights is not possible both because of and in spite of state sovereignty. The relationship between state rights and human rights is simultaneously one of conflict and of dependence (of the latter on the former), and refugees are the manifestation of this conflict-ridden, but dependent, relationship.

While it is not surprising that the interests of the state come into conflict with those of the individual, it is perhaps more perplexing that the democratic principle of people's sovereignty should also interfere with the rights of man, since together they form the basis of liberal democratic principles. However, Arendt notes that they do conflict in two important ways. First, the sovereignty of the people conflicts with the sovereignty of the individual. Both principles were declared by the French revolution, but the sovereignty of the people won out.

The main reason for this, says Arendt, was that the principle of "sovereignty of the individual" was based upon an abstract individual. The French Declaration of the Rights of Men and Citizens marked a turning point in history because it deemed man rather than God's command or the hierarchies of historical custom to be the source of human law.[14] "Man himself was their [the rights of man's] source as well as their ultimate goal."[15] Because they were seen as "inalienable," no higher authority was needed. But because no authority above man himself was invoked the entire human rights project is predicated on the liberal notion of an abstract natural individual who does not really exist, "for even savages live in some kind of social order."[16]

People's sovereignty was also proclaimed in the name of man (rather than God or tradition), so it was, in theory, reducible to man's individual sovereignty. All civil laws were supposed to rest on the rights of man, making man in the abstract and man in general the "sovereign in matters of law." However, after the French Revolution, it became clear that the so-called inalienable rights of men could only find their guarantee in the collective rights of the people to sovereign self-government because the source of government was the people of a particular territory, not individually and generally but collectively and specifically.[17]

So, almost from the moment of their establishment, the rights of man became entangled with the right of the people to self-determination. Within the classical liberal argument, each has a sovereign right to rule himself, but because all are equal, all have this right. In a collective context, this means that all have the right to share power. As Rousseau asserts, since no individual could have sovereignty over another, individuals must share in government by pooling their sovereignty to avoid any one man dominating. Because of this social feature of individual lives, "The whole question of human rights . . . was quickly and inextricably blended with the question of national emancipation [because] only the emancipated sovereignty . . . of one's own people, seemed to be able to ensure them."[18]

This meant that, philosophically speaking, "man had hardly appeared as a completely emancipated, completely isolated being who carried his dignity within himself without reference to some larger encompassing order, when he disappeared again into a member of a people."[19] Thus, in the nation-state system, it was man as a member of "the people" and not individual man upon whom rights were based. "The same essential rights were at once claimed as the inalienable heritage of all human beings *and* as the specific heritage of specific nations, the same nation was at once declared to be subject to laws, which would supposedly flow from the Rights of Man, *and* sovereign, that is, bound by no universal law and acknowledging nothing superior to itself."[20] This meant that "from then on human rights were protected and enforced only as national rights and that the very institution of a state, whose supreme task was to protect and guarantee man his rights as man, as citizen and as national, lost its legal, rational appearance . . ."[21] The state became an instrument of "the nation" rather than a protector of the individual. This fact only really became clear when masses of people appeared right in the middle of Europe as refugees from Nazism who could not be protected by the state because they did not belong to "the people" of the state. Membership of a people was then the prerequisite for rights, and a "people" in Europe had to be a nation with a territorial state and some notion of shared origins. This enabled, then and now, the portrayal of refugees as a threat to national identity, to seek their exclusion on the grounds of difference and, where refugees had to be accepted, to make assimilation the standard for successfully dealing with the "problem."

The conflict between people's sovereignty and individual rights posed further problems for individual rights because of a second conflict between the state and the nation. The people had to become a sovereign nation in order to protect itself from a potentially tyrannical state. This meant that the will of the people took precedence over both the state and the individual. These developments would come to have a huge impact on members of minority groups within the state whose lack of belonging to the people of the nation threw their citizenship into doubt. In this way, ethnicity quickly became a prerequisite for full citizenship, giving minorities a marginal status, which was much easier to transform into "no status" at a later date.

Arendt writes at length on the problem of minorities. Her discussion is based on the historical case of the 1919 Minorities Treaties, but many of her observations are still relevant today. The 1919 Peace Treaties established new nation-states in Central Europe to replace the fallen Austro-Hungarian Empire. The arbiters of Peace wanted to maintain the nation-state format, so they tried to draw the new territorial boundaries along ethnic lines. But they did not pay enough attention to the existing demographic map. They lumped together people from several nationalities in a single state, then dubbed some " 'state people' and entrusted them with the government, silently [assuming] that others . . . were equal partners in government, . . . and with equal arbitrariness created out of the remnant a third group of nationalities call 'minorities'. . ."[22] for example, in Czechoslovakia, the Czechs were the state power, the Slovaks were wrongly seen as the equal partners, while Sudeten Germans were an official minority. Special regulations were invented to protect these official minorities.

For Arendt, this case demonstrated three existing assumptions about nation-states within Europe. First, they should be ethnically homogenous; second, there should be a perfect match between nationality and territory; third, popular sovereignty can only be attained within one's own state. All of these assumptions have led to a situation in which minorities are in a sense stateless because the state belongs to "the people." This makes minorities easier to make into stateless refugees. If the members of an ethnic minority became fully assimilated and completely divorced from their origins, it may have been an easier matter to include them in the nation and apply state laws to them, but before that point, a law of exception was needed to protect them. In any case, assimilation meant nothing to purists who believed nationality to be a natural and objective quality that could not be altered.

A possible solution to the problems arising from conflicts among the sovereignty of the people, the state, and the individual was a better international agreement. Arendt argues that the refugee's problems are exacerbated (or at least not alleviated) by the current international system whose principle is state sovereignty. Unlike most of her contemporaries, Hans Morgenthau included, Arendt did not see the international situation as akin to a Hobbesian state of nature, although it was often characterized by power politics. Instead, she argued that the mere existence of reasonably secure states is evidence of some kind of loose agreement and sense of solidarity among states. It is this mutual agreement and solidarity that prevents states from imposing refugees on each other most of the time. For, if a state were to exercise its sovereign right to expel, it would be impinging upon another state's sovereignty by trying to force it to take new residents. However, where a state's dominant "people" either abandon this sense of shared norms or come to see the presence of a minority as a fundamental threat to its political project and expel them, then the refugees' lot is made even worse by the unwillingness of other states to pay what can be perceived as the cost of the originating state's refusal to accept its obligations.

This argument hints at the way that Arendt does recognize that the principle of state sovereignty contains a self-limiting mechanism. She argues that there exists a basic paradox in the principle of state sovereignty. The latter relies on the agreement of an international community, which both protects and constrains sovereignty. The mass deportation and denationalizations of various European groups (Russians, Armenians, Hungarians, Germans, and Spaniards) during the 1920s and 1930s revealed "what had been hidden throughout the history of national sovereignty, that sovereignties of neighbouring countries" could come into conflict in times of peace as well as in war. "It now became clear that full national sovereignty was possible only as long as the comity of European nations existed; for it was this spirit of unorganised solidarity and agreement that prevented any government's exercise of its full sovereign power."[23]

Without cooperation and mutual respect, states would have no lasting security whatsoever. Simply declaring a state as sovereign and monopolizing violence within borders to protect it, does not alone prevent the risk of invasion. It is international cooperation and recognition that turns a theoretical state sovereignty into a reality. For what else really prevents one state from invading another if not at least a tacit agreement not to invade? Once states are matched in physical might, fear of losing cannot function as the only deterrent.

So, agreements make state sovereignty possible. But at the same time, agreements make the exercise of *full* sovereignty—"in matters of nationality and expulsion"[24]—less likely. In the "European comity of nations" before totalitarianism, "practical consideration and the silent acknowledgement of common interests [had always] restrained national sovereignty."[25] In the same way that the liberal state both limits and guarantees individual sovereignty, so do international agreements both limit and guarantee state sovereignty.

But these limits on state sovereignty stem from fear and respect and rely upon the continued commitment to mutual inviolability. Thus, as Arendt points out, the more totalitarian a state, the more willing it was to exercise its "sovereign right of denationalisation."[26] Because the sovereign right to expel can only be used if a government ceases to respect the sovereignty of other states, the implication of this argument is that the exercise of full sovereignty in matters of exclusion is at the same time a denigration of the principle of sovereignty because it impinges on the sovereignty of other states.

Arendt thus identifies four main weaknesses of the international system that prevent the solution of the refugee problem. First, as we've already seen, the system is unable or reluctant to enforce human rights because of the principle of state sovereignty. Second, the modern refugee's displacement is made more permanent and insurmountable by the comprehensiveness of the nation-state system; there is no legal status left for the stateless person because there is nowhere else to go. The "new global political situation" in which we live in "One World," says Arendt, means that it is possible for millions of people to lose and not be able to regain the "right to belong to some kind of organized community . . ."[27] Becoming a stateless refugee means that the loss of the protection of one's own government leads to the loss of legal status in all countries. "Treaties of reciprocity and international agreements have woven a web around the earth that makes it possible for the citizen of every country to take his legal status with him no matter where he goes . . ." By the same token, the stateless person carries her political non-status with her wherever she goes. Because there is no longer a "no-man's land" into which a group or individual can escape, refugees cannot just go elsewhere and set up a new community. Only a state can provide the basic needs of a home and protection from harm, and without a state the refugee finds himself excluded from the family of nations altogether.

Third, the traditional solutions for the second problem have been naturalization and the right of asylum, but—again, because of the principle of state sovereignty—states cannot be forced to use these.

In addition, both are principles designed for individual exceptions, to allow states to apply the law of nationals to all its residents. But in an age of mass refugee movements, states are unwilling and unable to cope with numbers too large to be called exceptions.

For Arendt, the right of asylum was "the only right that ever figured as a symbol of the Rights of Man in the sphere of international relations." And just as the rights of man conflict with state sovereignty, the right of asylum is "in conflict with the international rights of the state."[28] In addition, the old asylum system, which had a history reaching back to the ancient city-states, worked for individual refugees who could be absorbed (and perhaps assimilated) into the body of the nation-state. Since ancient times, Arendt notes, the right of asylum functioned as protection both for refugees and the countries of refuge. It gave a status to the persecuted noncitizen who would otherwise be an outlaw, protecting the country of refuge from lawlessness and persons desperate enough to resort to crime. But the Peace Treaties of World War I, which created masses of refugees and stateless persons, began to lead to the erosion of the right of asylum.

In the contemporary world, a fear of large-scale "economic migration" and a perception that the asylum system is being "abused" by those searching for a materially more comfortable life, rather than fleeing persecution, exercises most of the governments of the industrialized world. Asylum and immigration are in danger of becoming further confused, with defense of the state's sovereign power to control immigration issues overtaking its obligation under international law and custom to offer even minimal protection to refugees. Since 9/11, antiterrorism laws have intersected with asylum laws. The popular press in Western countries such as the United Kingdom frequently equate refugees with crime or terrorism. Governments do little to dispel such impressions by repeatedly assuring the public that they are doing their best to control the asylum problem.

For Arendt, the importance of state sovereignty made the right of asylum problematic for states from the outset because state sovereignty is meant to apply to nationals even when they are outside their states (for example the United States extends the duty to pay income tax even to citizens living and working abroad). Strictly speaking then, it is an infringement on state sovereignty to give asylum to the citizen of another state. Under exceptional circumstances this was not such a problem. The right of asylum was also meant only for political refugees whose situation was seen as highly exceptional. It was meant to offer solace to individuals persecuted for political views and actions (the same criteria that would later be enshrined in the Geneva Conventions), not for vast numbers of people who were persecuted for reasons that had nothing to do with their own actions and opinions, but stemmed simply from their being Jewish, or Albanian or Roma or Tutsi.[29]

Arendt points out that the erosion of the right to asylum was further proven by the fact that, although it still existed as an ideal in the spirit of liberal democracy, it was not enshrined in the laws of any particular state, or in any international law as part of the post–World War I settlement. Even the Covenant of the League of Nations did not include it as a responsibility of member states. Because state sovereignty was the dominant principle in international relations, it remained the state's right to refuse entry and solace to foreigners.[30] The so-called right of asylum, therefore, carried an informal, nonlegal status. Arendt points out that it shared this fate in common with "the Rights of Man, which also never became law but led a somewhat shadowy existence as an appeal in individual exceptional cases for which normal legal institutions did not suffice."[31]

While the 1951 Geneva Conventions did establish a legal basis for asylum, the difficulty of naturalizing, assimilating, or repatriating refugees combined with the comprehensiveness of the nation-state system has led governments to find or construct places with a peculiarly "in-between" status, neither wholly in one state or another. These include refugee reception centers and waiting areas, asylum-seekers' detention centers, and the back rooms of immigration offices in airports. The most extreme recent case of this attempt by a state to avoid the responsibility of reception and later repatriation[32] is the Australian government's internment camp for asylum seekers on the island of Naaru. Arendt points out that because refugees could not be assimilated and the states didn't want them, "the only practical solution for a non-existent homeland was an internment camp,"[33] and from the World War II they became "the routine solution for the problem of domicile of the 'displaced persons.' "[34]

Arendt noted that a group made systematically "undesirable" in one country were more likely to be undesirable everywhere because of their impoverishment and lack of political status. "Once they had left their homeland they remained homeless, once they had left their state they became stateless; once they had been deprived of their human rights they were rightless, the scum of the earth . . ."[35] This is particularly the case if the minority is a majority in no state, like Jews and Armenians in the 1940s, the Kurds and Palestinians now, and the Roma in all ages. Arendt argues that the Nazis were so convinced of this principle that they used it as a strategy to spread anti-Semitism across Europe. Arendt quotes a Nazi source who in 1938 stated that, "if the world was not yet convinced that the Jews were the scum of the earth, it soon would be when unidentifiable beggars, without nationality, without money, and without passports crossed their frontiers."[36]

Fourth, there is no supranational law—only inter-state laws and treaties and guidelines. The UN's Universal Declaration of Human Rights (1948) was supposed to change the fact that only the state could guarantee and protect rights. Its creation represented a recognition that not all states could be trusted to recognize and guarantee the rights to life and freedom from coercion of their inhabitants. The UN's Charter also makes mention of the organization's commitment to human rights, in articles 55 and 56 in particular. But even in Arendt's time, as she argues, no one took the Rights of Man seriously. Although outlined in the Universal Declaration of Human Rights, they did not constitute law. While Charter articles have greater force in this regard, these were left to languish in terms of attracting the concerted attention of an organization, and a membership, focused upon the twin issues of decolonization and the cold war. Rather, they were guidelines upon which the civil laws of states are meant to rest. This is because the Rights of Man "had never been philosophically established but merely formulated, . . . never . . . politically secured but merely proclaimed. . . ." As such, they "have, in their traditional form, lost all validity."[37]

The strategic context of the Cold War, where the too active pursuit of human rights by those states ostensibly predicated upon them could have led to World War III, doubtless carries some of the burden here, but Arendt's point retains much of its force. Even in post–Cold War circumstances such as Rwanda, with no overwhelming geostrategic risks present, it appeared that the rhetoric of the rights of man was useless in the face of genocide. Indeed, Rwanda arguably demonstrated the weakness of international legal efforts to make meaningful, via legal institutionalization, notions of rights. The Genocide Convention is perhaps uniquely clear in establishing an obligation upon states to take action, an obligation the U.S. government sought to avoid by banning its officials from using the word "genocide" to describe events in Rwanda.

However, there was also a problem with the way human rights were formulated. Arendt argued that all attempts so far to define the universal rights of man have only succeeded in reiterating the legal rights of citizens. For Arendt, human rights are only those that cannot be protected by the state. The right of asylum is such a right, but, as we have seen, it is ineffective because it only applies to exceptional cases and because it (like all other human rights) relies on governments (who receive refugees) for its enforcement. Arendt's solution to the problem of statelessness was to create a supranational law that would only consist of one human right: the right to belong to a political community. "We became aware of the existence of a right to have rights . . . and a right to belong to some kind of organized community, only when millions of people emerged who had lost and could not regain these rights . . ."[38]

With the loss of a divine law, there was no higher moral law upon which to base rights. So, on what philosophical foundation can we base the rights of man? Arendt rejects both pragmatic and utilitarian solutions. As we saw earlier, eighteenth-century liberal rights were based on the " 'nature' of man," whether this came from natural law or divine command.[39] Natural rights would then exist even if there were only one man, and are therefore "independent of human plurality." However, in the twentieth century, nature was replaced by the idea of "humanity." The concept of mankind existed in the eighteenth-century notion of natural rights, but it "was no more than a regulative idea." Due to modern travel and communication technologies, increased global economic interdependence, and the possibility of mass destruction through nuclear weapons, the concept of mankind has now become a reality. So, humanity is now the basis on which to guarantee human rights, Arendt argues, but there is still no law of humanity. There is only inter-state law, a collection of "reciprocal agreements and treaties between sovereign states". A "sphere that is above nations does not exist."[40]

Neither would a world government solve the insurmountable problem of finding a universal moral law on which to base human rights. Like the Nazi government, a world government could also define what is right by what is good for "the people"—even if "the people" now meant the whole of humanity. Once we lost our absolutes, our standards that transcend us, we lost all authority. After that—as we saw in the nineteenth-century ideas, including utilitarianism—it became "inevitable that we would believe that what is 'right' is the same as what is 'good for'—good for the individual, for the family, or the people, or the largest number." Even "if the unit to which the 'good for' applies is as large as mankind itself . . . it is quite conceivable [and practically possible], that one fine day a highly organized and mechanized humanity will conclude quite democratically that for humanity as a whole it would be better to liquidate certain parts thereof."[41]

The only possible solution, then, is a new international agreement to create a supranational law. Agreements are only possible and, indeed, only necessary because of the human condition of plurality. Arendt concludes: "The concept of human rights can again be meaningful only if they are redefined as a right to the human condition itself, which depends upon belonging to some human community, the right never to be dependent upon some inborn human dignity which de facto, aside from its guarantee by fellow-men . . . does not exist . . ."[42] Such an agreement was absolutely essential in order to prevent the loss of the right to have rights. For, the contradiction within the formulation of human rights and the difficulties of enforcement meant that being a refugee constitutes an expulsion from humanity. Stateless refugees retain both life and even liberty in theory, but without a political context, they have no rights to these or any other aspects of the human condition. Whether or not they belong to a particular community is no longer a choice for them. They are deprived of the right to contribute anything to the world in any way. The "right to have rights . . . means to live in a framework where one is judged by one's actions and opinions."[43] A refugee by contrast is judged by his status within the laws of the receiving country—to be an "illegal alien," an "economic migrant," a "bogus asylum-seeker" or, if lucky, a "genuine" refugee.

By contrast, the concept of man upon which human rights have been based is man stripped of all worldly attributes; it is man in abstract nakedness. No one would want to be such a man as he represents a state of utter vulnerability.[44] To be stripped of citizenship is to be stripped of worldliness; it is like returning to a wilderness as cavemen or savages. "[A] man who is nothing but a man has lost the very qualities which make it possible for other people to treat him as a fellow-man."[45] Rightless people are "thrown back into a peculiar state of nature." It is peculiar because they are civilized, often well-educated people, but they have lost "all those parts of the world and all those aspects of human existence which are the result of our common labor . . . ," the outcome of the human artifice. They could "live and die without leaving any trace, without having contributed anything to a common world. . . ."[46]

Arendt describes what she and other refugees of Nazi Germany had lost by being forced to leave their homes: "We lost our home, which means the familiarity of daily life. We lost our occupation, which means the confidence that we are of some use in the world. We lost our language, which means the naturalness of reactions, the simplicity of gestures, the unaffected expression of our feelings. We left our relatives in the Polish ghettos and our best friends have been killed in concentration camps, and that means the rupture of our private lives."[47] The loss of a private place in the world, of their elementary usefulness to society, of their ability to participate in speech (and thus politics) came about through the loss of the right to belong to the place and community in which they had lived and, with it, their "right to have rights." With the loss of citizenship, one becomes a "human being in general" with no home, no occupation, no ability to have an impact on the world through speech and action.[48] Those who are fundamentally rightless are deprived "of a place in the world which makes opinions significant and actions effective."[49] "Only with a completely organized humanity could the loss of home and political status become identical with expulsion from humanity altogether."[50]

Thus, without citizenship one loses fundamental characteristics of the human condition: "the relevance of speech . . . and the loss of all human relationships."[51] Since Aristotle, these are seen as fundamental to human existence. Even a tyrant has difficulty taking away this social context. The only way to remove the conditions of human existence from living people is through expulsion from a political community—either through slavery where one is not considered human, or through exile. But even slaves are allowed to contribute something to the world through labour and to have a place in society (though not in politics). "Not the loss of specific rights then, but the right of a community willing and able to guarantee any rights whatsoever . . ." is what the stateless have lost. "Man, it turns out, can lose all so-called Rights of Man without losing his essential quality as man, his human dignity. Only the loss of a polity itself expels him from humanity."[52]

Attempts such as the Universal Declaration of Human Rights merely reiterated citizens' rights, which should, according to Arendt be properly defended by the state or "defended by citizens, organized in nations or in parties."[53] This is because rights only have meaning within a social context. As Arendt points out, refugees do not necessarily lose their right to free speech or association; they lose the context in which these things have meaning. Therefore, Arendt declares: "The only human right is the right to citizenship," that is, the right to belong legally to a state and have one's human status (and all that that implies) be guaranteed by its laws.

Arendt does not solve the many problems she raises. She does not deal with how to ensure that states obey the supranational law. Instead, she settles for a nod toward a concerted international agreement, suggesting a new supranational law and international court, springing from a loose, federated international system. But she does not discuss these in detail. Nor does she discuss in any depth the impact of inequalities among states. Indeed, this last omission points to a weakness in her thinking. For, just as individual citizens of a state need to come to the political sphere as equals, surely states constructing supranational agreements must do the same.

But the part of her argument that endures is this. First, refugees are the anomalies in the current political paradigm and, as such, they challenge the effectiveness of current political thought and practice. Second, we need to recognize that rights are conventions, the product of collective agreements, and, thus, part of the human artifice. That rights rely on human agreement and not on natural rights indicates the inherent fragility of all rights and of any product of human agreement; it also indicates the grave responsibility we all have to establish and maintain such an agreement. Finally, Arendt leaves us with a question whose relevance is increasing in recent years: is there such a thing as a right to belong? And if so, should we have a choice of where we belong and to what?

NOTES

1. Arendt, *The Origins of Totalitarianism* (London: Andre Deutsch, 1986), 277. Hereafter referred to as OT.
2. Ibid., 281. Arendt quotes Simpson approvingly, "all refugees are for practical purposes stateless." (ibid., 281, n. 28.).
3. Ibid., 288, n. 44a.
4. Ibid., 175.
5. Ibid., 288, n. 44a.
6. Ibid., 292.
7. Ibid., 269.
8. Ibid., 296.
9. Ibid., 283.
10. Arendt quotes Lawrence Preuss (1937), in OT, 278.
11. Ibid., 278–279.
12. Ibid., 279, n. 25.
13. Ibid., 280.
14. Ibid., 290.
15. Ibid., 291.
16. OT2, 291.
17. Ibid.
18. Ibid.
19. Ibid.
20. Ibid., 230 (emphasis in original).

21. Ibid., 230–231.
22. Ibid., 270.
23. Ibid., 278.
24. Ibid., 286.
25. Ibid., 278.
26. OT2, 278.
27. Ibid., 297.
28. Ibid., 280.
29. Ibid., 281, n. 27.
30. Ibid., 280.
31. Ibid., 280–281.
32. In some cases repatriation cannot be effected because asylum seekers have no passports and refuse to say where they are from.
33. OT, 1986, 284.
34. Ibid., 279.
35. Ibid., 267.
36. Ibid., 269.
37. OT3, 145.
38. Ibid., 295–296.
39. OT, 297.
40. Ibid., 298.
41. Ibid., 299.
42. Arendt, *The Burden of Our Times*, the first British edition of OT, 436.
43. Ibid., 296–297.
44. Ibid., 299.
45. Ibid., 300.
46. Ibid.
47. Arendt, "We Refugees," *The Menorah Journal*, XXXI (January 1943): 69.
48. OT, 1986, 302.
49. OT2, 297.
50. Ibid., 297.
51. Ibid.
52. OT, 1986, 302.
53. Arendt, *The Burden of Our Times*, 436.

CHAPTER 6

HANNAH ARENDT'S CRITICAL
REALISM: POWER, JUSTICE, AND
RESPONSIBILITY

Douglas Klusmeyer

Passionate interest in international affairs in which no risk and no responsibility are involved has often been a cloak to hide down-to-earth national interests; in politics, idealism is frequently no more than an excuse for not recognizing unpleasant realities. Idealism can be a form of evading reality altogether . . .

           Hannah Arendt, *Crises of the Republic*

In the intellectual sense as in the demographic sense, we are either a cosmopolitan nation, part of the world stream of thought and feeling, or we are nothing at all. Smaller nations, weaker nations, nations less exposed by the very proportion of their physical weight in the world, might be able to get away with exclusiveness and provincialism and an intellectual remoteness from the feelings and preoccupations of mankind generally. Americans cannot. It will never be forgiven if we attempt to do it.

           George F. Kennan, *Realities of American Foreign Policy*

Institutions have the pathetic megalomania of the computer whose vision of the world is its own program. For us, the hope of intellectual independence is to resist, and the necessary first step in resistance is to discover how the institutional grip is laid upon our mind.

           Mary Douglas, *How Institutions Think*

INTRODUCTION: ARENDT, THE REALISTS, AND THE HOLOCAUST

By the end of World War II, Hannah Arendt recognized that the emergence of Nazi Germany and Stalinist Russia had introduced state-organized terror and mass murder on a scale that defied comprehension. The "actions" of these totalitarian regimes, she observed, "have clearly exploded our categories of political thought and our standards of moral judgment."[1] From his study of the twentieth century's experience with such phenomena, the historian Eric Weitz has recently observed: "Genocides stand at the center of our contemporary crisis."[2] His work joins those by many others, including Zygmunt Bauman, Norman Naimark, and Omer Bartov, who have been exploring "the crucial relationship between war, genocide, and modern identity."[3] In the examples used to explore this relationship, the Holocaust remains the central point of reference. Philosophers, such as Susan Neiman and Richard Bernstein, have identified Auschwitz as the exemplar of "evil" in the modern era and one that has created a watershed in the history of western moral thought.[4]

All of these works emphasize the distinctively modern character of these phenomena of state-sponsored mass violence in the twentieth century. As the historian Christopher Browning has pointed out about the Holocaust: "The Nazi mass murder of European Jewry was not only the technological achievement of an industrial society, but the also the organizational achievement of a bureaucratic society."[5] In seeking to grapple with this century's experience with genocide and "ethnic cleansing," all of these works build—directly or indirectly—upon the insights of Hannah Arendt. Between 1945 and 1949, she wrote her magnum opus, *The Origins of Totalitarianism* in order to make the "unprecedented" character of the Nazis' use of terror and genocide comprehensible to her contemporaries as well as to herself. To comprehend for her meant "the unpremeditated attentive facing up to, and resisting of, reality—whatever it may be."[6] In short, she aspired to be a critical realist.

Arendt's remarkable originality and acuity as an analyst of Nazi totalitarianism and the Holocaust is apparent when one contrasts her work on these issues with the American realists' summary approach to these same phenomena.[7] Writing much of their seminal work in the 1940s and 1950s, this first generation of American realists were bitter critics of the liberal internationalists of the interwar years. The brutal coming of World War II seemed to make clear the dangerous fallacy of the internationalist's faith in international institutions like the League of Nations and international covenants like the Kellog–Briand Pact of 1928. Against this background, American realists like Hans J. Morgenthau (1904–1980) and George F. Kennan (1904–2005) emphasized the role of power and the primacy of national interests in the rivalries among sovereign states. They were sharply critical of what Kennan described as "the legal-moralistic approach to international problems," but equally so of nationalistic egotism and an excessive reliance on military force.[8] Recent scholarship on realist thought has persuasively depicted many of them as chastened idealists who were animated by strong moral convictions and a deep commitment to the responsible use of power.[9] The leading realists are properly regarded as influential insiders of the American foreign policy establishment, but many also distinguished themselves, at the same time, as principled and sometimes strident critics of that establishment.

Although the second volume of *The Origins of Totalitarianism* focused on imperialism, Arendt (1906–1975) never devoted much sustained space in her published writings to the study of international relations per se. Nevertheless, her emphasis on the anarchy of the sovereign state system and her skepticism about the regulatory capacity of international law and institutions showed marked affinities with the American realists of her generation. She shared their impatience with the "fog of ideological, hypocritical talk" that obscures the reality that "violence is traditionally the *ultima ratio* in relations between nations . . ."[10] Against those in the postwar era who placed their faith in international institutions like the United Nations and the International Court of Justice, she insisted that "sovereignty means among other things, that conflicts of international character can ultimately be settled only by war, there is no other last resort."[11] At the same time, her deep skepticism toward idealism in foreign policy did not simply stem from its failures during the interwar years, but also in reaction against the "idealism" she had observed in the foreign policy of totalitarian states. This "idealism" she explained, derived from "their unwavering faith in an ideological fictitious world . . .," which helped to "introduce into international politics a new and more disturbing factor than mere aggressiveness would have been able to do."[12]

Arendt had been part of a large migration of European refugee intellectuals who had come to the United States to escape Nazi persecution. Their ideas and methods had a major influence on the development of the American realist approach to the study of international relations. Perhaps the most influential of these realists, Hans Morgenthau was, like Arendt, a German Jew, who arrived in the United States in 1937.

He became a loyal friend of Arendt, and stood by her during the public controversy over her book *Eichmann in Jerusalem*. Morgenthau provided an important bridge for the import of German political and philosophical ideas into American political thought, but not the only one. Born to first generation German immigrant parents, Reinhold Niebuhr's (1892–1971) first language was German.[13] George Kennan himself had lived five to six years in Germany at various times starting from childhood. He became fluent in German, and trained in Russian studies at the University of Berlin. Years later, he recalled that "intellectually and aesthetically, Germany had made a deep impression on me."[14] From this experience, he developed a personal sympathy for the German people, whom he described in his memoirs as "the first victim of Hitler's madness and who suffered undeservedly from the tragedy he brought down on the heads of all Germans alike."[15] Many Germans expressed similar views after the war, but in characterizing the German people as "victims" Kennan remained strangely silent in his *Memoirs* about the millions of Jews and other targets of Nazi violence.[16]

Because they shared many common assumptions about the character of the modern international state system, the sharp contrast between Arendt's focus on the Holocaust as a defining event of the twentieth century with the realists' comparative neglect of this same event is instructive. It illustrates fundamental differences in their approaches to power, justice, and global politics. At the core of these differences, Arendt saw the problems of power and justice as inseparable and interdependent, while realists like Kennan and Morgenthau concentrated on the role of power at the expense of the problem of justice. As Morgenthau explained his approach to international politics, "realism assumes that its key concept of interest defined as power is an objective category which is universally valid."[17] This divergence in approach is closely tied to differences in the vantage points from which they observed international politics. Where the realists focused on the high politics of statecraft within the international realm, Arendt's perspective remained identified with the victims of state authority and the modern nation-state system. Consistent with their focus, the realists invoked the standard of "national interest" as their guiding norm for states in international affairs, while Arendt applied a cosmopolitan standard of justice that transcended the particular interests of individual states. She was no less an opponent of any form of idealism that ignored the harsh dynamics of power politics in the modern world than her realist contemporaries, but, unlike the realists, she did not equate this form of politics with the essence of all politics or explain it as an inevitable product of the dark character of human nature.

This essay is divided into five parts. It will begin by showing how Arendt's response to the Holocaust differed from that of realists like Kennan and Morgenthau, and how this difference reflects a more fundamental divergence in their perspectives on international politics. As the second part of this essay will demonstrate, this divergence is also evident in their approaches to international human rights. Although she shared the realists' deep skepticism toward the efficacy of such instruments, her guiding concern was always the vulnerability of victim-groups who could not depend on them rather than states that found them to be inconsequential. From this concern, she developed a far more searching critique of these instruments than did her realist contemporaries. Her analysis sought to expose how the basic failings of these instruments are rooted in the dysfunctional character of the modern system of nation-states. The third and fourth parts contrast the realists' understanding of power as essentially a mode of domination with her attempt to construct an alternative conception drawn from the republican and Lockean traditions. Both this search for an alternative, and her critique of command–obedience models of political authority, arose directly from her study of the origins and character of totalitarian forms of power. Likewise, she developed her cosmopolitan standard of justice as she grappled with totalitarianism, whose emergence in her view had shattered all of the conventional frameworks for evaluation. The fifth part of this essay focuses on her treatment of individual accountability and universal responsibility as the twin poles of this standard. Her application of this standard gave her both a normative and an analytical basis for addressing the problems of denazification and the re-building of democracy in postwar German life that her realist contemporaries lacked. As a result, while the realists' discussion of these problems remained at best cursory, she confronted them squarely, and developed a new framework for evaluation of these phenomena. Because she believed that the threats of totalitarianism, total war, and nuclear weapons posed a radical challenge to the very survival of civilization, she was determined to rethink the fundamental assumptions, conventions, and political norms of modern life from the ground up. This determination, as well as her analytical acuity, made her critical vision far more penetrating and sweeping than her realist contemporaries.

The Holocaust: Perspective and Understanding

Given the realists' reputed sensitivity "to dramatic, unheralded, and . . . unexpected outbursts of violence and their consequences," one would expect that they would have been foremost in grappling with the ramifications of Nazi genocide.[18] Like Arendt, Kennan and Morgenthau had personal and professional reasons for taking a heightened interest in Germany, as well as direct access to information about the reality of the death camps. Arendt completed her major work on the topic by the mid-1960s. Kennan and Morgenthau outlived her, while enjoying long, highly productive postwar careers. As university scholars, both had ample opportunity to consider this topic in later work if further reflection had prompted them to do so. Although the Holocaust was not an object of sustained attention for most of their contemporaries, one might expect that thinkers with the realists' reputation would be leaders rather than followers of public opinion in such an area, especially in light of their insistence that the true character of international politics was best comprehended by policy professionals like themselves.[19] In short, it might be expected that they would demonstrate perspicacity equal to their contemporary, Hannah Arendt.

The reasons behind the realists' failure to grasp the significance of the Holocaust and, more broadly, to address the issue of genocide in the twentieth century are complex, but at a minimum this failure raises serious questions about blind spots in their categories of analysis. Carried out as a central objective in a war for global domination and spanning the European continent, the Holocaust, in its scope and enormity, clearly could not be regarded as merely the domestic excesses of a "bad" state. Even when genocide occurs entirely within the boundaries of a state, its occurrence raises profound questions about honoring traditional prerogatives of a sovereign's right to exclusive jurisdiction and the duty of nonintervention by other states.[20] Similarly, "ethnic cleansing" by definition has an international dimension, because it necessarily involves the mass movement of people across state borders. Moreover, as Arendt pointed out, totalitarian states like Nazi Germany used the mass exodus of refugees as a "weapon" in their foreign policy.[21] Even for those thinkers primarily engaged with practical issues of international affairs, the staggering scale of Nazi-forced emigration and mass murder in the so-called heart of Western civilization might have been expected to command attention. That such an event would be deemed to fall outside the realists' definition of international politics reflects a methodological choice of how the boundaries of their field should be drawn. This definition was dictated not by some necessary internal logic of the subject matter itself but by the objects of interest to the realists themselves. A focus on the international realm, populated by states, as a universe unto itself also skews the modern problem of violence in politics generally, because it has not been war between states but the violence of governments against their own subject populations that has been by far the greatest source of mass death in the twentieth century. The political scientist R. J. Rummel estimates that "almost four times" as many people have been killed in genocides and mass murders within their home countries than have died on the battlefield during the past century.[22]

It seems likely that the realists' general working assumption that violence is an inevitable and normal—though of course regrettable—feature of international politics dulled their sensitivity to the extraordinary dimensions of the violence perpetrated in the Holocaust, but this explanation applies more readily to Morgenthau than to Kennan. For Kennan, World War I was the "greatest catastrophe of Western civilization in the present century," a world war "besides which even the miseries of the second look pale so far as western Europe is concerned."[23] With respect to Nazi mass murders, he referred to "German atrocities" in only the most general terms, and attributed them to the "customs of warfare which have prevailed generally in Eastern Europe and Asia for centuries and which presumably will continue long into the future."[24] Kennan was hardly insensitive to the human costs of violence, and he was always exceptionally wary of the use of force.[25] He wrote with great compassion and regret about the German victims of Allied bombings, but his perspective minimized the significance of Nazi violence by emphasizing its aberrational qualities.[26] His identification of "German atrocities" with practices native to Eastern Europe and Asia distances this form of systematic violence from western modernity by attributing its most horrifying dimensions to foreign influences, and more specifically to the barbaric practices of peoples outside the west.[27] To do otherwise would require, as Arendt recognized, a profound rethinking of the values and achievements of the civilization that had invented industrial mass murder. Kennan's perception of "German atrocities" as primarily a product of age-old "customs of warfare" was hardly unique during this period. In part, Arendt wrote *The Origins of Totalitarianism* to shake her contemporaries out of such conventional assumptions.[28]

The abstract standpoint of Morgenthau's approach to these issues is exemplified in his 1945 essay, "The Evil of Politics and the Ethics of Evil." Although published after the extremity of Nazi violence was known, Morgenthau never pauses to consider the question of whether the Nazi phenomena present any new or original perspectives on his theme.[29] Instead, situating his analysis against the theoretical background of Machiavelli and Hobbes, he reflects on the inevitable and timeless character of violence in politics. He treats "evil" here as largely a general abstract category, and frames the perennial problem of the statesman as primarily one of choosing between greater or lesser evils. Because at this level of analysis violence is a bloodless abstraction, such a schema tends to flatten out qualitative differences among its forms, reduce its victims to pawns sacrificed as a necessary cost of practicing politics, and defines its character as a quantitative matter of degree in a general economy of violence that informs all politics. By contrast, Arendt (in an essay also published in 1945) called attention to the irreducible qualitative difference between the totalitarian violence of World War II and the mass slaughter that characterized World War I. Writing with Nazi criminality foremost in her mind, she concluded that "the problem of evil will be fundamental to post-war intellectual life—as death became the fundamental problem after the last war."[30]

One of the primary factors that distinguishes Arendt's approach from Morgenthau's and Kennan's was that the latter viewed international politics through a top-down, state-centered lens. Jonathan Haslam has recently described the consequences of this perspective: "most realists developed or sought to develop a world-view from the balcony of statesmen; inevitably this meant a unit-level analysis in international relations and a natural identification with someone's idea of national interest."[31] Thus, for example, among the primary purposes Morgenthau conceived for IR scholars like himself, he emphasized their role as independent advisers to statesmen, whether in articulating the broader theoretical rationales for government policies with which they agreed or in sharply criticizing those that they found wanting.[32] For his part, Kennan approached foreign policy issues from the standpoint of a supremely gifted, but practical diplomat and later as a diplomatic historian. Both men played influential roles in shaping the postwar study of international politics as an applied policy field.

In appraising the early decades of IR as a distinct discipline within political science, Stanley Hoffmann has emphasized its American character and the correspondence of its rise with America's new global role after 1945. "If our discipline has any founding father," he added, "it is Morgenthau."[33] In explaining its rise, Hoffmann observed, that practitioners offered American policy-makers an expertise, a set of persuasive rationales, strategic advice, and an "intellectual compass" for charting this new role. One reason that political scientists were drawn to the field, he pointed out, was their fascination with power, and "in the postwar years what part of power was more interesting than the imperial bit?"[34] A key institutional nexus behind the rise of the discipline, he observed, "was the direct and visible tie between the scholarly world and the world of power: the 'in-and-outer' system of government, which puts academics and researchers not merely in the corridors of power but also in the kitchens of power."[35]

In thinking about the character and limits of this professional perspective, it is instructive to consider how the vantage point of state policy shapes the way the "real" world is comprehended; namely, what it privileges and what it obscures. In his book, *Seeing Like a State*, James C. Scott has emphasized the ways that state officials must by the nature of their duties, interests, and goals radically simplify the concrete and infinitely complex social facts that they confront. "The term simplification," he explains,

> is meant in two quite specific senses. First, the knowledge that an official needs must give him or her a synoptic view of the ensemble; it must be cast in terms that are replicable across many cases. In this respect, such facts must lose their particularity and reappear in schematic or simplified form as a member of a class of facts. Second, in a meaning closely related to the first, the grouping of synoptic facts necessarily entails collapsing or ignoring distinctions that might otherwise be relevant.[36]

As a function of their duties, state officials see "reality" at the aggregate level through the kind of abstract categories and classification mechanisms that make large scale administration, social measurement, and policy planning possible. Scott did not develop his thesis with IR theory in mind, but it helps to explain the strong tendencies in realist theory to reduce international politics to a closed and highly simplified universe organized around the interactions of abstract state units as well as its failure to come to grips with the horrifying particulars of events like the Holocaust.[37] What states see, Scott reminds us, is heavily conditioned and selectively fashioned by what is useful for their purposes. It should not surprise us that from these commanding heights, the comprehension of the concrete reality of violence should incline toward abstraction and the measure of utility.

In the international realm, a fundamental asymmetry exists between the democratic accountability to which governments like the

United States are subject and the foreign populations who may be the object of its policies. Here Scott's conclusions are particularly instructive. One of the main "barrier(s)" that has prevented modern governments from inflicting their most sweeping, highly abstract agendas of reform on their own populations, he contends, is the effective presence of representative political institutions "through which a resistant society could make its influence felt."[38] Moreover, the distance in perception between the agent and subject of policy in international affairs is likely to be exponentially greater than in domestic affairs. Where such institutional "barriers" are absent, Scott concludes, governing elites commit their worst excesses because there is little accountability. They are least inclined to learn from their own mistakes, because they are usually far removed from the actual effects of their mistakes. Emphasizing the emergence of this mismatch between the territorially bound, political model of the nation-state and the vast plurality of the international realm, Arendt pointed out that "before the imperialist era, there was no such thing as world politics . . .," and that in this era "the nation-state system proved incapable of either devising new rules for handling foreign affairs that had become global affairs or enforcing a Pax Romana on the rest of the world."[39] When the practice of politics is abstracted from the context of a given community, she argued, it tends to collapse into the mere exercise of power.

The importance of vantage point is illustrated in a disturbing anecdote Kennan recounted about his months of internment as a diplomat in Berlin following Hitler's declaration of war on the United States. In describing his frustration at how long he and his colleagues were forced to languish as internees, he complained how they lost their plane seats on one occasion to "Jewish refugees," who were not even American "citizens."[40] Summing up the significance of this episode, he observes how it was emblematic of "the obvious injustice of the approach of the government and large parts of the public to men of the Foreign Service in times of war."[41] Nowhere in this account (published in 1967) does he make any reference to the fate in store for those Jews who were unable to escape Germany. On a personal level, Kennan was not indifferent to the Nazi treatment of the Jews, which he condemned as "fantastically barbaric" in a personal letter to his wife during his tenure in Germany.[42] But his relative silence on this issue in his *Memoirs* recalling his years of professional service seems symptomatic of what Michael Barnett in another context has described as the tendency of government officials representing their country to assume a kind of "dual identity." As Barnett observes, "bureaucrats . . . have something of a dual identity: as members of a particular national community they draw symbolic boundaries between themselves and those outside the national state, and as members of a bureaucracy, they draw boundaries between the bureaucracy and society."[43] This "dual identity" is reflected in Kennan's emphasis on the fact that the refugees were not U.S. citizens and, therefore, did not merit preferential treatment from the American government. Kennan refers to his own sense of "dual identity" as drawn between the personal and the professional, between the "heart" and the "head." Kennan's condemnation of Nazi brutality toward the Jews falls into the personal category, and is included in a collection whose purpose and texture he expressly differentiates from the depersonalized "writing," such as the *Memoirs*, that has "constituted the backbone of my professional life."[44]

The ways that immediate policy considerations shape objects of interest is reflected in the realists' treatment of the postwar German issues. In his 1951 essay, "Germany: The Political Problem," for example, Morgenthau recognized how "the remembrance of past atrocities" inevitably inclines "us . . . to look at Germany with our emotions, with our heart rather than our minds." However, he cautioned that while as a personal matter "to cherish the memories of ancestors, friends, and teachers murdered by the Germans can even be a sacred thing," such remembrances should not obscure our understanding of "the problem of Germany" in "political terms."[45] As a political matter for American policy-makers, he argued, the overriding consideration is that "Germany has become both the battleground . . . and the main stake in the cold war."[46] In this period then, the central challenge from a policy perspective was to prevent the Soviet Union from acquiring dominance over all of Germany. However, since the United States was then an occupying power in West Germany responsible for overseeing its transition to a stable liberal-democratic order, this definition of the "political terms" seems rather reductive even "from the American point of view."[47] Like Kennan noting the Nazi persecution of the Jews in Berlin in a pivotal letter, Morgenthau confined addressing the implications of the Holocaust to the private sphere of personal life.

In contrast to the realists, Arendt never aspired to a place on the "balcony of statesmen," and was uncomfortable in the public arena.[48] She wrote from a cosmopolitan perspective rather than in terms of any particular national allegiance.[49] Having barely escaped a French internment camp for German refugees after the fall of France before coming to the United States, her vantage point was strongly influenced by her years as a "stateless refugee."[50] This difference in perspective gave Arendt and the realists very different starting points in their critical appraisal of the modern nation-state system. Where neither Morgenthau nor Kennan ever focused on the possible implications of statelessness, Arendt emphasized it as "the newest mass phenomenon in contemporary history," and regarded "the existence of an ever growing new people comprised of stateless persons" as "the most symptomatic group in contemporary politics."[51] This focus on the plight of individuals as a key to understanding the international system diverges sharply from any state-centered approach.

Whereas Arendt embraced a cosmopolitan standard of "universal responsibility" that focused on crimes against humanity and every individual's "right to have rights" at its core, Morgenthau and Kennan emphasized the particular responsibility of policy-makers to their own states as measured by a morally informed conception of "national interest." Their recognition of the relativity of moral judgments and their reluctance to apply sweeping normative criteria that inevitably reflected their own national allegiances to other nations showed a characteristic appreciation for boundaries and limits. "To know that states are subject to the moral law is one thing," Morgenthau pointed out, "to pretend to know what is morally required of states in a particular situation is quite another."[52] Morgenthau accepted the idea of universal moral norms, but never specified their content.[53] Kennan rejected this idea altogether.[54] Both men wrote in broad terms about the responsibility of political leaders, but never articulated "the concrete content of this ethic."[55] At the same time, both insisted that reformist impulses should always focus at home rather than abroad and shared an aversion to hypocrisy and moral grandstanding in foreign policy. Both believed that states would exert their strongest positive moral influence internationally if they led by the enlightened example of how they conducted their own domestic affairs. Kennan, in particular, criticized the American inclination toward national self-idealization. Like Arendt, Morgenthau and Kennan opposed the Vietnam War, and sharply criticized the rise of the "military–industrial complex" in the United States that followed World War II.[56]

In insisting that the pragmatic pursuit of national interest was a more reliable and responsible guide to foreign policy than a moralistic approach, the realists sought to emphasize the importance of reciprocity in international relations based on the recognition that other states had their own legitimate national interests to defend, which might reasonably conflict with those of other states.[57] Many scholars have called attention to the problematic character of the realists' notion of enlightened national interest.[58] Arendt has stated the problem most succinctly, observing: "Some experience plus a little reflection teach that it goes against the very nature of self-interest to be enlightened."[59] By elevating national self-interest into the guiding policy norm, the realists left states ultimately accountable only to themselves despite the character of their interdependent membership within an international community of states.

Comparing the approaches that Arendt and her realist contemporaries brought to their study of international politics makes it impossible to accept the self-description of "realism" as a tradition of thought at face value. Just like Arendt's, the realists' perspective depended on a set of normative assumptions that shaped the questions they posed, their categories of analysis, and the kind of answers they sought. Contrasting Arendt's perspective with her realist contemporaries shows just how decisive those normative assumptions are in defining any worldview. Moreover, the whole notion that the realists saw the world as it is, as opposed to how utopian dreamers would like it to be, is only credible if we assume that some form of utopianism is the chief alternative to their own pessimistic vision. In this sense, the conventional dichotomy drawn between "realism" and "idealism" is a false one. Even adding the qualifier "state-centered" to designate a particular form of realism does not in itself adequately convey just how selective the lens through which they perceived their world was. Indeed, Arendt was skeptical of the modern realist tradition because she deemed the realist picture of the world as being too abstract and even utopian in its premises and categories.

The failure of Kennan and Morgenthau to grapple with the significance of industrial mass murder and genocide as a phenomenon in the global politics of their day is still more striking when this neglect is compared with the work of the greatest classical chronicler of total war. Although Thucydides is often invoked as a key antecedent for twentieth-century realist thought, his vision was much broader than Arendt's contemporaries.[60] If judging merely from Thucydides' accounts of the civil war in Corcyra and the plague in Athens (among others), it is impossible to imagine that anyone truly following his example would have treated the Holocaust as incidental to the contemporary study of international politics, of the conduct, character, and effects of total war, or of the role of human nature in politics. Thucydides' emphasis on the interplay between foreign alliances and domestic factions in driving events like the Corcyraean civil war directly challenges drawing any neat boundary lines between the domestic and international realms as separate fields of study.

Moreover, his analysis reflects a constant awareness of how the corrosive effects of war on international standards of justice affect domestic politics. For Thucydides, power was no mere abstract category of analysis. He was acutely attentive to its moral effects within different states and within the international system of states. The breadth of Thucydides' vision may, in part, reflect the fact that he did not identify his analytical or normative perspective with the collective interests of any one city-state, including his native Athens. Likewise, his analysis was not shaped by an effort to distill policy lessons or prescriptions from his subject matter. It also seems worth noting that Thucydides did not require the benefit of much hindsight to recognize that events like the civil war in Corycra merited his close attention. He died shortly after the war he was chronicling had reached its end. In light of the intensity of her focus on the interrelationships of justice and power, Arendt should much more rightfully be regarded as the intellectual heir of Thucydides than either Kennan or Morgenthau. However, in her emphasis on the importance of judging, she stood at odds with the impartial, detached perspective presented by a historian like Thucydides, and never identified her work with his legacy.

SUBVERSIVE PARADOXES: NATIONAL SOVEREIGNTY AND INTERNATIONAL HUMAN RIGHTS

The realists were critical of the "legalistic-moralistic approach" to foreign policy for several reasons. While it might be reasonable to expect states to act in their own self-interest, the realists saw it as utopian to believe that they would honor any legal obligations deemed at variance with those interests, especially with respect to the application of universal human rights principles.[61] Moreover, in an era of democratic nationalism that invests warfare with an intense ideological dimension, realists like Morgenthau and Kennan sought to minimize a moralistic understanding of international affairs in order to discourage tendencies of states to absolutize their positions and demonize their adversaries.[62] They also assumed that nation-states bear primary, if not exclusive, responsibility for their own peoples, and that a state like the United States "ought to follow a policy of minding its own business to the extent that it can."[63]

Arendt was no less skeptical of the effectiveness of international human rights law and similar instruments than realists like Morgenthau and Kennan, but she developed her critique from a cosmopolitan perspective. In broadest terms, she interpreted this ineffectiveness as an expression of the pathology of the modern nation-state system that reached its extreme under totalitarianism. A key feature of this pathology involved the ways that whole segments of humanity were rendered "superfluous" and thereby disposable. She saw the destructive consequences of the self-absolutizing character of the modern nation-state as not simply evidence of this pathology, but also as a strong normative argument for the necessity of a cosmopolitan perspective that elevates the collective interests of humanity above the particular interests of individual nations. To accept the nation-state system as the de facto basis by which responsibilities for protection are allocated across the international realm ignores the degree to which the spread of this system has deprived vast portions of humanity of any effective protection.

For Arendt the problem of refugees in the twentieth century exemplified this dilemma, because the dynamics of modern nation-building has inevitably generated massive refugee flows in many parts of the world while the evolution of the state system has carved up the territorial space around the globe into ever more tightly bounded membership units. Because the nation-state model was predicated on the ideal of an ethnically homogenous national community, its application to ethnically mixed populations, which includes most of the world, has created strong exclusionary pressures.[64] At the same time, dividing the globe among sovereign units began to raise barriers constraining the freedom of people to move. "Theoretically, in the sphere of international law," she explained, "it has always been true that sovereignty is no more absolute than in matters of 'emigration, naturalization, nationality, and expulsion.' "[65] By the end of World War I, Western states had finally developed the capacity to control entrance and exit at their borders. As a result, she observed of the interwar years: "Suddenly, there was no place on earth where migrants could go without severe restrictions, no country where they would be assimilated, no country where they could found a new community of their own."[66]

In terms of the staggering scale of the refugee phenomenon during the first half of the twentieth century (and beyond), Arendt's emphasis on its importance as a new factor in international politics has been amply confirmed by subsequent researchers.[67] However, consistent with their focus on power politics among sovereign states, realists like Morgenthau and Kennan almost completely ignored the refugee problem in their writing. For example, in his textbook intended as a comprehensive introduction to the study of international relations, Morgenthau did not devote a single section to it in a fifth edition that numbered over 560 pages. He did include a section on "population" as a sociological and economic determinant of national power, in which he discusses (among other examples) how immigration contributed to the growing strength of the United States, but there was nothing on the significance of the movements of people fleeing persecution.[68] As an analytical category, "population" here is not only framed from the perspective of state interests, but also incorporates the same taxonomy through which states articulate those interests. Morgenthau's neglect of the refugee problem is hardly surprising. From a state-centered perspective, as Arendt pointed out, refugees are simply a burdensome anomaly who in no way serve the national interest of their host countries. In grappling with the refugee problem during the interwar period, she observed, the main interest of host countries was to find the most expeditious means of deporting them, which turned out to be very difficult to do.[69] In short, no segment of humanity was more "superfluous" in interwar Europe than the refugees. They were admitted as unwelcome aliens under systems of laws whose protections were designed for citizen-nationals. Under these circumstances, "an ever growing body of people [were] forced to live outside the scope of all tangible law . . ."[70]

Though devoting no more attention to the twentieth-century refugee phenomenon than Morgenthau, Kennan proved much more sensitive about the ways in which the concepts and categories that have been articulated in the language of states can reify their categories of analysis.[71] Much of international law, Kennan pointed out, for example, is premised "on a world comprised exclusively of sovereign nation states with a full equality of status."[72] Against this premise, he argued that

> the national state pattern is not, should not be, and cannot be a fixed and static thing. By its nature, it is an unstable phenomenon in a constant state of change and flux. History has shown that the will and capacity of individual peoples to contribute to their world environment is constantly changing. It is only logical that the organizational forms (and what else are such things as borders and governments?) should change with them.[73]

Consistent with this argument, he cautioned against a clear tendency in international law that "glorifies the concept of nationality and makes it the exclusive form of participation in international life."[74] Despite recognizing the dynamic relationship between concepts of nationhood and statehood, Kennan never developed these insights by thinking more deeply about the problems that had accompanied the emergence of the nation-state principle as the dominant organizational basis for the international order or about the effects of this transformation on the peoples involved. He never applied these insights to the refugee problem. With respect to the process of decolonization then underway, he advised in 1953 "view[ing] these resulting conflicts for what they are: tragic situations, in which the elements of right and wrong are indistinguishable." Given the magnitude of the difficulties and the hard choices this process entails, he urged "view[ing] this whole subject of colonization with humility, with detachment, with compassion for both sides."[75] Kennan moves briskly here to situate the issue on the moral plane without ever seriously engaging any of the analytical (and empirical) questions about the actual causes, character, and effects of colonization and decolonization. This kind of moral equivalency reflects Kennan's deeper normative commitment to the value of order and stability in the international realm.

Arendt's critique of international human rights began from the observation that: "No paradox of contemporary politics is filled with more poignant irony than the discrepancy between the efforts of well-meaning idealists who stubbornly insist on regarding as 'inalienable' those human rights, which are enjoyed only by citizens of the most prosperous and civilized countries, and the situation of the rightless themselves."[76] That she described the impotence of universal human rights at this historical moment as a "paradox" as opposed to dismissing these standards either as a sham or a relic is indicative of her concern with how the development of the modern nation-state had eroded this normative source of guarantees without providing any alternative basis for them. The "idealists" were seeking to address a real and serious problem, but had hopelessly inadequate tools by which to solve, or even fully comprehend, it. To understand this problem required seeing its roots in the structure of the nation-state system itself, so any effective and enduring solution would have to involve changing this structure. By ignoring this structural dimension, "the very phrase 'human rights' became for all concerned—victims, persecutors, and onlookers alike—the evidence of hopeless idealism or fumbling feeble-minded hypocrisy."[77]

For Arendt World War I and its aftermath had "sufficiently shattered the façade of Europe's political system to lay bare its hidden frame." This frame had been exposed through the "suffering of more and more groups of people to whom suddenly the rules of the world around them ceased to apply."[78] She traced the roots of this crisis to the French Revolution, to the pivotal moment in which the principle of absolute sovereignty became fused with the idea of the nation.

She argued that this fusion created an insoluble, though not always apparent, "conflict" from its inception. In explaining this conflict, she differentiated the *state* as a legal-political, institutional structure from the *nation* as a particular form of group identity. The former is an artificial organization of power that exercises exclusive jurisdiction over a fixed territory, and its "supreme function" is "the protection of all inhabitants in its territory no matter what their nationality."[79] By contrast, nations (in principle) have much more exclusive and ascriptive membership criteria that are identified with distinctive qualities of the persons and the groups to which they belong. The fusion of nation and state joined together the exclusive cultural membership model of the nation with the absolutistic sovereign organization of the territorial state. In the process, state membership became increasingly understood to require belonging to the same nationality or to a homogeneous national community.

For Arendt the glaring incompatibilities between the state's role as a legal-political institution whose raison d'être was providing security to all its inhabitants and its role as the home of the nation was embodied in the 1789 "Declaration of the Rights of Man and of Citizen."[80] In Arendt's view, the Declaration rested on two incompatible premises. On the one hand, it recognized (at the abstract level of principle) the universal existence of individual rights applicable to all persons irrespective of their particular nationality or territorial residence. On the other hand, the Declaration based the realization of these rights, as a concrete matter of enforceable guarantees and positive law, on the agency of the specific sovereign nation to which individuals belonged. As a statement of universal principles, the Declaration's proclamation of rights had no direct, practical effect, because these rights were not backed by any institutional enforcement mechanisms, nor could be since none existed at the international level. Such enforcement mechanisms existed only at the domestic level of sovereign states, whose governments, constitutions, and civil laws protected the rights of their citizens. Vesting sovereignty in the nation as a matter of principle increasingly transformed the institutional role of the state in the eyes of different nationalities from a general provider of security and justice over its territorial jurisdiction into a specific "instrument of the nation" for the achievement of a particular people's collective rights.[81] In short, the fundamental paradox of the French Declaration was rooted in how its affirmation of the principle of national sovereignty as a particular collective right of peoples undermined its proclamation of universal rights for individuals by depriving the latter of any means of realization on its premise of universality.[82]

Arendt's analysis of the failure of the interwar Minority Treaties offers a good illustration of her contextual approach. From a realist perspective, this failure could be simply added to the long list of well-intentioned international legal instruments that could scarcely match promise with performance. For Arendt this failure was largely a by-product of the misconceived application of the nation-state formula in the peace settlement ending World War I to the historically shaped, polyglot territories of eastern and central Europe. This settlement had to deal with the political vacuum left by collapse of the Austrian-Hungarian, German, Ottoman, and Russian Empires. However, the establishment of new successor states on the principle of national self-determination proved to be a recipe for chronic instability, resentments, and conflict. Because of the manner in which different nationality groups were heavily interspersed across these regions, the populations of these new nation-states were inextricably mixed. "The result," Arendt observed, "was that those peoples to whom states were not conceded, no matter whether they were official minorities or only nationalities, considered the [Peace] Treaties an arbitrary game which handed out rule to some and servitude to others."[83]

Far from providing effective protection to vulnerable groups, the Minority Treaties confirmed the norm that the purpose of states is to protect their own nationals and that only those members of a state that shared a common national origin are entitled to be treated as full and equal citizens. The resort to special international instruments to compel the protection of national minorities merely reinforced the idea that the presence of such groups is anomalous, so that extra-state measures are required to guarantee their basic rights.[84] Of course, any such measures infringe on the sovereignty of the states to which they apply. "The worst factor in this situation," Arendt argued,

> was not even that it became a matter of course for the nationalities to be disloyal to their imposed governments and for the governments to oppress their nationalities as efficiently as possible, but that the nationally frustrated population was firmly convinced—as was everybody else—that true freedom, true emancipation, and true popular sovereignty—could only be attained with full national emancipation, that people without their own national government were deprived of human rights.[85]

Since the sovereign as a political idea is understood to be indivisible and absolute within its territorial realm, two or more nations as real or potential bearers of this sovereignty cannot (in principle) occupy the same state without compromising the sovereign integrity of one or the other. The coupling of sovereignty and the nation then creates the modern ideological rationale not only for separatist and national liberation movements, but also for the mass population transfers of minorities across territorial borders and for even more brutal forms of ethnic cleansing.

The plight of refugees and minorities that emerged in this era, she contended, helped to shape the preconditions for the rise of totalitarianism and establish precedents for its exercise of power. Leaders of totalitarian regimes, Arendt observed, used the denial of nationality as a means to strip large classes of persons of any entitlement to a place in the world and any standing in their own communities. During the 1930s, "denationalization became a powerful weapon of totalitarian politics, and the constitutional inability of European nation-states to guarantee human rights to those who had lost their nationally guaranteed rights, made it possible for the persecuting governments to impose their standards of values even upon their opponents."[86] Rather than treating the exodus of refugees as an indictment against the regimes they fled or by whom they had been expelled, host states came to see the sheer number of refugees to be absorbed as the overriding policy problem and the refugees themselves as an increasingly intolerable burden on their societies. As a result, those persons and groups that the persecuting states had deemed "undesirable" by their own measures of human worth became similarly perceived across Europe.

Arendt argued that the identification of an absolutistic concept of sovereignty with a homogeneous cultural understanding of nationhood has proven lethal to the rights of minority nationals and to the stability of many modern states. Her approach emphasizes the importance of the political context in shaping the dynamics of ethnic conflict and the generation of refugees. In applying these insights to postwar Europe, Arendt argued in 1945 that the "problem of equal rights" for nationalities could not be solved through any formula that presupposed the "restoration" of the nation-state system. Various contemporary proposals to address the so-called German problem within the old logic of this system typically ignored the extent to which this problem was rooted in that system, and "show clearly the utopian character of 'realism' and power-politics in their application to the real issues of our time."[87] A postwar restoration based on that logic, she observed, would simply re-create the conditions for more nationalistic grievances and aspirations, for more ruinous ideological conflict, irrespective of any new guarantees for "collective security" or agreements over "spheres of interests." In particular, she pointed to the plans of the Czech and Polish governments in exile to cleanse their states of their German minorities. These brutal "population transfers" did occur with the connivance of the Allied governments.[88] Writing with the failures of the interwar Minority Treaties and other international human rights measures in mind, she contended that the only real, long-term solution lay in rejecting the abstract logic of the old nation-state system through the creation of a pan-European federation. "Within federated structures," she expressed the hope, "nationality would become a personal status rather [than] a territorial one."[89]

DOMINATION AND VIOLENCE: THE CRITIQUE OF POWER

Realists like Kennan and Morgenthau never glorified the pursuit of power for its own sake, nor romanticized the conduct of political leadership. Indeed, they emphasized the tragic limitations, costs, and unforeseeable consequences that any projection of force involved, so they urged that force always be highly disciplined, subject to strict principles, and pursuant to a carefully measured assessment of paramount national interest. They never ceased to call attention to the ways that developments in modern military technology had created a growing mismatch between the destructive potential of war and the limited (constructive) objectives any war, at best, could serve. Both men stressed the important role of professional diplomacy in avoiding violent conflicts between states and in cultivating areas for cooperation. However, their approach to the problem of power in war differed markedly from their approach to this problem in politics. By defining the essence of political power in a narrow, abstract manner, they elevated it to serve as a blunt master category in their analysis of politics. "Every man is the object of political domination," Morgenthau declared, "and at the same time aspires toward exercising political domination over others . . . Political domination, then, appears as a product of nature itself."[90] If power is conceived as quintessentially a form of domination, it will be assuredly so used. While such a conception may seem formally neutral, it has strong normative implications for understanding any exercise of power and its legitimate usages. Moreover, the core reality of politics is, by this premise, invariable and timeless irrespective of whether it is situated in a republic, monarchy, democracy, oligarchy, or tyranny. To grasp this essence then, context of any kind is irrelevant, because differences among various types of regimes are ultimately superficial. This insight into their essential similitude may come as news to many of the people actually living under these different types of regimes.

By the late 1940s, the "rhetoric of totalitarianism and the Nazi–Soviet comparison" had become a prominent theme in the Truman administration's foreign policy.[91] At a 1953 conference, Kennan proposed a provisional sketch of the principal elements of the totalitarian model.[92] These elements included its ruthless monopolization of political power, its extensive reliance on secret police, its subversion of every norm of the rule-of-law ideal, its dependence on modern technology, and its roots in nineteenth-century European romantic nationalism. At the same time, he made only a fleeting reference to the institution of the concentration camp system (in the context of the Soviet Union) as well as a passing reference to Arendt's study of totalitarianism. For his part, Morgenthau grimly characterized "mass exterminations" as an inevitable extension of the modern character of "total war," and Hitler's conduct of the war as an extreme example of a broader erosion of shared international standards of ethics.[93] Both Kennan and Morgenthau treated totalitarianism as primarily a problem in international relations, and so were understandably much less interested in exploring its origins or its character than in the practical problems of how to contain or combat it.

In neither case did their study of the phenomenon of totalitarianism alter their core conception of power as a matter of domination through the form of a command–obedience model. This conception remained the analytical standard against which they measured all forms of government and politics. In a 1953 essay, for example, Kennan called attention to the "diffused" character of political power in the American system, but portrayed this character as something of an aberration that had obscured to the American public the true essence of power. "We Americans have a strange—and to me disturbing—attitude toward the subject of power," he wrote. "We don't like the concept. . . . We like to feel that the adjustment of conflicting interests is something that can be taken care of by juridical norms and institutional devices, voluntarily accepted and not involving violence to the feelings of or interests of anyone."[94] In its "pure form," he observed, power is most typically institutionalized in a "national uniform police establishment functioning as the vehicle of a central political will."[95] Setting aside the totalitarian model as an extreme case, he reminded readers in a later essay that "the conservative authoritarian-state . . . has been the norm of Western society in the Christian era."[96] While acknowledging "differences" between this traditional "authoritarian" model and modern democratic ones, he described these "difference" as merely "relative" in a way that "do[es] not present clear-cut issues." Indeed, he highlighted their similarities thus:

> The authoritarian regime, despite its origins and sanctions, often rests on a wide area of popular acceptance and reflects popular aspirations in important degree. In democratic countries, on the other hand, such things as the aspirations of lobbies and political parties and the inevitable control of nominations by small groups of people tend to reduce the ideal representativeness of government and to make it hard to view the political process as much more than a negative expression of the popular will.[97]

This sweeping conclusion, advanced without any evidence or comparative examples, simply ignores the analytical need to delineate clear distinctions and definitions that would give it any weight or heuristic value. Even when in later writings, he expressly defends the advantages of institutional forms such as the separation of powers, he continued to emphasize that "the institution of government bears, in essence, no moral quality."[98] This sort of argument emphasizes the broad instrumental character of all governments with little regard for questions about the particular ends of justice that government is to serve. Some structure of government is a "necessity," he contended, and whether its external "form" is "liberal or oppressive" it stands between "civilized life" and "anarchy." Government provides order, and this necessity "flow(s) from the inability of men to govern themselves individually in a manner compatible with the interests of the entire community . . ."[99] This characterization emphasizes the generic role of government as an instrument of order while eliding important differences that may distinguish one government from another, such as the sources of any particular government's normative authority and the particular relationship between a government and its citizens.

While Kennan was always reluctant to engage in theory, Morgenthau sought to ground his approach to international politics on a clear set of universal postulates. His interpretation of the Nazi regime reflected these postulates. The "limitless character of the lust for power," he observed, for example, "reveals a general quality of the human mind . . . . The attempt at realizing it in actual experience ends always with the destruction of the individual attempting it, as the fate of all world-conquerors from Alexander to Hitler proves. . . ."[100] Consistent with a command–obedience model, Morgenthau defined "political power" in formal terms as being "a psychological relation between those who exercise it and those over whom it is exercised.

It gives the former control over certain actions of the latter through the influence which the former exert over the latter's minds."[101] He saw the drive for this kind of power rooted in human nature. "Man is born to seek power," Morgenthau explained, "yet his actual condition makes him a slave to the power of others. Man is born a slave, but everywhere he wants to be a master."[102] This postulate is unlikely to enhance anyone's respect for human dignity as a guiding norm. In the history of Western political thought which is replete with justifications for slavery, the master/slave relationship has nevertheless been commonly regarded as the paradigm for the most exploitive and debased form of power relationship, but here it is posited as the archetype for the human condition. Even Thomas Hobbes began from the premise that men were originally born free, and only later consented to their own subjugation. In using this archetype, Morgenthau is setting up the problem of politics in wholly negative terms that marginalize questions about the positive conditions that may promote human flourishing. Among the dangers that accompany this approach is that its adherents will be all the more inclined to live down to the bleakest expectations of human nature. It seems fair to ask whether this perspective is not corrosive to all but the most self-serving ethical standards in crafting public policy.

Morgenthau's pessimistic portrait of human nature follows in the tradition of Hobbes. The latter's portrait was designed to demonstrate that individuals could not cooperate effectively or govern themselves responsibly without the towering presence of an absolute sovereign. Hobbes's whole postulate of a "state of nature" assumes that human character is fundamentally the same irrespective of context. This assumption simply ignores the vast cultural and social diversity that also characterizes humanity. It also minimizes the role that the experience of living under different forms of government may have in shaping the particular norms and practices of the people in a given community. Moreover, as the example of Hobbes suggests, if one starts from a conception of human nature at its worst (as might be expected in a civil war environment), then any feasible basis for a solution to the problems of order and justice has already been established in the terms it was posed.

Consistent with his own description of human nature, Morgenthau also embraced the Hobbesian absolutist model of sovereignty. Like Hobbes, Morgenthau regarded this conception as fundamental to any form of government. As he observed:

> Democratic constitutions, especially those consisting of a system of checks and balances, have purposely obscured the problem of sovereignty and

glossed over the need for a definite location of the sovereign power. For while it is the main concern of constitutions to create devices for the limitation and control of personal power, the clearest case of a sovereignty, definitely located, is the unfettered authority of Hobbes' *Leviathan*, the source not only of law, but of ethics and mores as well . . . In their endeavor to make democracy "a government of laws and not of men" they forgot that in any state, democratic or otherwise, there must be a man or a group of men ultimately responsible for the exercise of political authority. Since in a democracy that responsibility lies dormant in normal times, barely visible through the network of constitutional arrangements and legal rules, it is widely believed that it does not exist, and that the supreme and law-enforcing authority, is now distributed among the different co-ordinate agencies of the government and that, in consequence, no one of them is supreme . . . Yet in times of crisis and war that ultimate responsibility asserts itself, as it did under the presidencies of Lincoln, Wilson, and the two Roosevelts and leaves to constitutional theories the arduous task of arguing it away after the event.[103]

Explicitly rejecting any notion of a mixed constitution in which political power is divided and shared among groups, Hobbes had argued that the only stable and enduring foundation for the preservation of order required that all power be concentrated in one unitary, supreme entity.[104] By Morgenthau's rendering here, all liberal-democratic checks on the abuse of power and measures for the accountability of officeholders become a kind of mask behind which the reality of power lies. The idea that, at least in liberal-democratic states, the citizenry bear some responsibility for the conduct of their government drops out in this account.

Where Morgenthau and Kennan approached totalitarianism from the perspective of waging the cold war, Arendt sought to investigate its sources, character, and dynamics, from its roots in the making of European modernity, the history of racism, and the experience with imperialism. From the many strands of this study, she traced the totalitarian idea of power back to a reconceptualization of power that accompanied the rise of the modern Western world. Through this reconceptualization, she argued "power became the essence of political action and the center of political thought when it was separated from the political community which it should serve."[105] In this way, she contended, the idea of power was stripped of any normative dimensions as it was abstracted from its concrete expression and role within specific communities. She saw this modern understanding of power exemplified in the political philosophy of Hobbes.

Where a realist like Morgenthau endorsed Hobbes's conception of power, Arendt sharply criticized it for elevating power to an end in itself.[106] She viewed Hobbes as a watershed figure who established the model of the sovereign state as a "power-accumulation machine" that operates wholly unaccountably in the world.[107] Hobbes had sought to show how this model derived from the character of men in their natural condition, whose basic contours he argued corresponded to the relationships among sovereigns in the international realm. His theory of human psychology provided a strong conceptual and normative foundation for the modern "idolatry of power" as an expression of the natural condition of human life, and he correctly "foresaw" that modern man "would be flattered at being called a power-thirsty animal."[108] In fact, she observed, this model of "commonwealth based on the accumulation and monopolization of power of all its members necessarily leaves each person powerless, deprived of his natural and human capacities."[109] Hobbes's reputed "psychological realism" strips human nature of any "capacity" for exercising "reason," "free will," "friendship," or "responsibility" by first isolating individuals from any actual bonds of membership in an existing community and treating this abstract, atomistic isolation as the natural condition of human life.

At the same time, she rejected drawing direct continuities between a Hobbesian conception of power and its radicalized totalitarian counterpart. Indeed, she emphasized the unique qualities that differentiated the latter from the former in order to clarify the precedent from the "unprecedented" aspects of totalitarianism. One reason that other Western states had not recognized the magnitude of the Nazi threat during most of the 1930s, she contended, was their failure to appreciate these differences. By contrast, Arendt sought to explore in a much more systematic way the distinguishing characteristics of the Nazi regime and to emphasize their "unprecedented" aspects. In their foreign policy, she argued, the states most opposed to Nazi Germany had failed to grasp the extent to which these characteristics were new and original. "The trouble with totalitarian regimes," she observed, "is not that they play power politics in an especially ruthless way, but that behind their politics, is hidden an entirely new and unprecedented concept of power . . ."[110] The old imperialist idea of political power had been predicated on the desire for expansion simply for the sake of expansion.[111] This new concept is built from the nihilistic principle that "everything is permitted," that no boundaries fixed in morality, nature or law exist that set limits to the goals, strategies, and methods of totalitarian rule. Earlier examples of tyranny, imperialism, military conquest, and racial domination reveal "precedents" and "intermediate stages" for various elements of totalitarian rule, but, given the opportunity, totalitarian regimes then substantially radicalize these elements in a wholly nihilistic direction.[112] She saw this new nihilistic ambition for "total domination" most fully expressed in the Nazi system of concentration and extermination camps.[113]

Having looked closely at a model of domination in its most extreme form, Arendt was much more critical than Morgenthau or Kennan of the assumptions behind this understanding of power and sought an alternative to any crude command–obedience model. Arendt saw the influence of this conception of power running throughout the modern tradition. Against this conception of power, she sought to recover alternative understandings from the classical republican tradition. She insisted on making a clear distinction between "forms of domination" on the one hand and "forms of government" on the other. Preserving this distinction requires recognizing that forms of rule based on "domination . . . are, strictly speaking, illegal."[114] Invoking Montesquieu in place of Hobbes, she observed that "constitutional or lawful government is established through the division of power so that the same body (or men) does not make laws, execute them, and then sit in judgment on itself."[115] For Arendt a chasm exists between lawfully constituted political authority that establishes a stable framework for political life and an arbitrary power that isolates individuals and reduces its subjects to fearful impotence. Likewise, she argued that power and law "did not rely on the command–obedience relationship," but rather on the idea of "support" for "the laws to which the citizenry had given its consent."[116] Behind this idea is a conception of government whose power does not rely on its capacity to compel compliance and enforce submission, but rather rests on the continuing sanction of its citizenry that is maintained in both an active and tacit sense.

By this view, political "power" reflects the positive ability of human beings to enter into cooperative relationships with one another and organize those relationships into enduring forms for mutual benefit. In an explicit effort to challenge the conventional terminology that she identified with the academic field of political science, Arendt attempted to redefine such "key words" as "power." As part of this effort, she proposed: "*Power* corresponds to the human ability not just to act but to act in concert. Power is never the property of an individual; it belongs to a group and remains in existence only so long as the group keeps together."[117] By forming groups, human beings generate their own power through which they can act more effectively and pursue ends beyond the reach of discrete individuals. Power in human affairs then is utterly dependent on the relationships among persons, whose collective solidarity enables them to act in concert.

She distinguished this relational concept of power from the idea of "strength" as a distinct quality of a singular person or an object. The "strength" of an individual may or may not have bearing on his/her relationships with others, but, she wrote, the "strength of even the strongest individual can always be overpowered by the many, who often will combine for no other purpose than to ruin strength precisely because of its peculiar independence."[118] Strength then is not the source of power, and the group that creates power is joined by some element of persuasion that motivates individuals to act in concert. Likewise, she argued, "power and violence are opposites; where the one rules absolutely, the other is absent."[119] Violence is an "instrument" by which those who use it may compel submission from others, but cannot earn their "support" since this involves freely given assent. A growing reliance on this "implement" is typically indicative of an increasing lack of support among those against whom it is applied. As a tactic, the use of violence can be very effective and "destroy power" understood in this sense, but it can never create power.[120] Of course, Arendt recognized that, in practice, governments exercise power in combination with the use of violence to varying degrees. However, she emphasized the importance of seeing "power" and "violence" as conceptually distinct. She sought to undermine any equation between political power and the monopolization of the legitimate means of violence by showing how the categories of "power" and "violence" are opposed in principle.[121]

In drawing such distinctions, Arendt sought to redress a gross imbalance in the modern understanding of power by sketching a vastly different model. Writing at the height of the cold war, she observed, it is not sufficient to know merely what we "fight against." If such a "fight is to be more than a mere fight for survival," we need to clarify, in positive terms, the nature of the cause we are "fighting for."[122] For Arendt the "*raison d'être* of politics is freedom . . ." and her appreciation for the ideal of a free political realm grounded on mutual consent in which citizens meet as equals stands as a direct counterpart to her diagnosis of the evils of totalitarianism.[123] In her view, freedom provides the opportunity for creative "action." This kind of activity is rooted in the uniquely human capacity for "spontaneity," which enables individuals to bring forth something new in the world with consequences that may be good or bad but whose full effects are always unforeseeable. Here again, her appreciation for this capacity had been heightened by her study of the dehumanizing character of the concentration camp system, which sought to destroy every element of human individuality that is expressed through this "spontaneity." Like equality, she argued, freedom is not given in nature, but rather is a collective good that can only be established and shared by members of a community. The exercise of freedom requires a bounded and protected space that only a community can provide. This space is the (public) political realm, and for Arendt real freedom is quintessentially political in nature. Over the course of human history, the creation of such spaces has always been far more the exception than the rule. In her view, recognition of this historical fact merely underscores the importance of seeking to understand more fully the specific positive conditions that have proven necessary for humanity to enjoy freedom in order to advance this cause. Arendt's discussion of the ideals at stake is often elusively abstract, but they nevertheless provide a set of positive terms that the realists' emphasis on the negative aspects of power conspicuously lack.

TOWARD A REPUBLICAN SOCIAL CONTRACT THEORY AND FEDERATIVE MODEL

Arendt, Kennan, and Morgenthau all recognized that the advent of nuclear weapons technology had profoundly altered the stakes in war and in peace. As early as 1950, Kennan opposed the adoption of nuclear weapons as a significant component of American military strategy and warned against the risks of an arms race.[124] By the early 1960s, Morgenthau had come to reject any distinction in strategy between the "limited" and "unlimited" use of nuclear weapons as predicated on a dangerous illusion. The recognition that any war between great powers, such as the United States and the Soviet Union, could easily spiral into a full exchange of nuclear weapons and thereby annihilate both sides threw into question a major premise of realism about the role of war as the inevitable final arbiter in the international realm.[125] In summarizing this dilemma, Arendt observed: "The technical development of the implements of violence has now reached a point where no political goal could conceivably correspond to their destructive potential or justify their actual use in armed conflict. Hence warfare—from time immemorial the ultimate arbiter in international disputes—has lost much of its effectiveness and nearly all of its glamour."[126] As Arendt pointed out, the risks of a nuclear exchange had undermined the old rationales that the great powers had traditionally used to justify war and gave the pursuit of peace a new imperative for global policy-makers.[127] Moreover, the realist assumption about the unalterable anarchical character of the international realm seemed to make full scale nuclear war an inevitable prospect sometime in the future. It is against the twin threats of totalitarianism and thermonuclear war that Arendt sought to rethink the core principles of modern politics. Both of these developments underscored for her that humanity shares a common collective interest that transcends any particular difference of nation, party, or culture. As an alternative to the sovereign nation-state model as the basis for the international order, she proposed federalism as a principle of political organization.

Against much the same background, realists like Morgenthau began to distance themselves from the core assumptions of their own approach and to embrace the merits of a cosmopolitan–utopian perspective. By 1961, Morgenthau had concluded that the "sovereign nation-state is in the process of becoming obsolete."[128] The time had come to prepare for "the abolition of international relations itself" as had been traditionally conceived.[129] To overcome the problem of anarchy in the international realm, Morgenthau saw the only possible solution to be some form of "world state," the prospects for which, he feared, remained doubtful. "The experience of two world wars within a quarter century and the prospects of a third one to be fought with nuclear weapons," he observed, "have imparted the idea of a world state with unprecedented urgency . . . . Reforms within the international society have failed and were bound to fail. What is needed, then, is a radical transformation of the existing international society of sovereign nations into a supranational community of individuals."[130] This model of the world state is based on the idea of "the transference of the sovereign over the individual nations to a world authority as the individual nations are sovereign within their respective territories."[131] At the same time, he also ruled out any prospect for the establishment of a world state "under the present moral, social, and political conditions of the world."[132] This solution then is offered less as a viable alternative or a guiding principle for reform than as a utopia that is completely out of reach for the foreseeable future.[133] Having explained the "urgency" for a "radical transformation" of international society, he then leaves us in an inescapable box with the problem. Morgenthau's vision of a world state shows that he never ceased to think in traditional terms of sovereignty to address the dangers he saw threatening international society. He explicitly rejected the prospect that federal principles could be applied to international society. Using the historical emergence of federal systems in the United States and Switzerland as his examples, he argued, that such systems are only possible where a "pre-existing community" exists upon which they may rest, though he did see some limited attractive potential in the emerging framework of the European Community.[134]

Both Kennan and Arendt rejected such a vision of a world-state as not simply unfeasible but also as undesirable.[135] "A supranational authority would either be ineffective or be monopolized by the nation that happens to be the strongest," she argued, "which could easily become the most frightful tyranny conceivable, since from its global police force there would be no escape—until it finally fell apart."[136] Kennan was always much more skeptical of the traditional model of sovereignty than Morgenthau, and also much more positive about the potential for new forms of federative associations. The traditional model, Kennan observed, assumes the "complete independence of the sovereign authority, wherever the quality of sovereignty might be said to reside—as an independence that no outside power [is] at liberty to challenge."[137] However, he pointed out, "a mere glance at the realities of international life will suffice to show that this is not really the way things work today. There are dozens of ways in which actions of a government, even where applicable in the first instance only to its own people and its own territory, affect the interests of other countries."[138] The sovereign model of political authority is vastly too blunt an instrument to deal with the realities of multiethnic and multilingual populations sharing territorial spaces. Alternative models are needed, he argued, "to find places for ethnic minorities in larger countries that will do justice to their own thirst for internal autonomy and international dignity, not to mention some control over their own economic resources. . . ."[139] As for the United States, he argued that "this country will not solve the problems of its developing world relationships except on the basis of a readiness to go in for an extensive merging of its life with other peoples."[140] As opposed to looking toward the ideal of world government, he urged along more federative lines that the U.S. government "start by tackling first the problem of our relationship with peoples nearest and closest to us. . . . The best way for us to move toward any form of unification is to try to make it so far as possible a living reality, or at least a living possibility, by unilateral actions affecting the nature of our own society before the problems of a formal contractual relationship are dealt with."[141] He offered the example of the European Community as the kind of model he had in mind.[142]

While advocating federalist arrangements as a practical measure, Kennan did not propose them as a panacea or as a means to overcome the anarchy of the international realm. Although he took the problem of nuclear weapons every bit as seriously as Morgenthau, Kennan did not believe that this anarchy could ever be overcome or that war could be eliminated as the "ultimate sanction for the protection of the national interest."[143] Instead he emphasized the importance of limiting the spread of nuclear weapons technology and radically reducing existing arsenals. He never linked his support of federalism with this effort or with articulating a new cosmopolitan vision to supercede a realist understanding of international relations. To the degree that Morgenthau believed that the advent of nuclear weapons had created a new imperative for some sort of cosmopolitan ideal, Arendt was much closer to Morgenthau than to Kennan. In a sense, she was simply echoing the former's own grim conclusions about many of the core realist assumptions when she observed in 1963 that "those who still put their faith in power politics in the traditional sense of the term and, therefore, in war as the last resort of all foreign policy may well discover in a not-too distant future that they have become masters in a rather useless and obsolete trade."[144] However, to the degree that she believed a solution could be found to this latest threat to human existence, she looked to federalism as the source for principles to transcend the anarchy of the state system. Under such principles, she imagined that a global system of federations of various shapes and sizes could possibly emerge that would be truly "*inter*national," and not "*supra*national." As opposed to the idea of a world-state, this kind of federative model would be decentralized, in ways that would accommodate autonomy and diversity among smaller member units that would provide the main locus for political participation. This kind of federal alternative to the state system, she hoped, would be built from the bottom up rather than the top down, according to a model "in which power would be constituted horizontally and not vertically."[145]

Beyond such speculative hints, Arendt never sought to develop any utopian plan for world federalism either in terms of how it could be achieved or how it would operate in practice. Rather than engaging in utopian theorizing from the top down, she focused on clarifying the principles through which political freedom, rooted in the structure of human communities, may be advanced from the bottom up. In the shadow of the twentieth century's experience with totalitarianism and nuclear weapons, she sought to emphasize that humanity is not helplessly marching toward oblivion but, in fact, at every step always has alternatives. Her whole approach to politics rested on a rejection of determinism. To whatever extent the actions of men and women are subject to processes and systems beyond their control, there also existed with the birth of each generation the possibility for new beginnings, for interrupting the causal flow of events from the past into the future with creative new initiatives. Consistent with the importance she attached to the role of beginnings as a source of alternatives and as evidence of humanity's capacity to remake its world, she turned to seventeenth-century social contract theory to articulate the alternative principles of political power and freedom, which she envisioned. Because the key move in this theory is explaining the transition from a "state of nature" to an organized political community, it offered her a useful vehicle to think through the conceptual basis through which new initiatives for advancing freedom may begin.[146]

In building upon this seventeenth-century theory, Arendt contrasted the two models of the social contract developed by Locke and Hobbes. Of these two models, she described the first form as a "horizontal" contract by which autonomous individuals bind themselves through mutual promises in order to establish a community. In Arendt's view, the most vivid example of this act of promising between equals occurred at the signing of the American Declaration of Independence. Their example illustrated for her the power that the binding act of promising can generate and the essential difference that distinguishes active pledging from passive consent.[147] Arendt derived this horizontal model from the social contract theory of John Locke.[148] His twofold distinction between an original social compact upon which the social order rests and a subsequent agreement from which government derives had enabled him to justify the right to revolution against a king while exempting the traditional social order itself from challenge. In contrast to this notion of a "horizontal" contract, Arendt distinguished a second form as a "vertical" contract. This form existed directly between the ruler and the ruled, the one and the many. She identified it in broad schematic outline with Hobbes. Under this kind of agreement, the many exchange their rights and powers in return for security and protection pledged from the one that is elevated above them. By this step, the individual "gives up his isolated strength and power to constitute a government; far from gaining a new power, and possibly more than he had before, he resigns his power such as it is, and far from binding himself through promises, he merely expresses his 'consent' to be ruled by the government, whose power consists of the sum total of forces which all individual persons have channeled into it and which are monopolized by the government for the alleged benefit of all subjects."[149] Through entering this contract, individuals do not acquire more power on a collective basis by combining themselves in an alliance structure, but rather establish a supreme power over themselves that takes its power from them. Accordingly, this new supreme power leaves them as isolated and impotent as before its establishment. Individuals move directly from their natural condition to political subjugation under a sovereign without the intermediary step of organizing themselves into a society that retains its organized structure apart from whatever government is then created.

Arendt argued that the first of these two forms of contract "contains *in nuce* both the republican principle, according to which power resides in the people" and "the federal principle . . . according to which constituted political bodies can combine and enter into lasting alliances without losing their identities."[150] Under this republican principle, individuals come together to establish communities on the basis of agreements that are freely entered and mutually made with one another for the benefits of association. As "political societies," these communities have organizational structures but claim no sovereign authority for themselves. By this federal principle, these independent bodies may unite with other such bodies while each retains internally their own separate, autonomous institutions and spaces for public life.[151] Through the effect of combination, the establishment of federal frameworks through which such bodies are united creates new sources of power rather than simply taking power away from its constituent units. In Arendt's view, the federal principle contradicts the idea that political power is indivisible and absolute, because it presupposes that political power can and should be divided through separation and distribution.[152] She identified the second form of this contract with the principles of absolute monarchy, whereby the ruler "is liable to be construed in the image of divine power, since only God is omnipotent." The most dangerous ramifications of this antipluralistic conception emerge when it is yoked to the principle of nationhood. According to the "national principle," she explained, "there must be one representative of the nation as a whole, and . . . the government is understood to incorporate the will of all nationals."[153] Because in her view it cannot be detached from these anti-pluralistic premises, she rejected the concept of sovereignty itself. As Hobbes's use of the "Artificial Man" as a metaphor for the sovereign suggests, the idea of sovereignty has traditionally emphasized the singularity of political power that is understood in terms of the unified person of the ruler who stands above and apart from the political community as a whole.[154]

The difference between these two forms of contract directly corresponds to the contrast Arendt draws between "power" and "strength." "Power," she observed, "can be divided without decreasing it, and the interplay of powers with their checks and balances is even liable to generate more power, so long as, at least, as the interplay is alive and has not resulted in stalemate. Strength, on the contrary, is indivisible, and while it, too, is checked and balanced by the presence of others, the interplay of plurality in this case spells a definite limitation of the strength of the individual. . . ."[155] Both are conditioned by the "plurality" that is fundamental to the character of human interaction. "Plurality," Arendt explained, "is the condition of human action because we are all the same, that is human, in such a way that nobody is ever the same as anyone else who ever lived, or will live."[156] This feature of the human condition is the basis by which individuals may distinguish themselves from one another. It presupposes that individuals are different from one another, but it also presupposes human equality that rests on the mutual interdependence of human beings in sharing a world together. Without this equality, she argues, individuals could not communicate with one another through speech.[157] "Plurality" is then, in Arendt's view, "the condition . . . of all political life," and living together is "the only indispensable material factor in the generation of the power" that supports this life.[158] They are bound together by the obligations of promise and by the common set of institutions they share.[159]

Arendt developed the groundwork for a model of political authority as an alternative to traditional concepts of sovereignty that is not simply adaptable to federative arrangements for certain purposes but presuppose them. Where Kennan and even to a lesser extent Morgenthau had recognized the possible advantages of various kinds of federative associations, these alternatives remained at the margins of their analysis and their focus on the power politics of existing states. Arendt's emphasis on plurality and spontaneity as necessary positive conditions for political life flows directly from her analysis of totalitarian terror that aims to eliminate both these qualities as well as the negative conditions that made the rise of totalitarianism possible, namely the atomization of modern society that undermines the reciprocal bonds between human beings.

Jürgen Habermas has observed that Arendt's concept of political power works best to explain the "generation" of power, but that it fails to take adequately into account its "strategic" dimensions in the competition for power and the modes of its "employment" within a political system.[160] This criticism has merit, but Habermas overlooks one of her central concerns to connect the problem of power with the problem of responsibility. The counter-model of political authority that she delineated emphasized the role of individual agents as being responsible for the terms of their cooperation and accountable to their promises.

In this way, she sought to build the principle of accountability into the very concept of power rather than treating it as some form of external restraint or normative expectation. She began from the recognition that portraying the command/obedience model of authority as simply a function of the way that power is organized necessarily obscures broader issues of individual accountability. Such a model assumes uncritically that "obedience" captures the essence of the relationship between leaders and their followers or the character of modern administrative organizations. By contrast, Arendt contended, "only a child obeys; if an adult 'obeys' he actually supports the organization or the authority of the law that claims 'obedience.' "[161] By setting an agenda, the leader may initiate a particular action, but those who work toward achieving the leader's goals are not merely "followers" but are also co-participants in a "common enterprise." Here she is setting a high standard, but one that she deliberately posed as a sharp counterpoint to what she saw as the dominant ethos of the modern era. More broadly, through this approach to power, she was seeking to emphasize the crucial importance of our taking active responsibility for the conduct and condition of the common world that we share rather than ceding or assigning that civic responsibility to governing elites.

Individual Accountability, Universal Responsibility, and the Cosmopolitan Ideal of Justice

"Moral rules operate within the conscience of individuals," Morgenthau observed. "Government by clearly identified men, who can be held personally accountable for their acts, is therefore the precondition for the existence of an effective system of international ethics." In emphasizing the importance of individual accountability, Morgenthau was not writing as an advocate for new and more stringent measures of accountability, but rather sought to call attention to an inescapable modern dilemma. "Where responsibility for government is widely distributed among a great number of individuals," he then explained, "with different conceptions as to what is morally required in international affairs, or with no conceptions at all, international morality as an effective system of restraints upon international policy becomes impossible."[162] This passage appears as part of a broader discussion that seeks to show how the democratization of an ever increasing number of governments destroyed the old aristocratic ethic of personal honor that had traditionally constrained statesmen and how the rise of nationalism had undermined any consensus over international norms that could regulate the conduct of governments. Having resigned himself to the impossibility of finding any solution to this dilemma, he thereby relegated the issue of international ethics to the background.

For his part, Kennan recognized that establishing the principle of an international "community of responsibility that unites men everywhere" and respects the "equal dignity of all nations" is "tremendously important" on the symbolic level.[163] He saw this symbol embodied in the United Nations, and held out the hope that "as interdependence and mutual responsibility grow among nations . . . the United Nations will provide one of the most important channels through which those changes can find practical expression."[164] However, he never sought to work out the implications of this notion of a "community of responsibility," and how he envisioned its practical bearing on the conduct of policy remained vague. This vagueness seems indicative of the marginality he attached to such notions as a factor in defining the national interest. "Instead of making ourselves slaves of the concepts of international law and morality," he observed, we should "confine these concepts to the unobtrusive, almost feminine, function of the gentle civilizer of national self-interest in which they find their true value . . . ."[165] In a final summation of his personal philosophy, Kennan remained skeptical, like Arendt, about the concrete benefit of international human rights instruments to the individuals they are designed to protect and the intellectual viability of any modern version of natural law. He acknowledged that in some instances the United Nations and national government's efforts to promote human rights had a "useful influence" in impressing on some offending states "a certain self-consciousness before world opinion."[166] However, he continued to see a certain "sanctimoniousness in American statements and demands about human rights," and reminded his readers that the government's "first duty is to the national interest."[167] In light of his many published criticisms of the shallowness, materialism, and profligacy of the culture of his fellow citizens, it seems fair to ask whether such moral judgments expressed at home are any less open to being interpreted as "sanctimonious"? To guide American foreign policy in a more responsible direction, Kennan's major institutional reform idea proposed the creation of a "permanent outside advisory body to the president" made up of "senior statesmen."[168] Whatever the merits of this idea on its own terms, it does not begin to address the problems of the corrupting influence of the "military–industrial complex" that he spelled out, but it does clearly reflect his own top-down perspective.

Arendt could never have been satisfied to leave the problem of international ethics and responsibility where Kennan and Morgenthau did. She might have pointed out that the latter's arguments help to show that modern developments have so fundamentally changed and magnified the problem of accountability that it has become too systematic and acute to ignore. The "rule by Nobody is clearly the most tyrannical of all," she observed, "since there is no one left who could even be asked to answer for what is being done. It is this state of affairs, making it impossible to localize responsibility and to identify the enemy, that is among the most potent causes of the current worldwide rebellious unrest . . . ."[169] From a perspective that focuses on the promotion of national interests of a superpower, the absence of effective measures of international accountability may seem regrettable in principle but not central to the policy questions of the day. Likewise, it is difficult to imagine that many people occupying the "balcony of statesmen" will especially welcome critiques that demand new measures enforcing their personal accountability. Arendt's approach to this problem stemmed from the fact that she saw the Holocaust as posing a radical legal and moral challenge at the international level that had to be met. "It is essentially for this reason," she contended, "that the unprecedented, once it has appeared, may become a precedent for the future. . . . If genocide is an actual possibility of the future, then no people on earth . . . can feel reasonably sure of its existence without the help and protection of international law."[170] From this perspective, Morgenthau's kind of resignation meant tolerating the prospect of new genocides in the future.

To address this danger, Arendt argued for the importance of modernizing criminal jurisprudence so that perpetrators of such "new crimes" could be effectively prosecuted. As a first step, this meant recognizing that acts of genocide represented a qualitatively different and more heinous category of crime from ordinary murder or war-related atrocities, because in seeking to eliminate an entire people from the earth it constituted a crime against the human diversity that is essential to the "order of mankind."[171] As a second step, she called for the creation of an "international penal code" under which such crimes could be prosecuted and an international criminal court in which their perpetrators would be tried.[172] In contrast to the symbolic character of the international human rights norms of her day, the clear advantage of a penal code and judicial body able to enforce it was the prospect that individuals would be subject to some measure of legal accountability. For this very reason—the specter of individual accountability—she was not optimistic that either an international penal code or an international criminal court would ever be established.[173]

In both his brief review of her book, *Eichmann in Jerusalem*, and in his longer retrospective review of her work, "Hannah Arendt on Totalitarianism and Democracy," Morgenthau did not address Arendt's treatment of these issues.[174] Like Arendt, he had been critical of the Nuremberg trials, but after dismissing them as victor's justice he did not take up the larger legal and moral issues that the Holocaust had posed.[175] He also dismissed the Allied denazification policy for resting on the "absurd idea" that "one could, through the medium of some superficial characteristics, objectively determine not only who was a Nazi and who was not but also to what degree one was a Nazi. . . ."[176] Arendt also sharply criticized the naiveté of Allied plans for denazification along similar lines, but that was only the starting point of her analysis.[177]

For his part, Kennan denounced the "crimes" committed by the Nazis as "immeasurable," and expressed his own preference that the top Nazi leaders should have been summarily executed at the war's end.[178] Like Morgenthau, Kennan was sensitive to the hypocrisy of the Allied governments, especially the inclusion of Stalinist Russia, at a trial judging the Germans for their crimes. The clear "implication," he argued, is that "such crimes were justifiable and forgivable when committed by the leaders of one government . . . but unjustifiable and unforgivable when committed by another set of governmental leaders."[179] He sharply criticized the Nuremberg trials, and opposed denazification on practical grounds. "The main purpose of our post-hostilities action on Germany is," he reasoned, "to assure that the country will not again become the seat of a program of military aggression which might threaten our security. For this . . . it must be demonstrated to Germany that aggression does not pay. But I do not see that this involves the artificial removal of any given class in Germany from its position in public life."[180] The blanket notion of "artificial removal of any given class" lumps together discrete individuals with different degrees of complicity into an abstract, homogenous category that shows how far removed issues of accountability were from his thinking here. The choices involved in determining appropriate punishment and identifying those to be subject to some form of punishment were not limited to the kind of stark either/or that his formulation implies. Although Kennan, like Morgenthau, was concerned with blunting American tendencies toward self-righteous moralism, the net result was to minimize the issues at stake. "That many Germans merited punishment was clear," Kennan acknowledged, "but their delinquency was not proof of our virtue."[181] The term "delinquency" is at best a curious descriptor to apply to those responsible for implementing the systematic criminality of the Third Reich.

Neither Kennan nor Morgenthau were dismissive of the scale and human costs of the brutalities that the Nazis had inflicted, but both tended to view the problem through the lens of state policy and to make American postwar national security interests their overriding consideration. Both saw the problem of accountability as too difficult to sort out in such circumstances, and hoped that the successful experience of democratic government in Germany would be the most effective means to discredit the Nazi past.[182] Both were also aware that the Germans were not alone in having committed atrocities, and saw almost all of the Allies as having dirty hands. This concern about hypocrisy is indicative of the intellectual integrity and critical discernment of both men. At the same time, because this issue centered on the conduct of governments, their concern with it also reflects how closely they identified their own perspectives with the state whose policies they sought to influence (and whom during this period Kennan served). "History, in judging the individual cruelties of this struggle," Kennan observed, "will not distinguish between those of the victor and vanquished. . . . If others wish, in the face of this situation, to pursue illumination of those sinister recesses in which the brutalities of this war find their record, they may do so. The degree of relative guilt which such inquiries may bring to light is something of which I, as an American, prefer to remain ignorant."[183] This quote is from a memorandum that Kennan wrote in 1947 and a passage from which he reproduced in his *Memoirs* to illustrate his thinking at that time, but he did not give any indication in the surrounding narrative that his thinking had changed in the light of new experiences or from retrospective reflection. It demonstrates a kind of moral high-mindedness that recognizes that no party to the war had a monopoly on guilt or innocence, but at the expense as a practical matter of suspending the whole question of responsibility for any particular acts or policies. Assigning the role of investigator and judge to "history" takes the problem of accountability out of the present and projects it into the indefinite future as a subject for historians rather than any contemporary forum of justice. Given that crimes involved genocide, this high-mindedness invokes a moral equivalence that amounts to an abdication of the responsibility toward both the victims and justice to find a principled basis for judgment.

Kennan also saw equivalence in the suffering that Hitler's regime had inflicted on Germans and non-Germans alike. For example, in his book, *Russia and the West under Lenin and Stalin*, he observed that Nazi rule "was a human tragedy, and one of which a great many Germans were sufferers no less than others."[184] In important ways, this kind of formulation invites closing off the myriad of questions that the issue involved rather than opening them up (if only to leave them for others to pursue). That the German people paid a heavy price for Hitler's policies is clear, but lumping all the different groups that suffered into one common whole flattens out any distinctions differentiating causes, acts, motives, knowledge, injuries, capacities, and agency that make any kind of moral or legal accounting possible. Without such distinctions, we are left as passive spectators to contemplate another sad "tragedy" that trapped its participants and defies human judgment. For this very reason, Arendt was at best skeptical of the usefulness in applying such "general notions" as "tragedy" to such episodes of violence.[185] However, the genre of tragedy may hold some lessons that Kennan did not consider. In Aeschylus's *Oresteia* trilogy, a cycle of violence spanning three generations is finally resolved by holding a court trial, a trial that in itself is intended to establish the precedent for the institutionalization of a new standard of criminal justice.

The difference between Kennan and Arendt here is not that one recognized the serious (and often insurmountable) difficulties involved in rendering justice while the other did not, but rather that Kennan immediately focused on these difficulties as a rationale to refrain from thinking any further about the problem. In part, his disinterest in this problem reflected a belief that, in the context of the cold war, the Germans were too valuable as allies against the Soviets to hold their past complicity in Nazi criminality against them. In fact, he goes to some length to attribute the main burden of this criminality to Hitler and his immediate circle of associates. Moreover, long before historians would conduct much research into this question, Kennan had reached the conclusion that the Nazis had drawn their support from the "lower middle class" and that the leaders that had emerged after the war in Bonn were men of an entirely different type.[186] While offering almost no evidence to support any of these conjectures about the character of popular support for the Nazis or the relationship of German elites to the Nazi regime during its years in power, he complained that the Allies during the war and its immediate aftermath had "misjudged" the German "conservative class." He lamented that the Allies failed to anticipate "what resources of courage and idealism the sons and daughters of just these people, scourged by the consciousness of Hitler's degradation of their country, would succeed in producing out of their bewildered midst."[187] The stance of moral high-mindedness that Kennan adopts in his *Memoirs* thus reflects the fact that he reached his own personal verdict on these issues of accountability and responsibility.

At the same time, Kennan's disinterest in these questions was also entirely consistent with his own basic priorities and intellectual commitments. As he observed in a later context, "humanity divides itself . . . between those who, in their political philosophy, place the emphasis on order and those who place it on justice. I belong in the first of these categories."[188] Moreover, in contrast to Arendt, Kennan approached such questions from a position of moral relativism whereby he was acutely conscious of the particularity of his own (American) values and skeptical about invoking any general normative standards to be applied outside his own context.

For Arendt the absence of any universal rules or "yardsticks" by which individuals can render judgments was one of the central difficulties anyone faces in comprehending totalitarianism. Nevertheless, she insisted that "we shall only come to terms with this past if we begin to judge and to be frank about it."[189] In her view, the absence of recognized universal rules makes the cultivation of an individual's faculty of judgment much more important now than ever before because without it there is ultimately nothing for the individual to fall back on in distinguishing between right and wrong. Arendt would have seen Kennan's high-minded distaste for the task of judging as characteristic of our era, but no less an "escape" from "personal responsibility."[190] The "fear of responsibility," she observed, "is not only stronger than conscience, but even stronger, under certain circumstances, than fear of death."[191] She dismissed "the reproach of self-righteousness raised against those who judge" as an "age-old" objection whose pedigree does not give it validity. "Justice, but not mercy," she observed, "is a matter of judgment, and about nothing does public opinion everywhere seem to be in happier agreement than that no one has the right to judge someone else."[192] When this right is abjured, the whole basis for holding any individual accountable is thereby undermined. In broadly advocating the importance of exercising this kind of judgment, however, she often seemed remarkably unconcerned about the other side of this issue, namely about those that may be uninformed, under-scrutinized, overzealous, or unprincipled. She also did not adequately consider whether the social practice of tolerance in a pluralistic society does not in some large measure depend on a willingness of its members to suspend at least the expression of judgment in numerous instances on a variety of issues.

No less than Kennan or Morgenthau, Arendt recognized the impossibility of finding a "political solution within human capacity for the crime of administrative mass murder," and, in fact, was considerably more conscious of the difficulties involved because, unlike them, she had grasped the full measure of the crimes involved.[193] From the beginning, she emphasized the insurmountable problems that any Allied program of denazification would encounter. As she observed of the Germans in 1945:

> the boundaries dividing criminals from normal persons, the guilty from the innocent, have so completely effaced that nobody will be able to tell in Germany whether in any case he is dealing with a secret hero or with a former mass murderer. . . . The number of those who are responsible and guilty will be relatively small. There are many who share responsibility without any visible proof of guilt. There are many more who have become guilty without being in the least responsible.[194]

Mass prosecutions of German perpetrators would not be effective, she contended, because (among other reasons) the overwhelming majority of Germans did not feel any responsibility for the crimes committed by their government. In principle, a criminal justice system rests on the assumption, she observed, that the verdict of "guilt implies the consciousness of guilt, and punishment evidence that the criminal is a responsible person."[195] Here, she contended, that consciousness at the individual level was largely absent and, given the circumstances of 12 years of totalitarian rule, understandably so. She rejected any notion of "collective guilt," because it ignores the conditions under which many persons had been drawn into complicity and because at that level of generalized abstraction the accusation of guilt has no purchase on the individuals to whom it is applied. "Where all are guilty," she observed, "nobody in the last analysis can be judged. For that guilt is not accompanied by even the mere appearance, the mere pretense of responsibility."[196] Along these same lines, she would later add: "confessions of collective guilt are the best possible safeguard against the discovery of culprits, and the very magnitude of the crimes is the best excuse for doing nothing."[197]

In her report on the 1961 Eichmann trial, Arendt developed her analysis of these issues. She saw the legal and moral challenges posed by the Third Reich exemplified in the Eichmann case in two crucial respects. First, though his crimes were monstrous, Eichmann's conscious intent in committing them had not been. He was neither "perverted" nor "sadistic," nor an ardent anti-Semite in his personal beliefs.

Rather he was "terribly and terrifyingly normal."[198] He was not "stupid," but simply "thoughtless," without the capacity or inclination to think through the moral implications of his acts, their real human consequences, in a way that encompassed the "enlarged perspective" of others. In short, he lacked any powers of "judgment." Second, though as a bureaucratic official in the Third Reich he had been responsible for the implementation and coordination of much of the Nazi deportation policy toward the Jews, he had not directly killed or injured anyone nor personally committed any specific atrocity. In his work as a bureaucrat, nearly all of his acts had been carried out lawfully pursuant to the orders of his superiors. This distance between the planning done by men like Eichmann and the actual crimes themselves enabled the whole chain of command to disassociate themselves as individuals from personal responsibility for genocide. The example of a mass murderer who did not recognize his acts as murderous because they were a function of his professional, administrative duties and not an expression of personal criminal intent encapsulated for her the peculiarly modern dimension of the Holocaust.

Arendt emphasized that the trial of Eichmann had one, and only one purpose, that is, to "do justice."[199] She criticized the prosecutor for seeking to use the trial to educate a wider public on the history of anti-Semitism, in which Eichmann's criminal conduct was depicted as the expression of a much longer and deeper historical pattern.[200] This strategy turns the perpetrator into a symbol and shifts the focus away from what he actually did. At the same time, she dismissed the cog in the machine "theory" that interpreted Eichmann as simply one small instrument within a vast bureaucratic apparatus. The latter is favored by political scientists and sociologists, she observed, who seek to explain the structural or systemic context in which human action occurs. Whatever their analytical merits, such explanations have the effect of removing the burden of responsibility from any particular individual by dispersing it across an entire organizational structure until the principle of responsibility itself is rendered almost meaningless. Her point is not to reject social science methodology as a general matter, but to highlight what is obscured through such approaches.

By bringing such functionaries to trial, she argued, "all the cogs in the machine, no matter how insignificant, are in court transformed back into perpetrators, that is to say, into human beings."[201] For Arendt the imperative of rendering justice had to be understood as distinct and independent from all other modes of seeking to comprehend and explain the phenomena like the Holocaust, such as through social scientific investigation. As opposed to "thinking" (or theorizing) which "deals with representations of things that are absent," she observed, "judging always involves particulars and things close at hand."[202] Both are necessary and "interrelated." The exercise of judgment is not (or should not be) confined to the courtroom or to matters of law, but there she found it best exemplified as the "one institution" in the modern world where issues of personal responsibility were "still" squarely addressed.[203] Arendt supported sentencing Eichmann to death, and she also endorsed the Israeli court's decision that "in general *the degree of responsibility increases as we draw farther away from the man who uses the fatal instrument with his own hands.*"[204] By emphasizing the courtroom setting as the exemplar for her notion of accountability, Arendt grounded this notion on the principle that agents should be directly and individually accountable to a general, external and public standard, namely the law, and not merely to their own private consciences or to some vague abstraction like the "judgment of history."[205]

In weighing accountability for crimes against humanity like genocide, Arendt argued that the law should treat the intent of perpetrator as ultimately irrelevant. The absolute character of such crimes creates an objective liability irrespective of the agent's subjective intent. As she explained, the genocidal policies of the Third Reich constituted "an attack upon human diversity as such, that is, upon a characteristic of the 'human status' without which the very words 'mankind' or 'humanity' would be devoid of meaning."[206] The Nazis had not simply persecuted a minority within their midst or murdered civilians as an ancillary tactic of war, but rather had sought with deliberate intent systematically to eradicate an entire people from the face of the earth. The nature of this intent makes this type of crime qualitatively distinct from—and far more "monstrous" than—even mass murder conducted on a vast scale. By using group difference like Jewishness as its criterion for extermination, Nazi genocide violates the most basic understanding of "humanity" as a multiplicity of peoples whose differences give this "idea" its defining character. In this sense, such a crime perpetrated against one people is a crime against all peoples, that is, against their right to exist as a distinct people and share the earth with others. Such crimes, Arendt contended, must be tried before an international tribunal, because anything less than that "minimizes" the universal threat.[207] Nevertheless, she defended the legitimacy of Israel's authority to try Eichmann in its own national courts as a necessary as well as lawful expedient.[208]

The normative basis for such an international court and the definition of crimes against humanity rests on a cosmopolitan ideal of justice.

This ideal, Arendt observed, "transcends the present sphere of international law which still operates in terms of reciprocal agreements between sovereign states."[209] It presupposes a conception of human "solidarity," based on a shared "community of interests," that recognizes an overarching principle of universal responsibility. This principle mandates "that in one form or another men must assume responsibility for all crimes committed by men, and that eventually all nations will be forced to answer for the evil committed by others."[210] Equally important for Arendt, recognizing this principle means "assigning a monopoly of guilt to no one."[211] However, this insistence of the absolute relativity of human guilt and innocence did not become, as it did for Kennan, an argument for suspending questions of accountability. Rather she saw it as an argument for taking seriously the full extent of one's moral implication in the common affairs of humanity, which included recognizing an individual's responsibility for both actions and judgments. Such a universalistic perspective, she argued, "is the only guarantee that one 'superior race' after another may not feel obligated to follow the 'natural law' of the right of the powerful, and exterminate 'inferior races unworthy of survival'. . . ."[212]

Her concept of doing "justice," which she emphasized in her report on the Eichmann trial, needs to be understood within this universalistic framework. This cosmopolitan ideal stands above any particularist understanding of justice that "identifies what is right with the notion of what is good for—the individual, or the family, or the people, or the largest number."[213] Such particularist notions of justice, she warned, can provide compelling rationales for societies to justify the inclusion or exclusion of groups in the name of "being good or useful for the whole in distinction to its parts."[214] Taken to an extreme, a majority of voters could decide on a democratic basis "that for humanity as a whole, it would be better to liquidate certain parts thereof."[215]

Because modernity has undermined the force of any common belief in the transcendent normative standards of the past, such as God or natural law, Arendt contended that the idea of humanity itself must take the place of these standards. "Humanity, which for the eighteenth century, in Kantian terminology, was no more than a regulative idea," she argued, "has today become an inescapable fact. This new situation, in which "humanity" has in effect assumed the role of history, would mean in this context, the right to have rights, or the right of every individual to belong to humanity, should be guaranteed by humanity itself.[216] At its core, this "right to have rights" is for Arendt the recognized entitlement of every individual or group to full membership in a political community, a right on which all other effective rights in her view are predicated. The deprivation of membership is so fundamental, she emphasized, that it is tantamount to being expelled from humanity itself.[217]

The conclusions that Arendt drew from her "idea" of humanity remain problematic. She was grimly aware that this "idea" had, in fact, guaranteed nothing in the immediate past and was not likely to guarantee much in the foreseeable future. Her concept of the "right to have rights" left unexplained the actual status of this "right" as a legal or normative entitlement. Such a right has little practical value without some specified institutional agency that has the recognized authority and capacity to enforce it. Her failure to address such issues left her perilously vulnerable to the very critique that she had applied to the French Declaration of the Rights of Man. To answer this kind of criticism, she might have argued that some sort of ideal perspective is necessary as a guide to the future. As she observed of her mentor Karl Jasper's own cosmopolitan ideal, "political philosophy can hardly do more than describe and prescribe the new principle of political action."[218] Nevertheless, her articulation of this idea of humanity remains incomplete even at the level of broad principle, especially with respect to explaining the basis on which it is grounded. Here it might have helped her to link it more directly with the norms that have been developed in postwar international human rights law. It is unclear how carefully she followed developments in this law after writing her critique of these norms in *The Origins of Totalitarianism*, but even here she failed to consider their potential contribution to the definition of standards, if only at the symbolic level.

Of course, realists like Morgenthau and Kennan had their own idealist standpoint based on their understanding of the true national interest and the overarching moral "purpose" of their society. On this normative basis, they routinely criticized the inclinations toward "national self-centeredness" that they believed so often marred U.S. foreign policy.[219] Arendt's own idealist standpoint was a universal one, and she recognized that her ideal needed some grounding in law and legal institutions to be effective. From this standpoint, she argued for the development of an international penal code and the establishment of an international criminal court.

CONCLUSION

It is scarcely ironic that today the United States, in the name of its own particular national interests and the traditional prerogatives of a sovereign, is the single greatest opponent of the international criminal court. This opposition would not have surprised Arendt (or Morgenthau and Kennan), but she would have been skeptical that it was rooted in any principled stand for preserving a state's right to sovereignty or concern for national interest per se. Rather she would have seen such rationales as being part of a larger pattern by which individuals attempt to shield themselves from personal moral responsibility (as well as potential criminal liability) for their acts in the name of the collective interests or group they claim to be representing.[220] The legal rationales that the Bush administration has developed to justify exemptions for the United States from the Geneva Conventions and the Convention against Torture not only help to explain the fervor behind its opposition to the International Criminal Court, but also highlight its determination to insulate officials acting under presidential authority from legal accountability, including federal criminal statutes, as well as from Congressional oversight.[221]

Arendt looked into the "balcony of statesmen" in the modern democratic era, and found a pattern of moral cowardice in leaders who sought to act without "risk"; namely, the "risk" of being held personally accountable for their own specific deeds or failures to act. She saw this problem not only in the ways that leaders too often seek to insulate themselves from "individual moral responsibility," but also in the flaccid standards of accountability by which publics "judge" their leaders' conduct in office.[222] Of course, this insight into the "power-hungry" world of governing elites pursuing their own goals in "an atmosphere of inflamed ambitions, rivalries, sensitivities, anxieties, suspicions, embarrassments, and resentments" would not come as any revelation to realists like Kennan and Morgenthau.[223] But the divergence in response between Olympian resignation over the tragic nature or fates of mortal men and an insistence on raising the standards of individual accountability for those in power reflects (among others) a fundamental difference in vantage point.

This difference in vantage point can have a profound impact on how "reality" is perceived, on the manner in which divergent kinds of questions or problems are prioritized, on how responsibility is conceived, and on the choice of criteria by which the various costs and benefits of policies are measured. Likewise, one's assessment of acceptable costs may depend a good deal on the degree to which one (as an individual) is directly bearing those costs, with whom one associates shared interests and loyalties, and the degree to which one identifies with the bearer(s) of those costs. As the anthropologist

Michael Herzfeld has cautioned in his study of the modern bureaucratic ethos, "(i)ndifference to the fate of 'others' becomes morally acceptable to those who would present themselves as the protectors of 'our own' interests."[224] With respect to the realists, their almost total neglect of the problem of refugees stands out as a case in point.

Realists have earned a reputation for tough-mindedness in contrast to those woolly-headed idealists who too often mistake their dreams for a better world for the one they actually live in. "Realist thought . . ." Jonathan Haslam has recently observed, "emerged and re-emerged at moments of crises when its lessons had been forgotten in happier times."[225] Although there is much to admire in the principled, sober-mindedness of American realists like Kennan and Morgenthau, such a characterization seems a bit glib when one recalls that the realists of the postwar generation missed the significance of the Holocaust in their approach to "crisis" management. Since then, it has not been the realists who have led the way toward grappling with such phenomena. It was Arendt, not her realist contemporaries, who offered the most cogent "lessons" for confronting genocide, punishing perpetrators of mass atrocities, and holding governing elites accountable. Haslam's assessment of the realists' insight leaves unquestioned the narrow instrumentalism of an intellectual tradition that had become so completely state-centered and policy-driven that industrial mass murder on a scale involving millions of people as part of an operation that extended across an entire continent simply did not fit into its analytical categories for understanding modern international politics. For the realists, the survival and welfare of states, rather than that of the peoples who inhabit them or flee them, became the overriding concern.

The sharp difference between Arendt's response to the Holocaust and those of the realists underscores the pivotal role that vantage point can play in our perceptions of "reality." This difference also suggests that recognition of the moral dimension of such phenomena, and not simply an abstract appreciation for the tragic role of violence in human affairs, is necessary to give them a meaningful frame of reference. It is this moral context that gives such phenomena their particular human significance, and which distinguishes them from just another violent event passing along in a history replete with "tragedies." Questions about "right" and "wrong" are quintessentially human ones; they do not arise in the world of nature. Posing such questions focuses attention on the specific character of the human activity involved, and addressing them requires exercising the faculty of judgment that differentiates among particulars.

Throughout her postwar career, Arendt emphasized the importance of addressing the moral dimension in facing up to the "reality" of totalitarianism and the Holocaust:

> For the moral point of this matter is never reached by calling what happened by the name of "genocide" or by counting the many millions of victims: extermination of whole peoples had happened before in antiquity, as well as in modern colonization. It is only reached when we realized that this happened within the frame of a legal order and that the cornerstone of this "new law" consisted of the command "Thou shall kill," not thy enemy but innocent people who were not even potentially dangerous, and not for any reason of necessity but, on the contrary, even against all military and utilitarian considerations.[226]

Like Thucydides' discussion of the inversion of moral values during the Corcyraean civil war, this sort of analysis presupposes that one begin with some general standard of justice as an object of guiding concern. "Our political life rests on the assumption," Arendt observed, for example, "that we can produce equality through organization, because man can act in and change and build a common world, together with his equals and only with his equals."[227] For Arendt, ethics is not an external goal or constraint to which the exercise of power ought to be subject, but rather constitutive of the process and basis of political life itself.

Coming to terms with what happened in Germany from the destruction of democracy in 1933 through the tolerance that the postwar German government had shown toward Nazi perpetrators meant for Arendt understanding these events as a moral catastrophe as much as a human calamity.[228] It meant grappling with them as unprecedented crimes reflecting an inversion and corruption of general moral standards, not just treating them as particularly egregious acts of organized violence. It presupposed recognizing that this catastrophe bore the deepest implications for "us" regarding the conditions of moral life and community in the modern world, and not just "them." It required seeing the problem of justice as directly related to, but still distinct from the problem of power, so that the former did not disappear into the latter. For Arendt, coming to terms necessitated tough-mindedness, not as an end in itself, but as a matter of applying individual accountability as a standard of judgment and taking active responsibility for the shape of the world that we share as human beings.

Arendt developed her positive ideal of political life from having looked deeply into the abyss of totalitarianism and from seeing in this abyss the component elements for new catastrophes in the future. Totalitarian rule, she argued, is only possible where large groups in a society can be treated as if they are "superfluous." Only then, can classes of persons or minorities become feasible targets for deportation, internment, or extermination on a large scale. The perception that large segments of any population are indeed "superfluous" fosters a "contempt for the value of human life."[229] On "an overcrowded earth" the conditions that breed such views will endure long after the totalitarian regimes of the twentieth century have fallen.[230] "The great danger arising from the existence of people forced to live outside the common world," she warned, "is that they are thrown back on their natural givenness, on their mere differentiation . . . they begin to belong to the human race much the same way as animals belong to a specific animal species."[231] Under these circumstances, such people feel their own "superfluity" because they have no community of which to feel a part, in which they have a stake, and which provides a protective framework for their activities. In the future, Arendt added, "the danger is that a global, universally interrelated civilization may produce barbarians from its own midst by forcing millions of people into conditions which, despite all appearances, are the conditions of savages."[232]

These developments, she warned in 1967, are creating the basis for the emergence of new forms of imperialism by the wealthiest and most powerful states. However, as the old imperialism had long ago revealed, the governing structures of the modern nation-state are ill equipped to carry out such roles effectively or justly. Their legitimacy depends upon the consent of the governed, a territorially defined principle contradicted by any extension of rule over colonial peoples.[233] To manage their imperial portfolios, these states will need to rely on an "invisible government" comprising the intelligence services as well as other national security agencies that fall outside the scrutiny and control of the "visible government" with its constitutional checks. "What seems uncomfortably clear even now," she observed, "is the strength of certain, seemingly uncontrollable processes that tend to shatter all hopes for constitutional development in the new nations and to undermine republican institutions in the old."[234] Accompanied by no proposed remedial strategies, the pessimism of this prognosis is daunting, but she insisted that humanity's best hope for the future lay in directly confronting the unpleasant realities of its present condition.

Coming to terms then also meant for Arendt facing up to facts, not as we want them to be but as they exist in the world. "Reason's aversion to contingency is very strong," she warned.[235] In their penchant for highly simplified and abstractly ordered models of reality, the ideologist, the technocrat, and the theoretician express this aversion in various ways. Reflecting on American policy in the Vietnam War, she saw a disturbing trend whereby a concern for projecting the correct image to the world and to the general public had gained primacy over attention to the realities on the ground and the actual stakes in the conflict. Lying in politics is hardly new, she observed, but the government's use of the modern tools of public relations and marketing to manipulate, conceal, and distort facts is a more recent phenomenon. Invested in asserting and defending their preferred image of reality, policymakers not only lose touch with the vastly more complicated world of facts behind that image, but can also become actually hostile to any inconvenient facts that challenge their version of truth. The practice of deception then encourages self-deception in the service of "image-making." The difficulty in challenging these deceivers effectively is that often they are the same ones who most ardently and sincerely believe in their own fallacious constructions of reality. In mounting challenges to these true believers, facts have little purchase.

For Arendt the problem of "defactualization" in policy-making is compounded by the confusion of theoretical representations of the world with hard empirical knowledge about it. What may be analytically valid and useful to posit in the form of theoretical hypotheses are too often converted into categorical statements of fact without any clear recognition of the substantial difference between these two types of claims. Real phenomena to be observed in the world are abstracted from their own particular, localized contexts to fit the broader theoretical framework imposed on them and are interpreted according to preexisting classificatory models. In the process, whatever is new or different about these phenomena escapes scrutiny, so nothing significant is learned from their appearance in the world. To grasp how this process happens, Arendt emphasized the importance of understanding the institutional context in which it happens. In her review of the *Pentagon Papers*, she observed:

> The internal world of government, with its bureaucracy on one hand, its social life on the other, made self-deception relatively easy. No ivory tower of the scholars has ever better prepared the mind for ignoring facts of life than did the various think tanks for the problem-solvers and the reputation of the White House for the President's advisers. . . . In the realm of politics, where secrecy and deliberate deception have always played a significant role, self-deception is the danger par excellence; the

self-deceived deceiver loses all contact with not only his audience, but also the real world, which still will catch up with him.[236]

Such a rarified environment, she concluded, undermines the "mind's capacity for judgment and learning," because it is so "shielded" from the "impact of reality."[237] Viewing international politics from these insulated but commanding heights invites ideological fantasying that obscures recognition of the real limits to power, the location of "tangible" national interests, and the incongruous features of the terrain below. A neo-Hobbesian approach to international politics exemplifies this kind of ideological thinking, because it mistakes a highly abstract and stylized construct of a "state of nature" for a "realistic" description of particular peoples with histories, cultures, and political agendas of their own. In her insistence on the importance of being attentive to facts and their contexts, Arendt, though a philosopher, shares far more with historians than with policy analysts trained in international relations theory.[238]

In contrast to the realists, Arendt did not reduce this sphere of politics to the study of the interrelations among states. As Kennan characterized this study, "international affairs are primarily a matter of the behavior of governments."[239] Arendt's confrontation with totalitarianism and the Holocaust led her to rethink the basic categories of the international system, such as the principle of sovereignty and the modern nation-state model, from the ground up. In the process, she developed an approach that places the problems of mass atrocities, refugee flows, minority rights, and state instability at its center rather than treating them as unfortunate by-products of a harsh world and consigning them to the fringe of a national interest-centered analysis.

By combining a deep skepticism toward international standards with an invocation of an easily manipulable concept of national interest as the guiding norm, realists such as Kennan and Morgenthau unwittingly gave a license to political leaders less principled than themselves to conduct foreign policy as if only their own interests mattered. This combination is a recipe for the most arrogant forms of unilateralism, which both Kennan and Morgenthau would have deplored.[240] Their own critiques of the "military–industrial complex" emphasized the ways that the national interest was becoming increasingly subject to manipulation. This complex, Kennan observed,

> is an establishment largely outside the perimeter of democratic control. . . . Constituting as it now does the greatest single purchaser in the American market, with all the power that implies, anchored in

long-term contractual obligations that defy normal annual budgetary discretion of Congress, its tentacles now reaching into almost every congressional district and distorting electoral decisions wherever they reach, this military–industrial establishment has become a veritable addiction of American society . . . .[241]

Writing these words in 1987, Kennan went on to predict that if the Soviet Union disappeared, this whole vast complex created to meet that threat would endure "until some other adversary could be invented" to justify feeding the addiction. Such critiques do not inspire much confidence in the guiding hand that an enlightened conception of national interest will exercise in policy-making. Moreover, it illustrates the importance of seeing how the particular domestic structures of government are interlinked on multiple levels with the goals and actions a government undertakes in the international realm. Despite sounding the alarm through such critiques, neither Kennan, nor Morgenthau developed any new conceptual framework for thinking through a response to the dangers that they identified. Whereas Kennan sought an institutional solution through the creation of some sort of advisory council of elder statesmen, Arendt emphasized the critical importance of an uncorrupted free press that could make the necessary information available to the public.[242]

In his retrospective assessment of her contributions, Morgenthau likened Arendt's thinking to that of a "poet," observing that she "tells us nothing about how freedom is to be preserved, how it is to be guarded against enemies within."[243] He was certainly right that Arendt did not solve many of the problems with which she grappled and that her approach had its limitations, but she never claimed to be trying to develop a blueprint for the future or to offer discrete policy prescriptions for the present. Morgenthau himself left many problems that he had identified unresolved, unless one thinks that the prospect of a sovereign world government is attractive and closer to realization than he did. His assessment suggests that he never entirely grasped the kind of questions to which Arendt was seeking answers or imagined that alternative political principles to his own were worth considering. At times, he identified the strength of his own approach in its recognition of the "objective laws" that govern "politics" as well as "society," and which "have their roots in human nature."[244] In fact, such summary statements do not do justice to the full complexity of his thinking about international affairs or his commitment to intellectual honesty, but nonetheless point to an unfortunate tendency toward highly reductive generalizations and categorical claims at the service of developing a policy-oriented discipline. Arendt's critical realism does not offer the statesman or -woman much in the way of a practical policy guide or instructions in cultivating the important arts of diplomacy, but her example does vividly demonstrate the limitations of an instrumental, state-centered perspective by drawing such sharp attention to the kind of fundamental issues that her contemporaries had neglected. At the core of her approach, she sought to grapple with the largest threats that the first half of the twentieth century had revealed to her by rethinking the principles of modern political life in both the domestic and international spheres. Morgenthau and Kennan, men of great intelligence and integrity, lacked the perspective that enabled Arendt so productively to rethink the principles of modern political life. She saw the inseparable connections between power, justice, and responsibility, and, in that, she saw the "real" nature of modern politics far more truly than Morgenthau and Kennan.

NOTES

The author would like to thank Julia Buckmaster, David Fagelson, Maryam Kamali, James J. Sheehan, and Astri Suhrke for their insightful comments on an earlier draft of this essay. Special thanks are due to Robert Kunath, Anthony Lang, and John Williams. All three offered extensive commentary on several different drafts, and their criticisms and suggestions have proven invaluable to the completion of the essay. Of course, the author alone is responsible for the opinions expressed herein and for any errors that remain.

1. Arendt, "Understanding and Politics (The Difficulties of Understanding)," in Jerome Kohn (ed.), *Essays in Understanding, 1930–1954* (New York: Harcourt Brace & Co., 1994), 307–327 at 310.

2. Eric D. Weitz, *A Century of Genocide: Utopias of Race and Nation* (Princeton, NJ: Princeton University Press, 2003), 8.

3. Omer Bartov, *Mirrors of Destruction: War, Genocide, and Modern Identity* (New York: Oxford University Press, 2000), 6; Norman Naimark, *Fires of Hatred: Ethnic Cleansing in Twentieth Century Europe* (Cambridge, MA: Harvard University Press, 2001); Zygmunt Bauman, *Modernity and the Holocaust* (Ithaca, NY: Cornell University Press, 2000).

4. Richard J. Bernstein, *Radical Evil: A Philosophical Investigation* (Cambridge, UK: Polity Press, 2002), 1; Susan Neiman, *Evil in Modern Thought: An Alternative History of Philosophy* (Princeton, NJ: Princeton University Press, 2002), 1–9.

5. Christopher Browning, "The German Bureaucracy and the Holocaust," in Alex Grobman and Daniel Landes (eds.), *Genocide: Critical Issues of*

168   Douglas Klusmeyer

the Holocaust (Los Angeles: The Simon Wiesenthal Center, 1983), 145–149 at 148.

6. Hannah Arendt, "Preface to the First Edition (1950)," *The Origins of Totalitarianism*, new edn (New York: Harcourt Brace & Co., 1979), viii.

7. Jack Donnelly, *Realism and International Relations* (Cambridge: Cambridge University Press, 2000); Jonathan Haslam, *No Virtue Like Necessity: Realist Thought in International Relations since Machiavelli* (New Haven, CT: Yale University Press, 2002); Joel H. Rosenthal, *Righteous Realists: Political Realism, Responsible Power, and American Culture in the Nuclear Age* (Baton Rouge: Louisiana State University Press, 1991); Michael Joseph Smith, *Realist Thought from Weber to Kissinger* (Baton Rouge: Louisiana State University Press, 1986); and, Samantha Power, *"A Problem from Hell": America and the Age of Genocide* (New York: Basic Books, 2002). One searches in vain for any record of the realist response to the Holocaust or genocide generally in the standard accounts of this tradition. Likewise, the voices of the American realists are notably absent in Power's recent chronicle of the making of American policy toward genocide and ethnic cleansing in the twentieth century. Moreover, in his highly influential and erudite study, *Man, the State and War: A Theoretical Analysis* (New York: Columbia University Press, 1954/59), the neorealist Kenneth N. Waltz also does not address the implications of totalitarianism and the Holocaust.

8. George F. Kennan, *American Diplomacy: 1900–1950* (1951; repr., New York: Mentor Books, 1962), 82.

9. Joel H. Rosenthal, *Righteous Realists*.

10. Hannah Arendt, "Tradition and the Modern Age," in Hannah Arendt (ed.), *Between Past and Future* (New York: Penguin Books, 1993), 22.

11. Hannah Arendt, "Thoughts on Revolution and Politics," in Hannah Arendt (ed.), *Crises of the Republic*, 229; and, Arendt, "On Violence," in *Crises of the Republic*, 107.

12. Hannah Arendt, *Origins of Totalitarianism*, 417–418. Arendt points out that Adolf Eichmann described himself as an "idealist" in the sense of being "a man who lived for his idea . . . and who was prepared to sacrifice everything and, especially, everybody . . . The perfect 'idealist,' like everybody else, had of course his personal feelings and emotions, but he would never permit them to interfere with his actions if they came into conflict with his 'idea.' " Hannah Arendt, *Eichmann in Jerusalem: A Report on the Banality of Evil*, rev. and enl. ed. (New York: Viking Press, 1969), 42.

13. Richard Wightman Fox, *Reinhold Niebuhr: A Biography* (Ithaca, NY: Cornell University Press, 1996), 15.

14. George F. Kennan, *Memoirs: 1925–1950* (Boston: Little, Brown & Co., 1967), 415.

15. Ibid. Elsewhere, he attributed key "responsibility" for the ultimate collapse of the Weimar Republic and the Nazi takeover to Stalin and the German Communist party. George F. Kennan, *Russia and the West under Lenin and Stalin* (Boston: Little Brown & Co., 1961), 290–291.

16. Michael L. Hughes, " 'Through No Fault of Our Own': West Germans Remember Their War Losses," *German History*, 18, no. 2 (2000): 211; Robert G. Moeller, *War Stories: The Search for a Usable Past in the Federal Republic of Germany* (Berkeley: University of California Press, 2001), 6. Minimizing attention to the victim groups that had been the actual target of Nazi policies was consistent with the postwar West German self-understanding of themselves as a "victim community."

17. Hans J. Morgenthau, *Politics Among Nations: The Struggle for Power and Peace*, 5th edn, rev. (New York: Alfred A. Knopf, 1978), 8.

18. Haslam, *No Virtue Like Necessity*, 252.

19. Peter Novick, *The Holocaust in American Life* (New York: Houghton Mifflin Co., 2000), 1–2, 103–123; and, Neiman, *Evil in Modern Thought*, 250–251. In general, the specter of the Nazi death camps attracted little public comment throughout the first decades after the war. The Holocaust did not emerge as a potent public symbol of transcendental human suffering until the 1970s.

20. Leo Kuper, *Genocide* (New Haven, CT: Yale University Press, 1982), 161; and, George J. Andreopolous, ed., "Introduction: The Calculus of Genocide," *Genocide: Conceptual and Historical Dimensions*, (Philadelphia: University of Pennsylvania Press, 1994), 1–28 at 18–19.

21. Arendt, *Origins of Totalitarianism*, 269, 278.

22. Referring to such regimes as Nazi Germany, the Soviet Union, Mao's China, and Cambodia under the Khmer Rouge, he concludes: "These fifteen *megamurderers*—those states killing in cold blood, aside from warfare, wiped out over 151 million people, almost four times the almost 38,500,000 battle dead from all century's international and civil wars up to 1987." R. J. Rummel, *Death by Government* (London: Transactions Publishers, 1994), 3.

23. Kennan, *Russia and the West*, 47, 202; George F. Kennan, "The Price We Paid for War," *The Atlantic Monthly*, 214, no. 4 (October 1964): 53.

24. Kennan, *Memoirs*, 179.

25. Kennan, *American Diplomacy*, 88.

26. Kennan, *Memoirs*, 427–441.

27. Zigmunt Bauman, "Holocaust," in David Goldberg and John Solomos (eds.), *A Companion to Racial and Ethnic Studies* (Oxford: Blackwell Publishers, 2002), 46–63 at 47.

28. Arendt, "Understanding and Politics," 309.

29. Hans J. Morgenthau, "The Evil of Politics and the Ethics of Evil," *Ethics*, LVI (October 1945): 1–18.

30. Hannah Arendt, "Nightmare and Flight," in Jerome Kohn (ed.), *Essays in Understanding, 1930–1954* (New York: Harcourt Brace & Co., 1994), 133–135 at 134.

31. Haslam, *No Virtue Like Necessity*, 237.

32. Hans J. Morgenthau, "The Intellectual and Political Functions of Theory," in Hans J. Morgenthau, *Truth and Power: Essays of A Decade, 1960–70* (New York: Praeger Publishers, 1970), 258–259.

33. Stanley Hoffmann, "An American Social Science: International Relations (1977)," in Stanley Hoffmann, *Janus and Minerva: Essays in the Theory and Practice of International Politics* (Boulder, CO: Westfield Press, 1987), 6; George Schultz, "Morality and Realism in American Foreign Policy," *Department of State Bulletin* (December 1985).

34. Hoffmann, "An American Social Science: International Relations," 10.

35. Ibid., 12.

36. James C. Scott, *Seeing Like a State* (New Haven, CT: Yale University Press, 1998), 81.

37. George F. Kennan, *Realities of American Foreign Policy* (Princeton, NJ: Princeton University Press, 1954), 93; Scott, *Seeing Like a State*, 92; and, Bauman, *Modernity and the Holocaust*, 18, 70. Both Bauman and Scott point to the "metaphor of gardening" as "capturing much of the spirit" of this "high modernist" perspective. Kennan uses this same metaphor to explain his preferred approach to international relations. "If there is any great lesson we Americans need to learn with regard to the methodology of foreign policy," he writes, "it is that we must be gardeners . . . in our approach to world affairs."

38. Scott, *Seeing Like a State*, 102.

39. Arendt, "Preface to Part Two (1967)," in *Origins of Totalitarianism*, xxi.

40. Kennan, *Memoirs*, 139.

41. Ibid., 140.

42. George F. Kennan to wife, October 21, 1941, in *Sketches from a Life* (New York: W.W. Norton & Co., 2000), 75; George F. Kennan, *From Prague to Munich: Diplomatic Papers, 1938–1940* (Princeton, NJ: Princeton University Press, 1968). Kennan observed the growing campaign against the Jews from his diplomatic posts in Czechoslovakia and Berlin.

43. Michael N. Barnett, "The UN Security Council, Indifference, and Genocide in Rwanda," *Cultural Anthropology*, 12, no. 4 (1997): 563.

44. Kennan, *Sketches from a Life*, viii–ix, 364. Apparently, his memoirs have served the purpose he intended. Colin Powell, "Remarks on the Occasion of George Kennan's Centenary Birthday," speech at Princeton University, February 20, 2004, http://www.state.gov/secretary/rm/29683.htm. U.S. Secretary of State Colin Powell observed: "Above all, Ambassador Kennan has grasped the link between diplomacy and human nature. And that's why his memoirs

have been treasured for so many decades by generations of Foreign Service officers."

45. Hans J. Morgenthau, "Germany: The Political Problem," in Hans J. Morgenthau (ed.), *Germany and the Future of Europe* (Chicago: The University of Chicago Press, 1951), 77. When focusing on National Socialism itself, Morgenthau likewise did not address its genocidal policies. See, e.g., "Nazism (1946)," *The Decline of Democratic Politics* (Chicago: The University of Chicago Press, 1962), 227–240.

46. Morgenthau, "Germany: The Political Problem," 81.

47. Ibid., 76.

48. "Curiously enough, the thing about it [teaching] I really can't tolerate is, of all things, the political aspect—being in the public eye every day," Arendt to Karl Jaspers, July 1, 1955, in *Correspondence: Hannah Arendt and Karl Jaspers, 1926–1969*, no. 165, ed. Lotte Kohle and Hans Saner, trans. Robert and Rita Kimber (New York: Harcourt Brace & Co., 1992), 260; and, Arendt to Karl Jaspers, March 26, 1955, in *Correspondence*, no. 167, 258–259. (I am indebted to Robert Kunath for drawing my attention to these letters.)

49. As she once observed, "I have never in my life 'loved' any people or collective . . . I indeed love 'only' my friends and the only kind of love I know of and believe in is the love of persons." In expressing her views, she added, "I do not belong to any organization and speak only for myself." Arendt to Gershom Scholem, July 24, 1963, in Hannah Arendt, *The Jew as Pariah: Jewish Identity and Politics in the Modern Age*, ed. Ron H. Feldman (repr., New York: Grove Press Inc., 1978), 246, 250.

50. Arendt, "We Refugees (January 1943)," in *Jew as Pariah*, 55–66.

51. Arendt, *Origins of Totalitarianism*, 277.

52. Morgenthau, "The Problem of the National Interest," *Decline of Democratic Politics*, 106; Hans J. Morgenthau, *Human Rights and Foreign Policy* (New York: Council on Religion and International Affairs, 1979), 4.

53. Hans J. Morgenthau, "Symposium," in *Human Rights and Foreign Policy* (New York: Council on Religion and International Affairs, 1979), 9–43 at 10.

54. George F. Kennan, "Morality and Foreign Policy," in George F. Kennan, *At a Century's Ending: Reflections, 1982–1995* (New York: W.W. Norton & Co., 1996), 271; George F. Kennan *Around the Cragged Hill: A Personal and Political Philosophy* (New York: W.W. Norton & Co., 1993), 51.

55. Smith, *Realist Thought*, 216.

56. George F. Kennan, "Foreword to *The Pathology of Power* by Norman Cousins," in Kennan, *At a Century's Ending*, 118; and, "American Democracy and Foreign Policy," in Kennan, *At a Century's Ending*, 131–132. For Morgenthau's views of this issue, see his essays: "Truth and Power," "What Ails America," "How

Totalitarianism Starts: The Domestic Involvement of the CIA," "Modern Science and Political Power," and "Government and Private Enterprise," in Morgenthau, *Truth and Power*, 13–39, 51–55, 215–240, 262–278. For Arendt, see Hannah Arendt, "Lying in Politics," in Arendt, *Crises of the Republic*, 1–47.

57. Kennan, *Russia and the West*, 188.
58. Smith, *Realist Thought*, 218–238; Daniel Warner, *An Ethic of Responsibility in International Relations* (Boulder, CO: Lynne Rienner Publishers, 1991), 37–48, 61–81; Donnelly, *Realism and International Relations*, 44–47, 164–166.
59. Arendt, "On Violence," 175.
60. Smith, *Realist Thought*, 4–11.
61. Morgenthau, *Human Rights and Foreign Policy*, 7.
62. Morgenthau, *Politics among Nations*, 196; Kennan, *Russia and the West*, 5–6.
63. "From Containment to . . . Self-Containment: A Conversation Between George F. Kennan and George Urban," in Martin F. Herz (ed.), *Decline of the West? George Kennan and His Critics* (Washington, DC: Ethics and Public Policy Center of Georgetown University, 1978), 11–37 at 13.
64. Morgenthau, "The Political Problems of Polyethnic States," in Hans J. Morgenthau (ed.), *The Restoration of American Politics*, vol. 3, *Politics in the Twentieth Century* (Chicago: The University of Chicago Press, 1962), 342–347. Morgenthau recognized the often destabilizing consequences of the nation-state model, but never applied this insight to refugees, and it remained at the margins of his analysis of international politics.
65. Arendt, *Origins of Totalitarianism*, 278.
66. Ibid., 293.
67. Michael R. Marrus, *The Unwanted: European Refugees in the Twentieth Century* (Oxford: Oxford University Press, 1985), 3–5; Claudena M. Skran, *Refugees in Inter-War Europe: The Emergence of a Regime* (Oxford: Clarendon Press, 1995), 13–14, 31, 60–61; Aristide R. Zolberg, "The Formation of New States as a Refugee-Generating Process," in Elizabeth G. Ferris (ed.), *Refugees and World Politics* (New York: Praeger Publishers, 1985), 26–42; Aristide R. Zolberg, "Global Movements, Global Walls: Responses to Migration, 1885–1925," in Wang Gungwu (ed.), *Global History and Migration*, (Boulder, CO: Westview Press, 1997), 279–307.
68. Morgenthau, *Politics Among Nations*, 130–134.
69. Arendt, *Origins of Totalitarianism*, 284.
70. Ibid., 293.
71. Kennan, *The Realities of American Foreign Policy*, 108–110; Kennan, *Around the Cragged Hill*, 151–156. Like Morgenthau, Kennan approached migration issues from the perspective of state national

interest. Accordingly, he was primarily concerned with how immigration and the threat of a rising global population might affect the strength and welfare of the United States.

72. Kennan, *American Diplomacy*, 84.
73. Ibid., 84–85. Parentheses in the original.
74. Ibid., 84.
75. George F. Kennan, "Foreign Policy and Christian Conscience," *The Atlantic Monthly*, 203, no. 5 (1959): 46; George F. Kennan, *Russia, The Atom and the West* (New York: Harper & Brothers Publishers, 1958), 74–75. Here, without citing any supporting evidence for this conclusion, he simply dismisses the "claim . . . that colonialism invariably represented a massive and cruel exploitation of colonial peoples. I am sure that honest study would reveal this thesis to be quite fallacious. Advantages, injuries and sacrifices were incurred on both sides. Today these things are largely bygones. We will do no good by scratching around to discover whose descendents owe the most to the descendents of the other. If we are to help each [other] in this world, we must start with a clean slate."
76. Arendt, *Origins of Totalitarianism*, 279.
77. Ibid., 269.
78. Ibid., 267.
79. Ibid., 230.
80. Ibid. Emphasis in original.
81. Ibid.
82. Ibid., 290–294.
83. Ibid., 270.
84. Ibid., 274–276.
85. Ibid., 272.
86. Ibid., 269.
87. Hannah Arendt, "Approaches to the 'German Problem,' " in *Essays in Understanding, 1930–1954*, 106–120 at 120; Arendt, "Power Politics Triumphs," in *Essays in Understanding, 1930–1954*, 156–157.
88. Naimark, *Fires of Hatred*, 136–137. In explaining the circumstances surrounding these "transfers," the historian Norman Naimark has observed, "throughout Europe and the Soviet Union, nationalism appeared to be the dominant motif of the new stage of state-building that accompanied the end of World War II. Recognition of minority rights, a principle that was at least formally accepted as part of the post–World War I settlement, had come crashing to an end." With respect to the expulsion policies undertaken by the Czech and Polish governments, he observes, "a major motivation . . . for expelling the Germans derived from the desire of the new postwar governments (and their predecessors in London) to rationalize and control their societies by making them ethnically homogeneous and fully responsive to the needs and goals of the dominant nationality."

89. Arendt, *"The Nation,"* in *Essays in Understanding, 1930–1954,* (New York: Harcourt Brace & Co., 1994), 206–211 at 210.

90. Hans J. Morgenthau, *Scientific Man vs. Power Politics* (Chicago: The University of Chicago Press, 1946/57), 177–178.

91. Abbot Gleason, *Totalitarianism: The Inner History of the Cold War* (Oxford: Oxford University Press, 1995), 81–82.

92. Kennan, "Totalitarianism in the Modern World," in Carl J. Friedrich (ed.), *Totalitarianism* (Cambridge, MA: Harvard University Press, 1954), 17–31.

93. Morgenthau, *Politics among Nations,* 176–177, 181–183, 187–196.

94. George F. Kennan, "Training for Statesmanship," *The Atlantic Monthly,* 191, no. 5 (May 1953): 41.

95. Ibid.

96. George F. Kennan, "Foreign Policy and the Christian Conscience," *The Atlantic Monthly,* 203, no. 5 (May 1959): 45.

97. Ibid.

98. Kennan, *Around the Cragged Hill,* 53.

99. Ibid., 54.

100. Morgenthau, *Scientific Man,* 194.

101. Morgenthau, *Politics among Nations,* 14.

102. Morgenthau, *Scientific Man,* 168.

103. Morgenthau, *Politics among Nations,* 260–261.

104. Likewise, Morgenthau concluded: "The simple truth [is] that a divided sovereignty is logically absurd and politically unfeasible." Ibid., 260.

105. Arendt, *Origins of Totalitarianism,* 138.

106. Ibid., 141–142.

107. Ibid., 146.

108. Ibid.

109. Ibid.

110. Ibid., 417, 437.

111. Ibid., 125.

112. Ibid., 440.

113. Ibid., 437.

114. Arendt, "On the Nature of Totalitarianism: An Essay in Understanding," in *Essays in Understanding: 1930–1954,* 328–360 at 330.

115. Ibid.; Hannah Arendt, *On Revolution* (New York: Penguin Books, 1990), 150–151.

116. Arendt, "On Violence," 139–140.

117. Ibid., 143. Emphasis in original See her discussion of this theme in: Hannah Arendt, *The Human Condition: A Study of the Central Dilemmas Facing Modern Man* (Garden City, NY: Doubleday & Co., 1959), 178–186.

118. Arendt, "On Violence," 143.

119. Ibid., 155.

120. Ibid., 152.

121. Ibid., 134, 150–151.
122. Arendt, "Understanding and Politics," 310.
123. Arendt, "What is Freedom?" in *Between Past and Future*, 146.
124. Kennan, "Foreword to *The Pathology of Power* by Norman Cousins," 116–117, 120–121; Rosenthal, *Righteous Realists*, 83–86.
125. Campbell Craig, *Glimmer of a New Leviathan: Total War in the Realism of Niebuhr, Morgenthau, and Waltz* (New York: Columbia University Press, 2003), 74–116.
126. Arendt, "On Violence," 105; Hannah Arendt, "Europe and the Atom Bomb," in *Essays in Understanding: 1930–1954*, 417–422 at 418–422.
127. Arendt, *On Revolution*, 16.
128. Hans J. Morgenthau, "The Intellectual and Political Functions of a Theory of International Relations," in *The Decline of American Politics*, vol. 1 of *Politics in the Twentieth Century*, 75.
129. Morgenthau, "International Relations," in *Restoration of American Politics*, 174.
130. Here he is characterizing the argument for world government, but later concludes: "Our analysis of the problem of domestic peace has shown that the arguments of the advocates of the world state are unanswerable." Morgenthau, *Politics Among Nations*, 491–492, 499.
131. Ibid., 492.
132. Ibid., 503.
133. Ibid.
134. Ibid., 507, 520–523.
135. Kennan, *Russia and the West*, 276; Kennan, *Memoirs*, 129–130.
136. Arendt, "Thoughts on Politics and Revolution," 230.
137. Kennan, *Around the Cragged Hill*, 88.
138. Ibid.
139. Ibid., 92.
140. Kennan, *Realities of American Foreign Policy*, 105–106.
141. Ibid., 106.
142. Kennan, *Around the Cragged Hill*, 92–93.
143. George F. Kennan, *The Nuclear Delusion: Soviet-American Relations in the Atomic Age* (New York: Pantheon Books, 1982), xxviii.
144. Arendt, *On Revolution*, 18. Compare here Craig's assessment of the "conceptual breakdown" that Niebuhr and Morgenthau encountered as they tried to rethink their understanding of international relations in the face of nuclear war. Craig, *Glimmer of a New Leviathan*, 110–116.
145. Arendt, "Thoughts on Politics and Revolution," 230, 233. Emphasis in original.
146. Arendt, *On Revolution*, 19–20.
147. Ibid., 130, 175–177.
148. Ibid., 170; Arendt, "Civil Disobedience," in *Crises of the Republic*, 86–87. Morgenthau, "The Right of Dissent," in *Truth and Power*,

40–44. Although without the same kind of philosophical elaboration, Morgenthau also explicitly supported this right.

149. Arendt, *On Revolution*, 170; Arendt, "Civil Disobedience," 86.
150. Arendt, *On Revolution*, 171.
151. Ibid., 168.
152. Ibid., 152–153, 245.
153. Ibid., 171.
154. Arendt, "What is Freedom?" 164–165; Arendt, "Freedom and Politics," in Albert Hunold (ed.), *Freedom and Serfdom: An Anthology of Western Thought* (Dordrecht: D. Reidel Publishing Co., 1961), 191–217, 204–205.
155. Arendt, *The Human Condition*, 180.
156. Ibid., 10.
157. Ibid., 23, 155–156.
158. Ibid., 10.
159. Arendt, *On Revolution*, 76.
160. Jürgen Habermas, "Hannah Arendt's Communications Concept of Power," trans. Thomas McCarthy, *Social Research*, 44, no. 1 (1977): 3–23.
161. Hannah Arendt, "Personal Responsibility Under Dictatorship," in Jerome Kohn (ed.), *Responsibility and Judgment* (New York: Schocken Books, 2003), 17–48 at 46; Arendt, *Eichmann in Jerusalem*, 278–279.
162. Morgenthau, *Politics Among Nations*, 254.
163. Kennan, *Realities of American Foreign Policy*, 45.
164. Ibid., 46.
165. Kennan, *American Diplomacy*, 50.
166. Kennan, *Around the Cragged Hill*, 72.
167. Ibid., 72, 210.
168. Kennan, "Foreword to *The Pathology of Power* by Norman Cousins," 121.
169. Arendt, "On Violence," 137–138; Arendt, "Personal Responsibility Under Dictatorship," 31.
170. Arendt, *Eichmann in Jerusalem*, 273.
171. Ibid., 272.
172. Ibid., 269–270, 274–275.
173. Ibid., 298.
174. Morgenthau, Book Review, *Chicago Tribune*, May 26, 1963; Hans J. Morgenthau, "Hannah Arendt on Totalitarianism and Democracy," *Social Research*, XLIV (Spring 1977): 127–131.
175. Morgenthau, "The Nuremberg Trial," in *Decline of Democratic Politics*, 45, 377–379; Arendt, "Understanding and Politics," 310. Arendt described the Nuremberg Trials as an "abysmal failure."
176. Morgenthau, "Germany: The Political Problem," 78.
177. Hannah Arendt, "The Aftermath of Nazi Rule: Report from Germany," in *Essays in Understanding, 1930–1954*, 248–269 at 256–269.

178. Kennan, *Memoirs*, 260.
179. Ibid., 261.
180. Ibid., 177.
181. Ibid., 429.
182. Kennan, *American Diplomacy*, 121; Morgenthau, "Germany: The Political Problem," 85.
183. Kennan, *Memoirs*, 179.
184. Kennan, *Russia and the West*, 368.
185. Arendt, "Lying in Politics," 33.
186. Kennan, *Russia and the West*, 367–368.
187. Ibid., 368.
188. George F. Kennan, *Democracy and the Student Left* (New York: Bantam Books, 1968), 149.
189. Arendt to Gershom Scholem, 24 July 1963, in *Jew as Pariah*, 49, 248.
190. Arendt, *Eichmann in Jerusalem*, 297.
191. Hannah Arendt, "Social Science Techniques and the Study of the Concentration Camps," in *Essays in Understanding: 1930–1954*, 232–247 at 242.
192. Arendt, *Eichmann in Jerusalem*, 296.
193. Arendt, "Organized Guilt and Universal Responsibility," in *Essays in Understanding: 1930–1954*, 121–132 at 126.
194. Ibid., 125.
195. Ibid., 127.
196. Ibid., 126–127; Arendt, *Eichmann in Jerusalem*, 278.
197. Arendt, "On Violence," 162.
198. Arendt, *Eichmann in Jerusalem*, 276.
199. Ibid., 254.
200. Ibid., 19.
201. Ibid., 289.
202. Hannah Arendt, "Thinking and Moral Considerations," in *Responsibility and Judgment*, 159–162 at 189.
203. Arendt, "Personal Responsibility under Dictatorship," 21.
204. Arendt, *Eichmann in Jerusalem*, 247. Emphasis in original.
205. Warner, *Ethic of Responsibility*. Warner presents a sharp critique of the realist approach to accountability and responsibility.
206. Arendt, *Eichmann in Jerusalem*, 268–269.
207. Ibid., 269.
208. Ibid., 258–266.
209. Arendt, *Origins of Totalitarianism*, 298.
210. Ibid., 236; Arendt, *On Revolution*, 88.
211. Arendt, "Organized Guilt and Universal Responsibility," 131.
212. Ibid., 131.
213. Arendt, *Origins of Totalitarianism*, 299.
214. Ibid.
215. Ibid.
216. Ibid., 298.
217. Ibid., 297.

218. Arendt, "Karl Jaspers: Citizen of the World?," in Hannah Arendt (ed.), *Men in Dark Times* (New York: Harcourt Brace & Co., 1983), 93.
219. Kennan, *Realities of American Foreign Policy*, 4, 15.
220. Arendt, *Eichmann in Jerusalem*, 298.
221. "Working Group Report on Detainee Interrogations in the Global War on Terrorism: Assessment of Legal, Historical, Policy, and Operational Considerations," unclassified document, http://online.wsj.com/public/resources/documents/military_0604.pdf (March 6, 2003).
222. Ibid., 296–298; Hannah Arendt, "Home to Roost," in *Responsibility and Judgment*, 257–275 at 266.
223. Kennan, *Around the Cragged Hill*, 55, 58.
224. Michael Herzfeld, *The Social Production of Indifference: Exploring the Symbolic Roots of Western Bureaucracy* (Chicago: The University of Chicago Press/Berg, 1993), 167.
225. Haslam, *No Virtue Like Necessity*, 252.
226. Arendt, "Personal Responsibility Under Dictatorship," 42.
227. Arendt, *Origins of Totalitarianism*, 301.
228. Hannah Arendt, "Some Questions on Moral Philosophy," in *Responsibility and Judgment*, 49–146 at 53–64.
229. Arendt, *Origins of Totalitarianism*, 311.
230. Ibid., 457, 460.
231. Ibid., 302.
232. Ibid.
233. Ibid., 125. Compare with Kennan, *Russia and the West*, 276.
234. Arendt, "Preface to Part II," in *Origins of Totalitarianism*, xx.
235. Arendt, "Lying in Politics," 12.
236. Ibid., 35–36.
237. Ibid., 40.
238. Ibid., 6–7.
239. George F. Kennan, "Training for Statesmanship," *The Atlantic Monthly*, 191, no. 5 (May 1953): 41.
240. For my views on this problem in connection with the Bush policy toward terrorism, see Douglas Klusmeyer and Astri Suhrke, "Comprehending 'Evil': Challenges for Law and Policy," *Ethics and International Affairs*, 16, no. 1 (Spring 2002): 27–42.
241. Kennan, "Foreword to *The Pathology of Power* by Norman Cousins," 118.
242. Arendt, *"Lying in Politics,"* 45.
243. Morgenthau, "Hannah Arendt on Totalitarianism and Democracy," *Social Research*, XLIV (Spring 1977): 129, 131.
244. Morgenthau, *Politics Among Nations*, 4.

CHAPTER 7

GOVERNANCE AND POLITICAL ACTION: HANNAH ARENDT ON GLOBAL POLITICAL PROTEST

Anthony F. Lang, Jr.

In the last few days of November 1999, a meeting of the World Trade Organization (WTO) in Seattle collapsed, in part, because of protests taking place in the streets outside. Various non-governmental organizations (NGOs) had been meeting and planning ways to halt the negotiations through nonviolent protests since January 1999. Their actions, including dressing up like turtles and blocking traffic at key intersections in Seattle, created enough chaos in the streets outside the meeting areas that some delegates were blocked from attending the meetings.[1]

Underlying the protests is a tension between the desire to act politically and the need to create structures of governance. This tension exists at the local, national, and global levels, but it is heightened at the global level for reasons I explore later in this chapter. In short, the tension between political action and governance that occurs within functioning political systems, that is, at the local and national levels, is lessened by the fact that political actions can be channeled into means for sustaining and improving methods of governance. For example, political actions such as voting, advocating specific causes, and attaining positions of leadership feed into existing modes of governance.

At the global level, however, there remain questions about what constitutes governance. Scholars and even institutions continue to debate whether or not international and regional institutions actually constitute a qualitatively different level of governance or whether they are simply institutions that collect the interests of nation-states. Many would argue that the sovereign state is losing its ability to govern, especially as problems arise that cannot be addressed through national mechanisms. The European Union, the World Trade Organization, the International Monetary Fund, the United Nations, and the International Criminal Court all "govern" in different ways. These institutions have increased their reach and influence, but they remain, in many ways, subordinate to the nation-states that created them.

More importantly for the purposes of this chapter, these institutions do not provide mechanisms for political action by individuals. If institutions of global governance continue to increase in size and number, this lack of space for political action will become more and more problematic. Two possible responses to the lack of opportunities for political participation at the global level have recently appeared: activism through transnational NGOs and political protests against international institutions. Both actions allow citizens to engage in politics in a way that satisfies the human need to act publicly. Yet, neither form of action has a direct bearing on institutions of global governance. The disconnect between these forms of political action and the creation and sustenance of institutions of global governance reveals an important lacuna in the international system.

The work of Hannah Arendt speaks directly to these challenges. As detailed in the introductory chapters of this volume, Arendt wrote on issues of politics more broadly defined, but in ways that make her work clearly relevant at the global level. The dilemma between political action and governance was at the heart of Arendt's work. In this chapter, I draw on two works, in particular, to explore how Arendt might help us understand the tension between political action and governance: *The Human Condition* and *On Revolution*. In the former, Arendt articulates a theory of political action that does not necessarily require a sense of what the outcomes that action might produce are going to be. This is relevant to the protests in Seattle because the diverse groups engaged in the protests did not work together closely, leading some critics to argue that the protests were pointless. Arendt's notions of political action suggest ways in which we might evaluate these actions more positively. In *On Revolution*, Arendt suggests some ways in which diverse political actors do create certain types of institutions. These institutions, in particular, revolutionary councils and political parties, are not institutions of governance but are structures that give individuals the means to engage in political action. While the protests in Seattle may not have created new formal institutions or even changed radically existing institutions, they did create something like revolutionary councils, making them spaces in which Arendtian political action can be seen as having a long-term effect.

In the next section, I explore the relationship between governance and political action through Arendt's work. I then examine the protests against the WTO in November and December 1999 and evaluate them based on the Arendtian framework I develop. The chapter concludes with some suggestions on how political action at the global level can lead to forms of governance by returning to Arendt's views.

ARENDT, POLITICAL ACTION, AND GOVERNANCE

What is the relationship between political action and governance? One answer comes from Aristotle. In *Politics*, Aristotle—upon whom Arendt draws extensively in *The Human Condition*—sets out a theory of political action and governance that ties the two together. Beginning with the assumption that the human person is inherently political, he goes on to describe different types of political systems. Book III, in which he describes the citizen, provides an answer to the problem identified above:

> He who has the power to take part in the deliberative and judicial administration of any state is said by us to be a citizen of that state; and, speaking generally, a state is a body of citizens sufficing for the purposes of life.[2]

For Aristotle, political actions—that is, deliberations in an assembly or judgments in a court—are to be considered political actions performed by all citizens. In so describing the political system and the citizen, Aristotle neatly connects the individual's political actions to outcomes of governance.

But an essential element of the Aristotelian political community was that it was limited in size.[3] Today's nation-states simply do not conform to the Aristotelian limit on size. Even in cases where political systems do, such as local politics, they tend not to be direct democracies but rather representative ones. At the level of global governance, the focus of this chapter, the Aristotelian limits on size quite clearly do not apply. At the global level it appears even more difficult to make connections between political action and governance. Those institutions formally constituted to "govern" the international system comprise states, so the distance of representation from the individual citizen is even further. One theorist of democracy notes: "To handle these broader matters, the democratic unit might be enlarged; but in doing so the capacity of the citizen to participate effectively in governing would be diminished."[4]

One result of this disconnect between governance and political action is that individuals at the global level advocate more often for their rights than they do for being able to participate in global governance. Indeed, it is only rational for individuals to focus on protecting themselves from the powers of states and other powerful entities at the level of the international system. David Held, whose work has explored questions of global governance and cosmopolitan citizenship, concludes that democratic global governance should focus primarily on achieving autonomy rather than creating means to influence the global political system.[5]

Is political action absolutely disconnected from governance at the global level? Can cosmopolitan citizens play a role in governing themselves, or should they only focus on protecting their rights in an unfriendly and dangerous international system? Hannah Arendt's work moves us closer to an answer through her development of a theory of political action.

The Human Condition lays out Arendt's theory of political action in most detail. Like many of her works, it uses ancient philosophy to confront current politics. The focus of the work is the *via activa*, or that aspect of human life, which is concerned with doing rather than thinking. She divides human action into three realms: labor, work, and action. Action is the most important realm in terms of politics; for action is that activity in which human persons reveal themselves in moments of interactions with others. It is the way in which we assert who we are, in which we create ourselves by presenting ourselves in public. Politics, which provides the constructed stage of a parliament or town meeting, provides the paradigmatic instance of moments in which the human person can be revealed. Arendt develops this concept of action in an engagement with Greek and Roman philosophers who sought to define the realm of the political. That realm, combining a Homeric *agonal* spirit with an Aristotelian notion of speech as the quintessentially human characteristic, results in a public space that allows for competition and conflict.

According to Arendt, the public realm is the place where persons distinguish themselves, the arena in which "everybody had to constantly distinguish himself from all others, to show through unique deeds or achievements that he was best of all."[6] Since political action is a public presentation of the self, there must be a community to whom this presentation is made. She notes that action occurs within a "web of human relationships," a place composed both of other people acting and speaking and of the "common world" that surrounds and anchors human interaction: "most words and deeds are about some worldly objective reality in addition to being a disclosure of the acting and speaking self."[7] Politics thus requires a public realm, one composed of fellow humans with an agreed upon equality, not one of merit but one of agency.

Arendt moves from conceiving of political action as occurring within a web of human relations to action within a *polis*, or a political community. But political action, according to Arendt, cannot be confined within the walls of the *polis*. Political action is similar to a miracle—something one cannot expect and cannot contain. Action tends to go beyond the boundaries within which we attempt to contain it:

> Action, moreover, no matter what its specific content, always establishes relationships and therefore has an inherent tendency to force open all limitations and cut across all boundaries. Limitations and boundaries exist within human affairs, but they never offer a framework that can reliably withstand the onslaught with which each new generation must assert itself.[8]

While the *polis* is an attempt to create a physical space for political action, action forces itself beyond those boundaries.

Ultimately, action does not just create spaces and institutions for politics, it creates the agents themselves. It is here that Arendt's work moves to the ontological realm. For in her argument, humans exist as fragmented, alienated and acquisitive entities until they engage in political action. Once they appear on the public stage, either through words or deeds, human agents become a definitive "who" as opposed to a "what."

For Arendt, action reveals being through narration. Only when stories are told about the actions in which persons engage can those actions contribute to the revealing of who they are. According to Paul Ricouer, "The political enterprise, in [Arendt's] sense, is the highest attempt to 'immortalize' ourselves."[9] In acting and narrating, persons are revealed. Selya Benhabib finds in Arendt's work two modes of political agency, which she calls the *agonal* and the narrative:

> [W]hereas action in the *agonal* model is described through terms such as "revelation of who one is" and "the making manifest of what is interior," action in the narrative model is characterized through the "telling of a

story" and "the weaving of a web of narratives." Whereas in the first model action appears to make manifest or to reveal an antecedent essence, the "who one is," action in the second model suggests that "the who one is" emerges in the process of doing the deed and telling the story. Whereas action in the first model is a process of discovery, action in the second model is a process of invention. In contemporary terms, we may say that the first model of action is essentialist while the second is constructivist.[10]

Benhabib uncovers in Arendt an alternative to the *agonal* politics of the Greeks. Instead of securely constructed individuals contesting each other in a competitive atmosphere, we find in Benhabib's reading of Arendt a theory of political agency that relies on the history of an event. The meaning we give to a political action comes not just from the intention of the agent, but also from the interpretation of that agent and his action.

The narrative model of action forces us to reconsider political history as well:

> The meaning of a committed act is revealed only when the action itself has come to an end and become a story susceptible to narration. Insofar as any "mastering" of the past is possible, it consists in relating what has happened; but such narration, too, which shapes history, solves no problems and assuages no suffering; it does not master anything once and for all.[11]

For Arendt, action does not exist just in the moment of doing; it is as much, or rather more, in the narration of the event. In one of her essays, Arendt provides us with a powerful critique of history, arguing that history has become a means of limiting political freedom and action by adopting a deterministic outlook.[12]

Benhabib's exploration of Arendt's thought not only links it to narration, it also demonstrates how political agency can lead to the creation of a less confrontational political space. But the public good is difficult to uncover at the global level. In fact, the more *agonal* contest between states at the international level does not give much hope for a dialogue that might lead to public policies that are good for the whole. Does this lack of a public good mean that Arendt's theory of political agency is ultimately one that will simply reinforce the power politics of the international system?

There appear to be two answers to this question. The first arises from a more critical engagement with Arendt's work, one suggested by feminist theory. This approach accepts the lack of an articulation of a public good but can still lead to a democratic engagement, an argument developed by Bonnie Honig. Honig argues that Arendt "theorizes a democratic politics built not on already existing identities or shared experiences but on contingent sites of principled coalescence and shared practices of citizenship."[13] In other words, Arendt not only assumes that political actors assert their identities in certainty and confidence. Instead, only when they act do they take on an identity, and not an identity that is fixed but one that is fluid and changing with each political engagement.

> When they act, Arendt's actors are reborn. . . . Their momentary engagement in action in the public realm engenders identities that are lodged forever in the stories told of their heroic performances by the spectators who witness them. Prior to or apart from action, this self has no identity; it is fragmented, discontinuous, indistinct, and most certainly uninteresting.[14]

Honig's formulation thus moves Arendt's argument from an ontological to a normative one. For she has presented an Arendt who is not simply identifying a politics of contest and competition, but a politics that, when it does not rest on stable identities, will lead to a more democratic engagement of agents.

This ontological/normative analysis of Arendt leads in one direction. A second direction can be found in Arendt's book, *On Revolution*. In this comparison of different revolutionary traditions, Arendt provides the most sustained reflection in her writing on how political action can lead to governance. She begins the work by comparing the French and American revolutions, asking why one leads to a stable form of government, while the other soon collapses. This leads to her well-known critique of the "social question"—an argument that political engagement should not be sullied by addressing social questions such as poverty. She faults the French revolutionaries for being driven by compassion for the poor rather than seeking to create a lasting, constitutional government.[15] In contrast to the French revolution, Arendt argues that the American revolution led to the creation of a lasting, constitutional government because its founders did not need to worry as much about social inequality and poverty. The American revolution, focused as it was on questions of political governance and constitutional structure, led to a more secure structure.

More importantly for the argument of this chapter, Arendt develops here a notion of collective political agency that is lacking in *The Human Condition*. Quoting Thomas Paine, Arendt reminds us

"A constitution is not the act of a government but of a people constituting a government."[16] It is this creation of a constitution— a constitution in the Aristotelian sense of a structure of governance and not simply a piece of paper—that embodies corporate political action. In this moment of founding, individuals exhibit power, a power that can only come through joint action:

> To [the American founders], power came into being when and where people would get together and bind themselves through promises, covenants and mutual pledges; only such power which rested on reciprocity and mutuality was real power and legitimate, whereas the so-called power of kings and princes or aristocrats, because it rested only on consent, was spurious and usurped.[17]

Power comes through corporate action, a power that depends on binding individuals to each other through promises and covenants— exactly the type of bond that a constitution creates.

But how does this relate to her analysis in *The Human Condition*, an analysis that posits a much more fluid and noninstitutional politics? Indeed, *On Revolution* stands in contrast to some of the arguments in Arendt's other works that highlighted the overemphasis on "ruling" and institutions in the study of politics.[18] Clearly, Arendt understood that politics could not take place without institutions; as described above, political action needed the constructed space of the *polis* to be meaningful. But Arendt's idea of a "web" captures a middle ground between a rigid, formalized institution and a loose congeries of political actions with no connection to past and future. Webs do create links among individuals, but in a way that does not bind them permanently.

Having laid out her understanding of corporate political action, Arendt concludes *On Revolution* with a discussion of two different institutional political forms: political parties and revolutionary councils. She notes that both forms arose from modern, post revolutionary politics. Councils allow individuals to act for they are institutions that do not elect representatives but act directly in the public sphere. Unfortunately, according to Arendt, the councils in most systems have been directed toward running economic enterprises (i.e., taking over the factory) rather than engaging in the political sphere. Political parties do not directly act in the political sphere; rather, they nominate representatives to the parliament. As Arendt notes, while councils seek to act on their own, parties support a parliamentary system of governance.

While she argues that councils are preferable because they give direct access to the political sphere, Arendt laments that neither parties nor councils, as they are currently constituted, allow true political action: "The trouble, in other words, is that politics has become a profession and a career, and that the 'elite' therefore is being chosen according to standards and criteria which are themselves profoundly unpolitical."[19] The current political system has solidified into a system that does not create opportunities for individuals to engage in politics in the ways in which Arendt desires.

Yet, the fact that revolutions continue to occur supports another, perhaps most important observation of Arendt's. One of the defining elements of the human condition is its natality—its ability to act anew, to create new structures, to move beyond the boundaries of those spaces that confine us. So, while political parties, councils, parliaments, and governments quickly solidify into seemingly unmovable blocs, Arendt reminds us that new political actions are always possible. Her concerns that the social will overwhelm the political in a revolution need to be kept in mind, although some have criticized her for an overemphasis on this point. If there is a final point to take from Arendt on this topic, however, it is that the future is always open to new possibilities, that political action can create new structures, new webs in which individual political action can arise.

Three important points can be drawn from Arendt: First, political action must be connected to narration. This means that action must be accompanied by explanation and articulation of the ideas that motivate the individual and/or group. While agents cannot control those journalists and historians, they should be provided with space in which not only to engage in actions but to describe those actions as well. The link between action and governance then must include the creation of governing structures that protect and nurture the ability to speak freely. Second, the interpretations of Arendt offered by Benhabib and Honig stress that agents should not be seen as unified, clearly focused individuals prior to their actions. Agents, a category that could include both individual persons and corporate entities, need not have settled identities or even aims prior to their actions for those actions to be considered worthwhile. In evaluating political action, such as political protests, then, I would argue that demanding a clear agenda prior to action is not the most important factor. Third, politics always allows the potential for new action, the creation of new structures. Actions do lead to new frameworks; both those frameworks should not be seen as final, as solid structures that can never change.

Arendt and Global Political Protest

Arendt's account of political action and its potential to produce "webs" of governance was conceptualized in terms of national and local politics. As with other chapters in this volume, however, the goal of this chapter is to move Arendt's thinking to the global level. This section will explore how Arendt's arguments provide a better understanding of these movements, with a focus in particular on the protests in Seattle in 1999.

Scholarly interest in transnational networks and global NGOs has been growing in recent years.[20] These works have demonstrated that international politics cannot be confined to interactions between nation-states or even international organizations; rather, global political movements play an essential role in bringing issues to the world agenda, providing information and advice to governments and international bureaucrats, and advocating for political positions. These organizations and networks, while largely composed of citizens from developed countries, also try to give individuals access to global politics that have traditionally been confined to diplomats and national political elites.

This literature, however, focuses primarily on how these movements arise and their work as transmitters of information to national and international governing elites. Keck and Sikknik, for example, evaluate transnational networks primarily in terms of how they facilitate new frames of reference for international elites and how they push those elites to change their behavior.[21] While evaluating these groups on this basis is important, it does limit our evaluative tools to a nation-state context. Rather than think critically about how they might create new "webs" of political action, these works focus primarily on the structure as it currently exists.

These works also tend to focus on the organizational structure of the movements rather than on moments of political action.[22] This focus, while important for understanding the origins and impact of these movements on international politics, moves attention away from those moments in which potentially disruptive protests may generate new structures.

In other words, most analyses of global NGOs and transnational networks remain confined to the nation-state system and its structures of governance. The 1999 anti-globalization demonstrations in Seattle turned attention away from the structures of NGOs to the moments of protest themselves. For this reason, this protest moment, and some that followed suggest that an Arendtian analysis might elucidate more clearly ways in which these networks may do more than simply provide information and advocate policies to governments. In this case, protesters took to the streets in a mass political action that did not appear to have a single purpose. But, for a moment, it demonstrated that political action can erupt in ways that give access to the global political realm.

In the following, I provide a brief description of what happened, including how the events were described, or "narrated," by the press. I conclude with some suggestions on how an Arendtian analysis of the events might help to see them in a new light, especially in light of the disconnect often seen between political action and governance.

The *Los Angeles Times* reported during the protests:

> Not since the days of the Vietnam War and the civil rights movement has the entire downtown core of a major American city been seized by popular political uprising; rarely has so diverse an array of groups linked elbows against a common enemy, in this case the faceless forces of globalization.[23]

Other protests against international financial institutions have taken place in Prague, Melbourne, Davos, Geneva and Washington, DC. Some contend that this trend indicates a worldwide crises in citizenship. As Smith and Smyth maintain in their paper on globalization, citizenship and technology, "the ascendancy of [global] markets [has] erode[ed] the political dimension of citizenship and becomes a substitute for political decision-making, narrowing the scope of the public and collective decision-making."[24] Indeed, it is telling that the Seattle protesters chose to target the WTO, an international body that is not accountable to any citizens but its member states.

The protests in Seattle started during the last week of November and lasted through the first week of December 1999. An estimated 50,000–100,000 people participated in the demonstrations. The WTO was in Seattle to convene a ministerial meeting for their Millennium round of trade talks. Their goal was to set an agenda for lowering tariffs and removing other trade barriers among their member-states. Some of the specific issues on the agenda were greater access to U.S. and European markets for textiles from developing countries; possible linkages of minimum labor and environmental standards to trade; and possible inclusion of China into the WTO.

Among the more well-established organizations that protested were the Sierra Club, the National Wildlife Federation, Public Citizen, as well as a variety of trade unions including the American Federation of

Labor-Congress of Industrial Organizations (AFL-CIO) and the United Steelworkers of America. There were smaller activist groups who focused on similar causes as these organizations, as well as a variety of groups who mixed and matched their interests to create organizations like the Alliance for Sustainable Jobs and the Environment. The Alliance, formed by California environmental groups and locked-out Kaiser Steel workers, protested the WTO's undermining of environmental and labor laws in the United States. Many individuals who claimed no ties to any activist groups were also drawn to the protests after coming across anti-WTO websites on the Internet.

To organize groups for the Seattle talks, NGOs such as Global Trade Watch, Seattle99, and the Ruckus Society created websites featuring a variety of resources: literature concerning the WTO and its policies; links to issue-related sites; mechanisms for obtaining free or inexpensive housing; information on free car-rides; and a system for organizing a corps of volunteers to direct activists on the ground. Such coordination was possible because the groups relied heavily on the Internet, which was relatively inexpensive and because there was an ethos of cooperation against a common foe.[25]

Different groups initiated the planning for the protests. In February 1999, the local representative of Public Citizen, the NGO headed by Ralph Nader, organized local groups in Seattle to prepare for the arrival of the WTO.[26] The initial meetings brought together primarily local groups, but those groups soon connected to national and international organizations. The point at which the protests moved to a "global" level is not clear, something that deserves further investigation. And, although Public Citizen played an important role in the initial organizing process, and Lori Wallach of Public Citizen became a spokesperson for many protesters as they developed, it is difficult to pinpoint a single organizing group or person as the leader. Janet Thomas suggests that it was not until an animal rights activist suggested that all the groups were linked by a concern with health and food safety that they really coalesced into a single unit, a point that Wallach might not see as the primary impetus of the protests.[27]

As the planning progressed, other groups began taking on a more active role. The Ruckus Society, a group founded by a former member of Greenpeace who had been involved in protests and wanted to support diverse forms of direct political action, held a meeting north of Seattle in September 1999 to orient protesters in forms of nonviolent direct action. The focus of this planning stage seemed oriented less toward the issues and more toward the forms of direct political action.

As described by a report in the *Guardian*,

> At the Ruckus training camp, direct action techniques were taught. Workshops were held in political theater and WTO delegates will be greeted by an army of thousands of colorful puppets. Activists were taught about the ethics of non-violence and practiced de-escalating violent situations.[28]

A series of forums, teach-ins and religious services were held in the days leading up to the meetings. The protests themselves began on November 30. Groups organized into different coalitions, and undertook different forms of political action. One group donned "turtle" outfits and marched in favor of environmental rights. This group, less because of their cause and more because of their method, attracted a great deal of the media's attention. Other groups undertook sit-ins and blocked traffic.[29]

On November 30, after two days of delay in the talks due to protesters' blockades, Seattle officials brought in the National Guard and used riot-control tactics to deal with activists who blocked the delegates and clogged the streets. Tear gas, rubber bullets and other crowd-control tactics were used against the protesters. A strict curfew was also imposed for most of the talks. The Seattle streets had not been set up prior to the meeting with crowd-control measures such as barricades, an oversight which drew criticism from the delegates who had witnessed similarly disruptive protests at the 1998 WTO meeting. The Seattle officials were, as a result, put in the difficult position of imposing often heavy-handed police tactics to control the protests, which were being reported by journalists from around the world. During the last days of the WTO ministerial meeting, Seattle authorities closed down the streets near the WTO's convention center, leaving the immediate area comparatively desolate after so much protest activity. Meanwhile, protests continued in other parts of downtown Seattle.

The protesters affected the WTO talks in many ways. In addition to blocking the ministers' entrance to the talks, they were also able to get leaders and ministers, most notably, President Bill Clinton, to respond to the protesters messages. Clinton "gave two impassioned pleas . . . for nations of the world to use trade agreements to protect the rights of laborers and the environment, and delivered a pointed attack on the WTO for the secrecy of its operations."[30] (After Clinton left Seattle however, U.S. Trade Representative Charlene Barshefsky told WTO delegates that his statements were not actually reflected in the U.S. negotiating position.)

Antiglobalization demonstrations used what has been dubbed the "hubs and spokes protest model."[31] Naomi Klein, in wondering "Does protest need a vision?" asserts that because the movement was primarily driven by the internet, the protests "mirror[ed] the organic, decentralized interlinked pathways of the internet" by including a series of "affinity groups" in "coalitions of coalitions."[32] Klein sees advantages and disadvantages to this protest method. One advantage, says Klein, is that this network of activist organizations does not have fixed leaders, per se, so they can work more fluidly; they can respond quickly to blockade entrances of meetings as was the case in Seattle, where protesters gave the police a real challenge by using their numbers and cooperative tactics to elude the authorities. But the Seattle authorities ultimately overcame the protesters' tactics, and succeeding antiglobalization protests have met similar but much quicker fates. Klein sees another disadvantage in that the inclusiveness of these networks allows a great deal of variety in ideology to replace singularity in purpose. It is not that they lack vision, Klein says, but there is no driving ideology that binds all the protesters. Yet Klein is not convinced that the hurdle of a missing binding ideology will hamper antiglobalization groups. Indeed, books, essays and websites have been created to flesh out the plan for an alternative vision to a WTO-led globalization—"globalization from below."

According to Lori Wallach the general goal of the Seattle protests was to get a critical mass of people to communicate to the world at large that the WTO must be reformed because it undermines the protection of human rights, the environment, jobs, and agriculture around the world.[33] If their decision-making process does not become more accountable for the effects of its policies, Wallach contends, protesters will demand its demise. Whether protest groups really have the power to "sink" the WTO is questionable; but as it stands, without such reformation of the WTO, the globalization of markets will continue to develop—without any input or control by citizens.

Wallach's organization espouses a variation of the idea of "globalization from below." In the model Global Trade Watch champions, the WTO, as the primary engine of globalization, would become "accessible to people" as a result of citizens becoming activists against, and not simply subjects of, the current economic trends of globalization. At the center of this movement is the concept of the "public citizen": "a person who, once empowered with the information and tools to affect change, makes being an activist part of daily life."[34] Global Trade Watch wants to launch country-based campaigns around the world whereby groups band together in their own countries to pressure their national governments to demand reforms in the WTO within a pre-set time frame. If the WTO does not espouse these reforms, Global Trade Watch would then launch another series of campaigns to demand withdrawal of state-membership, or what Wallach's group calls the "de-funding" of the WTO. It has yet to be determined, however, whether such a campaign will have any impact, by threat or by action, on the WTO.

Critics of these movements and the protests in Seattle have focused on their lack of coherence, tactics that appeared to be without purpose, and on the anarchist elements. While such elements existed among the protesters, they cannot be reduced to these elements. Rather than avoid these elements, however, it is important to explore them. Because of the approach I set out in my exegesis of Arendt, I believe the protesters should not avoid criticisms such as those suggested, but, rather, embrace them as defining their political actions. For at the base of these criticisms is a more fundamental critique: the actions of these protesters are not tied to the creation of future systems of global governance and, as a result, do not advance the causes of world peace and justice. I want to suggest here that (1) the protests can be a positive thing simply by the fact that they happened and (2) they do advance certain ideas and contribute to global governance, but that governance is continuously open to contestation and debate. Like Arendt, I believe that political actions must be seen as interventions into the public space and contributors to the creation and sustenance of that space. But, they cannot be reduced to that. They must be seen as moments in which identities are constituted and revealed, where the human need to act politically is played out.

Drawing on Arendt, I suggest three modes of evaluation: (1) Did the protests create new forms of governance? (2) Did the protests create spaces in which not only action but also speech could be conducted? (3) Did the protesters develop new identities as they undertook their actions?

DID THE PROTESTS CREATE NEW FORMS OF GOVERNANCE?

The protests certainly altered the conduct of negotiations at the Seattle meeting. Delegates were unable to attend the ministerial meetings and many felt that the protesters had forced a change in the public perceptions of the WTO. The fact that the U.S. president felt compelled to respond to the concerns of the protesters indicates that they had some influence. Also, later meetings of the WTO were surrounded by a greater degree of security in anticipation of further protests.

But, these changes seem largely confined to protecting delegates at future meetings. The substance of the WTO and its procedures do not seem to have been affected in large part by the protesters. If we define global governance as the structures that rule the lives of individuals, the protests in Seattle seem to have had very little effect on the structure of the WTO.

It is important, however, to consider Arendt's comparison of the councils and parties in thinking about governance. Did the protests contribute to or create new forms of political engagement that look like the council or party system? Some have critiqued NGOs because of their lack of representation, especially because they do not represent the developing world as well as the developed. But, this assumes that these groups are more like political parties, on the Arendtian model, that should be evaluated on how well they represent their constituents. This also assumes that the group will create a political "elite" who can then interact with other skilled politicians to craft legislation and change policy.

But, if we consider these groups on the model of the council, we begin to see them in a new light. According to Arendt, the value of the councils was that they provided a means for group action, for direct engagement in the public sphere. Clearly, according to this model, the protesters in Seattle were successful; they provided an opportunity for political action in a group context that would not have otherwise been available.

Did the Protests Create New Spaces in Which not Only Action but Also Speech Could Be Conducted?

The protests not only engaged in street theater and direct political action in the streets of Seattle, they also sought to explain and justify their actions through the creation of a large number of websites. These sites, originally created to provide logistical information about getting to and finding housing in Seattle, have become sources of information about future meetings of international institutions and descriptions of their policies. Critical evaluations of these institutions have become an important part of the web presence of many of those who were involved in the protests.[35]

The protesters also sought to use the media to advance their cause. Organizations like the Ruckus Society teach activists not only how to scale buildings and create puppets but also how to use the media to advance their cause. Lori Wallach's interview in *Foreign Policy* played an important role in explaining the purpose of the protests to the foreign policy-making elites in the United States. This active media presence demonstrates that the protesters were interested and were successful (in part) in creating a space for speech as well as action.

DID THE PROTESTERS DEVELOP NEW IDENTITIES AS THEY ENGAGED IN POLITICAL ACTIONS?

Many individuals and groups came to Seattle with only the goal of responding to the power of the WTO. As they planned and began their protests, however, they developed a level of solidarity that was unexpected for many. Moments at which they needed to plan strategies and develop responses to police actions focused their energies and allowed them to develop alliances and even new identities.

At the same time, it does not appear that there has arisen a single organization that brings together these diverse groups and which has outlasted the protests. Different groups continue to engage in protests without much cohesion in either means or ends. Protests in New York against the World Economic Forum demonstrated a certain amount of dissonance among the groups involved, indicating that a single, permanent identity had not coalesced as a result of these disparate actions.

This lack of a single identity, however, does not mean that the political actions in Seattle did not create new identities for the protesters. If the actions they undertook in Seattle "revealed" the "who" of these different groups, then their actions match the model of political action that Arendt laid out. Indeed, according to Honig, if those identities did remain rigid and bound in a single framework, they might have left an Arendtian realm to become something else. By remaining fluid and contingent upon the protests in which they engaged, the various groups and individuals who conducted the protests can be seen as truly Arendtian political agents.

CONCLUSION

This chapter has sought to examine the political actions of a group of protesters in terms of the Arendtian category of political action. In so doing, I have sought to identify whether or not those groups and individuals created new forms of global governance, created new spaces for political speech, and created new identities. I have found that they succeeded on all three accounts.

The fact that the protesters did not create new forms of global governance in the context of the WTO needs to be considered in terms of Arendtian categories of political action. While the WTO may not change its policies, the protesters were able to create something like the "councils" that Arendt saw as part of the revolutionary heritage. Even if their overt desire was to change or destroy that institution, the fact that they created new spaces for speech and may have developed new identities that depend on further political action will influence global governance in the long run. In fact, the need for free speech and political actions may be more important at this point than the creation of new institutions for governing the globe. The international system already contains a large number of institutions that claim to govern. What it lacks are active cosmopolitan citizens who agitate for their rights and who fulfill their responsibilities. While many will continue to condemn protesters as incoherent and anarchic, my Arendtian reading of their actions suggests that we need more such actions not less.

NOTES

This chapter benefited from research by Janice Gabucan and feedback from participants at the National Endowment of the Humanities and Carnegie Council on Ethics and International Affairs' Faculty Development Seminar on Supranationalism, held at Columbia University, New York, NY, Summer 2001. John Williams and Joel Rosenthal also provided useful feedback.

1. The meetings also failed to reach a conclusion because of conflicts among delegates, although this is not the focus of my analysis here. Elizabeth Olson, "Patching Up Morale at the World Trade Organization," *New York Times*, October 30, 2000, http://www.nytimes.com/2000/10/31/business/31WTO.html.
2. Aristotle, Stephen Everson (ed.), *The Politics* (Cambridge: Cambridge University Press, 1996), book III, chapter 1, 1275^b20, 63.
3. Aristotle, *Ibid.*, book VII, chapter 4, 1326^b15–20, 173. In this passage, Aristotle suggests that a *polis* must not be so large that citizens do not know each other's names.
4. Robert Dahl, "Can International Organizations be Democratic?" in Ian Shapiro and Casiano Hacker-Cordon (eds.), *Democracy's Edges* (Cambridge: Cambridge University Press, 1999), 22.
5. David Held, *Democracy and the Global Order: From the Modern State to Cosmopolitan Governance* (Stanford, CA.: Stanford University Press, 1995).

6. Hannah Arendt, *The Human Condition* (Chicago, IC.: University of Chicago Press, 1958), 41.
7. Ibid., 152. Interestingly, this "common world" does not only arise from action but also from work, which creates physical objects that persist beyond the individual lives of persons, giving the world a permanence necessary for us to live. But, although work creates this common world, it is also affected by political action.
8. Ibid., 190–191.
9. Paul Ricouer, "Action, Story, and History: On Reading the Human Condition," in Reuben Gardener (ed.), *The Realm of Humanitas: Responses to the Writing of Hannah Arendt* (New York: Peter Longman, 1990), 151.
10. Selya Benhabib, *The Reluctant Modernism of Hannah Arendt* (Thousand Oaks, CA: Sage Publications, 1996), 125–126.
11. Hannah Arendt, "The Concept of History: Ancient and Modern," in Hannah Arendt (ed.), *Between Past and Future: Eight Exercises in Political Thought* (New York: Penguin Books, 1968).
12. Arendt, "The Concept of History: Ancient and Modern."
13. Bonnie Honig (ed.), *Feminist Interpretations of Hannah Arendt* (University Park, PA: University of Pennsylvania Press, 1995), 3.
14. Honig, *Feminist Interpretations of Arendt*, 141.
15. Hannah Arendt, *On Revolution* (New York: Penguin Books, 1963), 86.
16. Ibid., 145.
17. Ibid., 181.
18. See introduction to this volume for an elaboration of this point as it relates to the IR emphasis on the state.
19. Ibid., 277.
20. See Margaret E. Keck and Kathryn Sikknik, *Activists Beyond Borders: Advocacy Networks in International Politics* (Ithaca: Cornell University Press, 1998); Jackie Smith, Charles Chatfield, and Ron Pagnucco (eds.), *Transnational Social Movements and Global Politics: Solidarity Beyond the State* (Syracuse: Syracuse University Press, 1997); Thomas Risse-Kappen (ed.), *Bringing Transnational Actors Back In: Non-State Actors, Domestic Structures, and International Institutions* (Cambridge: Cambridge University Press, 1995); Robert O'Brien, et al., *Contesting Global Governance: Multilateral Economic Institutions and Global Social Movements* (Cambridge: Cambridge University Press, 2000).
21. Keck and Sikknik, *Activists Beyond Borders*, 201.
22. Although, see Roland Bleiker, *Popular Dissent, Human Agency and Global Politics* (Cambridge: Cambridge University Press, 2000) for a sophisticated theoretical account of political action. Bleiker, although not drawing on Arendt, concludes with some strikingly similar conclusions: "A discursive notion of human agency is grounded precisely in this recognition that there is no end to circles of revealing and concealing, of opening and closing spaces to think and act. Revealing is always an act, not something that remains stable," 282.

23. Kim Murphy, "In the Streets of Seattle, Echos of Turbulent 60s," *Los Angeles Times* (December 1, 1999).

24. Peter Smith and Elizabeth Smythe, "Globalization, Citizenship and Technology: The MAI meets the Internet," Manuscript, International Studies Association Convention Los Angeles (March 14, 2000).

25. See Craig Warkentin, *Reshaping World Politics: NGOs, the Internet, and Global Civil Society* (Lanham: Rowman and Littlefield Publishers, 2001) for an account of how the Internet can provide resources for those engaged in transnational NGO work.

26. Janet Thomas, *The Battle in Seattle: The Story Behind and Beyond the WTO Demonstrations* (Golden CO: Fulcrum Publishers, 2000), 21. See also, Greg Miller, "WTO Summit: Protests in Seattle," *Los Angeles Times* (December 2, 1999): 24.

27. Compare Thomas, 21–30 to Lori Wallach and Moises Naim, "Lori's War," *Foreign Policy* (Spring 2000).

28. Andy Rowell, "Faceless in Seattle," *The Guardian* (October 6, 1999): 4.

29. See Steve Greenhouse, "A Carnival of Derision to Greet the Princes of Trade," *New York Times* (November 29, 1999): A12.

30. David E. Sanger, "Talks and Turmoil: The Overview; President Chides World Trade Body in Stormy Seattle," *The New York Times* (December 1, 1999).

31. Naomi Klein, "Does Protest Need a Vision?" *New Statesman* (July 3, 2000).

32. Ibid.

33. Naim Moises, "Lori's War," *Foreign Policy* (Spring 2000).

34. See http://www.citizen.org.

35. See Warkentin, *Reshaping World Politics: NGOs, the Internet, and Global Civil Society*, for an elabortion of this point.

CHAPTER 8

HANNAH ARENDT AND THE INTERNATIONAL SPACE IN-BETWEEN?

John Williams

INTRODUCTION

This chapter attempts to use Hannah Arendt's idea of politics as taking place in a "space in–between" people as a starting point for thinking about politics in a nascent or emerging global civil society that is typically characterized in liberal terms.1 This liberal version has many benefits and attractions, but this chapter suggests that we should not take for granted the idea that liberalism offers the only, or an unproblematic, account of what such a new political space could or should look like. Arendt's critique of politics within the modern state offers a potentially rich and insightful way of thinking about these transnational political forms in a way that relies less on law, institutions, and "ruling," and instead sees them as offering scope for a politics of freedom via the active involvement, through dialogue, of individuals who bring with them a rich identity and rootedness, rather than a thinner status as a rights-holding citizen.

This bald statement disguises a number of problems involved in such an exercise, problems that influence the structure and approach of this chapter in important ways. First, there is the problem that Arendt does not address this kind of issue directly and extensively in her work. This chapter is therefore not meant as a straightforward exegesis and analysis of a number of texts, although the first section does offer an account of the idea of the space in-between. The second, connected, problem is that Arendt discusses the idea of the space in-between almost entirely in the context of a territorially bordered political space. The idea of global or transnational civil society, of course, is that it does not have geographically fixed territorial borders understood in terms of sovereignty. Arendt is a theorist of the bounded community, but this chapter tries to suggest that even though a global civil society is not bordered in a territorial and sovereign sense it does contain other sorts of boundaries and borders that make her understanding of the space in-between applicable, with some license asked for and granted in terms of Arendt's original exposition of the ideas. Finally, Arendt's account of the space in-between is tinged with sadness about its decline and pessimism about is future in a modern politics that, as discussed in the introduction to this book, its dominated by "ruling." Reinterpreting a story of decline in terms of opportunity and potential is not always a straightforward task and, again, requires a filling in of gaps and an amount of speculation about and flexibility in the use, and, doubtless in the eyes of some, abuse, of concepts and categories.

The chapter proceeds in three main sections. The first offers a brief account of Arendt's idea of the space in-between. In the interests of brevity this assumes some limited prior knowledge of Arendtian concepts, but hopefully no more that can be gained from the book's introductory chapter. The second section looks at reasons why Arendt may have felt uncomfortable attempting to extend the idea of the space in-between to the international arena, focusing upon the problem of violence and especially the role of war in international relations. It also addresses the flaws in one initially temping way of trying to think about an international in-between by seeing states as analogous to the individuals who potentially constitute an in-between among themselves within the state. The idea of an "international society" of states, borrowed from the English School of IR theory is used to illustrate these problems. Finally, the third section looks at the virtues of an international in-between in relation to the emergence of a transnational or global civil society. Here the benefits of an Arendtian critique of a liberal version of this emergent political form comes through most clearly, with a stress on the need to respond to the diversity of human beings and their communities, and the likelihood of communities wishing to withdraw from the world, as well as to engage in it.

THE SPACE IN-BETWEEN

Arendt's analysis of what a properly political life would be like, offered in *The Human Condition*, carries with it a tone of despair for the decline of a different sort of politics—the politics of the *agora* and the *polis*.[2] This despair is echoed elsewhere. Her analysis of revolution stresses how it is the pursuit of a freedom that is freedom into politics, rather than freedom from it, that is the defining feature of the revolutionary ideal, and one almost never preserved in the institutionalization of the postrevolutionary state.[3] Her account of totalitarianism also stresses how it is active and engaged individuals, rooted in real communities and identities that are the bulwark against the terror and loneliness of totalitarianism and its juggernaut of permanent, boundary and border shattering dynamism.[4]

Within the modern, liberal state Arendt sees an ideal politics threatened by the emphasis on "ruling." However, with the ideal of the *agora* irrecoverable, it is within the state that Arendt sees any remaining potential for "true" politics to take place. The modern state, insofar as it is the heir to the *agora* and the Aristotelian and Republican tradition, stands for her as the closest incarnation of the ideal of the *polis* and it is on the reinvigoration of an active, participatory form of politics within the state that her normative vision focuses.[5] Freedom, the political goal to which she attaches the highest priority, appears most strongly within the ideal political community that is the republican state and it comes with participation. And participation takes place in the space in-between.

The idea of the space in-between or the space of appearance takes on great importance in the Arendtian vision of an ideal politics, and its imperfect and fragile manifestation in the modern world. The space in-between is ephemeral, intersubjective and laden with immanent potential and unpredictability.[6] It is thus the opposite of the structured, institutionalized, reified and determined models of ideal political situations that she argues have dominated the Western political tradition since Plato.[7]

Thus the space in-between does not possess an institutional form, indeed to try and institutionalize it in any but the loosest of ways is to demolish it. The institutional requirements are equal access in the sense that the participants need to be able to bring themselves to political encounter as equal political beings.[8] The *agora* is the inspiration, where citizens gathered as equals to debate the issues of the day and to take decisions about their collective interests, goods and future. Given the practical impossibility of re-creating actual meeting places in modern states, it is the principles behind the *agora* which inform the space in-between. The equality of citizenship, the right to contribute to debate, discussion and decision, the opportunity to place oneself into the public realm—to appear as a political individual—are what animate Arendt's vision.[9]

This, for Arendt, is freedom. The chance to take the political stage is the chance to act in the world, and it is action that is the highest form of human activity and politics is its quintessential manifestation.[10] Politics is an act of creation—an opportunity for a new beginning, giving reign to the potential Arendt sums up in the idea of "natality." This is action that goes well beyond the day-to-day necessities of life—what Arendt calls labor—or even the creation of enduring physical artifacts, even works of art—the idea of work. Instead action is about asserting the essential human characteristics through speaking, revealing ourselves to others in ways that may be in the context of the everyday but which establish the connections between peoples that enable the mutual recognition of our deeper humanity. To act is to be free and freedom therefore requires politics and the minimal institutional frameworks necessary to be free from overweening cares about survival or the exhausting burdens of living and working in the social realm. We need to be citizens, we need protected access to and possibilities for political engagement with fellow citizens and we need the shared bases of recognition and understanding upon which interaction can be meaningful.

The requirement for citizenship helps to explain Arendt's assumption that the modern, if deeply imperfect, inheritor of the legacy of the *polis* is the state. This is, to be sure, citizenship of a different character to that accorded the male heads of household in classical Athens, but as we attempt to trace the move from an unrecoverable ideal to the compromised world of contemporary political reality citizenship offers one useful signpost. Citizenship has, until recently, been something that is understood almost exclusively in relation to the state, and Arendt does not seriously challenge this assumption. In the classic liberal account of the development of citizenship, provided by T.H. Marshall, the development of citizenship is seen as a mechanism for mediating, defining and limiting the respective rights, duties, and responsibilities of the state and its inhabitants.[11] Arendt would not sign up to a liberal vision of citizenship, arguing that it brackets too many things into the private sphere that ought to be public matters, for example.[12] She nevertheless goes along with the idea that our political status as citizens, the status that provides the basis for our potential political actions, must be understood in relation to the state, "all inhabitants of a given territory are entitled to be admitted to the public, political realm."[13]

Protected access is something that is usually associated with the rights to vote, to stand for public office, to join political parties, and to engage in public lobbying and pressuring of the political process.

Arendt's account of political action is very different from these conceptions, of course, but it does retain the requirement that access is protected. That protection normally comes from the state as a limited institution, one that is the product of the individuals who inhabit it and which reflects the community that these individuals have been able to forge.[14] Indeed, unlimited state power in the form of totalitarianism is the greatest threat to the prospect of real and true politics because it destroys the possibility of trusting, open, political engagement with fellow citizens. It creates the condition of "lonelines"—a condition whereby the space in-between cannot exist because lonely individuals cannot experience the trust and familiarity that is necessary if they are to project themselves into the political realm of the in-between, to engage in a public way with their fellows.[15]

This points to a further requirement, idealized in the *polis* and struggling for space in the modern state: a basis for meaningful interaction. This is understood by Arendt as requiring a political community—the trusting company of one's equals, people with whom we can share assumptions, understandings, ideas, and ideals. This is not to see community as totalizing, homogenizing, and rendering individual human beings into an amorphous bloc.[16] Arendt's whole political philosophy rests on the plurality of individuals, but it does recognize that history, culture, language, religion, experience and so on build groups of people. The state, too, has a role in this. In its ideal, republican form it is in part protector and nurturer of the community, with the good state in turn being owed the loyalty and commitment of the people.[17] Even in the nonideal world, the extent to which states match this ideal makes them necessary and valuable to the possibility of a politics taking place in-between active, equal, familiar citizens.

Thus the space in-between is framed by a view of politics that sees individuals in the light of what Arendt regards as Aristolte's two greatest insights—man is a political, or *polis*-living, animal; and man is a speaking animal—one who engages in political action through the mechanism of speech.[18] Coming together to speak—to debate and discuss—with one's familiar but distinct fellow citizens of a community is where politics occurs and where people are free. This is the space in-between—the ephemeral and intersubjective moment of dialogue between people taking on a public face and presenting themselves in the public role of active and engaged citizens.[19] In addition to its ephemeral intersubjectivity, the space in-between is laden with immanent potential. The potential consequences for people engaging in this activity are limitless.[20] Arendt stresses how politics of this kind is untrammeled by institutional restrictions; instead the limitations to it are those that can come out of a dialogue among equals in this sort of situation—the limitations are those of promising and forgiveness.[21]

Promising establishes some sort of reliable expectations among politically acting people, reflecting their shared trust and identity as members of a community. Forgiveness enables them to deal with the unexpected and unpredictable outcomes and consequences that are a part of almost any action. The space in-between thus has to be created and re-created continuously among individuals. They affirm and reaffirm their recognition of one another as equals and as valued members of the community to which they belong, to which they make their contributions as active citizens and from which they draw their sense of identity and rootedness in the world.

It is the act of constituting a republic, through the promulgation of a constitution, that is the basic act enabling freedom. The goal of a political community should be the constitution of a republic, or at least contributing to its restoration through its reform or reconstitution.[22] The ideal republic, though, has proven historically difficult to maintain, difficulties that are unlikely to abate, and thus, maintaining the virtues of the republican form is a struggle. Thus, while communities which do not take on this republican form seem to be ruled out as being possible sites of a properly political in-between, this is too harsh a conclusion. A political location where the issues of the public realm are central and where individuals can act in the Arendtian sense of embarking on a public dialogue is not an impossible dream in the modern state, but it is one not easily created and not to be taken for granted. Thus Arendt's view of the nature of politics and the place where politics happens, the space in-between, is encompassed within and aimed at the creation of a republic, or at least at the creation of republican moments and sites within the nonideal state. This is one where individuals can be safe in the company of their fellows with whom they share an identity and a sense of purpose, where they can gather together under the conditions that enable the space in-between to exist.

This is a narrow definition of what politics is and can be. Arendt's critique of the institutionally focused political craftsmanship that is dominant in the social world of "really existing" politics extends to ruling out almost any of what takes place under the label of politics as being politics.[23] The ephemeral, intersubjective, truly political world of individuals inserting themselves into a dialogic public space is under so great a threat in the modern world that it is becoming almost imperceptible in this ostensibly political realm. What we would term "civil society" offers some hope, as Arendt's commentary on the civil rights movement suggests, but even here the goal of institutions, of legal rights, of entry to the formal political process seem to undermine her idealized world of the space in-between.[24] At the same time, though, what else can such groups hope to do if they are to maintain themselves as communities within a framework where the opportunities for revolution are few and far between and dependent on the decrepitude of the existing state? If the (republican) state is the precondition for communal freedom and the existing state is not decrepit then gaining a place and a space within it, demonstrating one's position within the community, is the goal of political action, the necessary prerequisite for freedom.

Thus the boundaries of state, of community, the limits of understanding and the intersubjectivity of the space in-between help us to understand why Arendt is a theorist of the bounded community. She is dismissive of the possibility of universal principles and ideas such as the ideal of the sovereign individual in liberalism[25] and of the possibility of resisting totalitarianism, for example, through an appeal to universal humanity as opposed to the fraternal spirit of human collectivities and communities.[26] Her writings on revolution and her critique of human rights also stress the need for limitations, for borders and boundaries not just in a territorial sense but in establishing the network of locating places and spaces, ties and understandings, beliefs and identities which are what, for Arendt, make us human.[27] It is these characteristics that make the space in-between possible.

The good republic stands at the pinnacle of this bounded, bordered, located existence. The republic gives us freedom and requires of us responsibility for its nurturing through our engagement with it. The modern state, though, may also be a means to the ends of human freedom through action, and it is a necessary if imperfect means and one without which the hopes for freedom and action are scuppered. This is the state as the inheritor of the legacy of the *polis* in this regard—the human artifice that is nevertheless necessary for us to fulfill ourselves as humans.[28]

THE IMPOSSIBILITY OF AN INTERNATIONAL IN-BETWEEN?

This account of the in-between in Arendt's thought has already pointed to substantial problems with trying to translate her idea of the in-between as the site of politics to the international level. A strict fidelity to the texts may have to be set aside. The seemingly unavoidable centrality of the state and her close connection of the state to the communities which enable the space in-between to exist in a meaningful fashion are two that we shall return to shortly, but first I want to point to one external constraint that Arendt arguably overstates.

Arendt's account of international relations is sparse and patchy. A limited defense of a narrowly construed international law can be adduced in *Origins of Totalitarianism*. The start of *On Revolution* offers a dismissal of the deterrence dominated strategic discourse that monopolized the academic study of IR in the 1950s and 1960s.[29] These are indicative of the absence of focused and systematic enquiry. Arendt regarded international relations as being constituted by the relations of states pursuing power and security in an anarchic environment where the threat of war and other forms of violence was ever present, rendering international relations politically mute in a true sense.[30] Such a view explains her seeming disregard of international relations as a source or site of politics in any sense that she could regard as recognizably connected to the idealized version she defined and defended, or even its imperfect manifestations in the domestic politics of contemporary states.[31]

Law offered some potential salvation from this Realist view. Legally codifying and controlling the relations of states would enable international relations to be civilized and controlled, but it would not necessarily become properly political. "Treaties and international guarantees provide an extension of this territorially bound freedom for citizens outside of their own country, but . . . the elementary coincidence of freedom and a limited space remains manifest."[32]

Arendt does not attempt, for example, to utilize the domestic analogy to put forth a normative vision of a properly political international relations in which states, or more particularly their representatives, take on the roles filled by individuals within the domestic political condition. There is no sense of states as "big people" able to construct a space in-between themselves in which dialogue might be heard and where the limitlessness of human diversity might be negotiated and the human potential for freedom might be furthered. The international is too suffused with violence, too lacking in security, too inaccessible to people and too diverse in its communities for a space in-between to be possible. There is no chance for the human voice to sound in the form of dialogue among diverse yet familiar equals in the largely empty places and spaces of the international. "If we equate these [spatially limited] spaces of freedom . . . with the political realm itself, we shall be inclined to think of them as islands in a sea or as oases in a desert. This image, I believe, is suggested to us . . . by the record of history."[33]

Thus, for Arendt, an approach to understanding international relations that does offer an account of the accommodation of plurality—the "pluralist" strand of the "English School," for example—is not an adequate or potentially properly political account.[34] The idea of a society of sovereign states that have instituted a set of rules, norms and principles of behavior that are accepted as not just being in the interests of the individual states but in the interest of them all—an international common good—is not enough.[35] The seeming parallels between the loosely institutionalized fora of international society—symbolized by the practices of diplomacy—and the *agora* are misleading. States' representatives may be able to appeal to the same notion of equality as Athenian citizens, via the doctrine of sovereign equality. They may enjoy something much closer to the freedom of dialogue or debate than is present within the congested world of domestic politics. But this line of enquiry is ultimately sterile. The failure of the domestic analogy to hold, the rootedness of the state in its international manifestation in the violence of war and the diversity of the communities imperfectly manifested in states means that we cannot have an interstate in-between.

This rather bleak impression, and an impression rather than a fully thought-out picture is what we have, returns us to the state-centricity of Arendt's view of politics as a whole and the way in which she views the potential for real politics to be contained within the state. However, if we can unravel some of the limitations that are present in this account, we may be able to discern a potential route into an international space in-between.

The first stage here is to offer an alternative understanding of international society as being not just the normatively constituted and rule-governed arena in which states engage in international relations. Instead, while the focus of international society is on the management and regulation of the relations of states, it also offers potential political space for other actors. By controlling the use of violence, amongst other things, the constitution of an international society helps to quell this politically mute force and create the potential, under-explored and underexploited though it may be, for politics. Clearly the principal actors and beneficiaries of international society are states, but it needs to be remembered that the system exists to preserve itself and not just whatever states happen to exist at the time. It thus does enjoy a certain degree of autonomy, at least as being an object of value in international politics. International society is an enduring human artifice, and one created with the goal of enabling politics among states to escape the abyss of a, presumed to be Hobbesian, state of nature. It has within it the potential to be a site where other political actors and entities may find room, too.[36]

The anarchic international arena is not the barren wilderness of violence that Arendt rather assumes when she says, "Violence is traditionally the *ultima ratio* of relations between nations."[37] It lacks well-developed and authoritative institutions but this may be an advantage for an Arendtian view of politics that takes an institutional focus as being a positive disadvantage. In opposition to a domestic political arena that Arendt sees as becoming more hostile to the creation of an in-between where true politics can happen because of the over institutionalization of modern politics in a social world, international society lacks such congestion. It has other serious problems—especially those of violence and a structure which formally restricts access by non-state actors—but these may not be insuperable, especially the latter as all kinds of non-state actors take their place alongside states in the conduct of an increasingly global politics.[38]

The centrality of the state in Arendt's portrayal of international relations is linked to her conception of the community, which contributes to her state-centrism and seeming inapplicability to international politics. Both state and community, as we have seen, are vital to Arendt's conception of the space in-between where true politics can take place. We cannot analogize our way to an international in-between among states for reasons discussed above. If we want to find a way of bringing Arendt's account of politics to bear in international relations then we need to find a way to break down her linkage between the community and the state and the state and the ideal of the *polis*.

Arendt's emphasis on community is nevertheless potentially of great use here. She stresses the importance of community to individuals as ethically and politically significant beings. Indeed, it is this kind of significance that makes us human. From this starting point, Arendt offers us a route into one of the key issues of international relations: the mediation of the plurality of individuals and the pluralism of communities.[39] There is no straightforward jump to the pluralism of an English-School-approach, as exemplified by Robert Jackson, but there is a way in which the English School's recognition of diversity is helpful.[40] For the pluralists among the English School, diversity is one of the reasons for the existence of international society and one of the reasons why it is a valuable institution.[41] The ability to control violence, in particular, is vital to enabling the reasonably orderly coexistence of diverse communities, institutionalized and partially manifested in sovereign states.[42] Arendt recognizes this in part, but, as argued, would accept that while this opens the possibility for politics within the state it does not enable it among states. However, this account of diversity is deeply problematic as it underestimates diversity, reifies the community as state and establishes one set of boundaries as being of supreme importance.[43]

Arendt's cementing of community within the state places the possibility of the in-between within the territorial borders of the state. The territorial borders of sovereignty thus delimit the possibility of real politics. This is because of both her understanding of the nature of politics between states and because of her essentializing of the state as the inheritor of the role of the *polis* and as the prerequisite for people to fulfill their nature as political and speaking animals.[44]

THE VIRTUES OF AN INTERNATIONAL IN-BETWEEN

Arendt's nods toward the importance of civil society as an arena where true politics can still take place within the modern, industrial state, points to an area where her thought may be profitably applied to international politics—the realm of an emerging global civil society.[45] Here we may appeal to changes that have taken place in the world since Arendt's death as being important.

The significance of the end of the Cold War for the structure of the international system has been much debated. Many have argued that it has had no significant consequences for anarchy as the structural principle of the system and thus the power and security logic engendered by anarchy operates with undimmed power.[46] However, a more positive interpretation of the consequences of such an event can have significant implications for an Arendtian interpretation of international relations and the potential for the existence of an international space in-between. This is because of the ideational impacts of the end of the Cold War and the potential for change that it demonstrated.[47]

Clearly a single chapter cannot address the end of the Cold War debates in detail. Where I want to highlight their consequences are in the way they have served to draw attention to aspects of international, or global, politics that are not necessarily overshadowed by the inescapable threat of a politically mute violence. Eastern Europe, with the partial exceptions of Russia and Romania and the tragic one of Yugoslavia, enjoyed generally peaceful transition from Communist rule. Peaceful yet profound change in international relations can and did take place. The efforts to expand the west European zone of peace eastwards, although not as straightforward as hoped in the first flush of the early 1990s optimism, has had significant success. There are other examples of individuals and groups in civil society, working together and acting within and across both states' borders and established political institutions, effecting peaceful international political change. Democratic transition in South Africa, the Philippines, Indonesia, Kenya, reform in Iran and elsewhere are indicative. As Anthony Lang argues, new social movements are also engaged in global governance, reinforcing the idea that a significant post–Cold War shift in ideas about the structures and possibilities of international relations is unfolding.[48]

The phenomena of globalization provide a catch-all term for changes that have the potential to revolutionize the nature and content of political activity in ways that threaten Arendt's schema.[49] The idea, or ideal, of global civil society has received a great deal of attention in recent years. It has been posited as the basis for a cosmopolitan democracy that could bring effective government to an increasingly globalized world where the political authority and effectiveness of the sovereign state are being undermined by transnational forces, notably of capital and capitalism.[50] Global civil society has also been seen as a less institutionalized force for the control of globalizing capitalism, using social movements and protests as a device for exerting accountability over transnational corporations, capital markets, international economic governance bodies like the WTO and so on.[51] Also, global civil society has been seen as a basis for an emerging cosmopolitan ethical community that will propagate, promote and protect ideals like universal human rights, overcoming, or at least mitigating, the problem of ethical diversity.[52] This emerging global community has seen ideas such as global and/or cosmopolitan citizenship gain prominence.[53]

These are non-state forms of politics, but they are, surely, politics, even by a standard as demanding as Arendt's. The nature and extent of democracy, the control of capital, the constitution of community and its relation to territorial space are clearly public issues dealing with the sort of collective interests, goods and futures that provide the core of an Arendtian political agenda. They also posit, or attempt to posit, alternative constitutional arrangements, putting them at the heart of a politics of diverse conceptions of freedom. Even more striking, from an Arendtian perspective, is the desire of many protagonists to use new forms, institutions, and methods to revitalize a sclerotic politics of the state in ways stressing participation, dialogue, and active involvement. However, it is worth noting here Arendt's mistrust of mass movements as a corrective to one line of enquiry that could be followed in this context.[54]

Thus political will formation can and does take place even in the absence of either the state itself or the kind of republic that offers, for Arendt, the ideal conditions for individuals to act in a properly political way. By extension, because of the way that Arendt understands political action, the basis exists for communities that are at least in part de-territorialized and that aim at forms and processes of politics not exclusively tied to or aimed at constituting, or reconstituting, the territorially delimited state.

An international in-between can appeal to the core idea of Arendt's understanding of the space in-between—that it is about the active political engagement of rooted individuals enjoying the company of their familiar equals. If we take a view of the public realm as existing beyond the reified borders of the sovereign state, because we recognize that political issues exist in international society and a nascent global political space, we can nevertheless retain community. To assume that the community of state citizenship trumps all others is to underestimate the extent and importance for politics of the manifestations of human plurality. Multiple community memberships generating multiple senses of obligation, rights and duties can locate rooted individuals in places and in ways that are not only, principally or even significantly territorially defined.[55] The new guarantee of freedom via territorial borders that Arendt appealed to will no longer do. If freedom is based upon an act of constitution then the political communities that are being constituted need not be territorially specific.[56] It is the nature of the authority constituted—limited, participatory, republican and responsive to community needs—that is more important than its territorial specificity. The acts of promising and forgiving, of entering into the public realm of the space in-between that forms collective will, collective identity, and founds effective political authority are processes that do not have to be tied to place. Freedom may continue to be limited and may continue to be about participation in government and governance as Arendt argues, but such limitations and goals need not always possess a fixed, geographical character.[57]

The space in-between may even be more secure in the international and global spaces of the human artifice of politics, because of the relative lack of institutions in these arenas.[58] The social world is increasingly dominating the classic political space within sovereign states, making it harder to protect, let alone promote, the active engagement of rooted individuals in a political experience like the space in-between.[59] The more open spaces of the international and global offer a greater opportunity for ephemeral, intersubjective spaces in-between to manifest themselves in a way that is less overshadowed by the monolithic political structures of the social world that has populated the politics of most states. The diversity of political forms, actions, groupings, manifestos, goals, and purposes to be found among social movements in a nascent global civil society, including the interlinkage of those groups that continue to exist wholly within and to focus upon "domestic" issues, reinforces this point. If we are plural, but social, beings, able to build politics through speech, action, promising, and forgiving, then our plurality and ability to seek and engage in public, social dialogue in the in-between can be fostered through an international in-between. This need not reduce plurality to state citizenship understood as the prerequisite for the manifestation of plurality, but which, in the social world, privileges only one version of human plurality.

For there is no need for these emerging forms of public politics to result in homogeneity. The unpredictability and limitless potential of action, rooted in natality, that characterizes the space in-between is surely more closely approximated in fora such as these than in the predictable, stereotypical maneuverings of the average constitutional democracy, let alone authoritarian state.[60] The communal reactions to the cosmopolitan aspects of globalization and global civil society can thus also be included in this account of an international in-between. The response to globalization and the decline of territoriality may well be a defense or restatement. A search for a new bordering of politics, whether by culture, identity or old-fashioned lines on the map, is far from ruled out. An international in-between, as a site of politics, should not close them off or deem them illegitimate. We need limits and borders; there may well be groups or individuals with whom we cannot engage, or whom we cannot understand at present. However, such potential engagement and understanding is always immanent and should be sought. Arendt's cosmopolitanism—the essential nature of plurality—allows for the possibility of individuals being "open" in some aspects of their thought and "closed" in others. She dismisses the ideal of the "sovereign" individual and thus allows for opening and closing aspects of the in-between via natality, promising, and forgiveness. We might also allow for this process to work at multiple levels for individuals enjoying multiple community memberships and operating with territorially and non-territorially constituted spaces. This also helps us respond to the power of the idea of human rights in contemporary political discourse, while recognizing Arendt's critique.

The prominence of ideas such as universality, cosmopolitanism, and human rights in the accounts of a nascent, or emerging or even existing global civil society are problematic for an Arendtian approach. Arendt's analysis of human rights stands as a powerful example of her dismissal of appeals to universal principles, statements, or pronouncements. In *Origins of Totalitarianism* she describes how the universalization of rights into an abstract realm marked the end of their usefulness in offering meaningful protection to individuals.[61] Her account stressed the linkage of rights to citizenship of a state and membership of a community. Rights formed part of the institutional structure granting access to the space in-between and also a part of the social fabric of a community that enabled individuals to enjoy the trusting company of their equals. Ending this institutional, social, and personal aspect of rights ended their utility, argued Arendt, because without their rootedness and internalization within a community they could not operate effectively and properly.

Whilst Arendt's account of rights is a distinctive one, her analysis of community retains, via the immanent potential of the in-between, a radical and transformative edge.[62] This is vital in distinguishing her from a conservative account of rights that treats them as being exclusively social products, rooted in communities, and historic understandings of the liberties and obligations of citizens. The radical edge is what enables Arendt's account of the in-between to be of use in offering an alternative view of global civil society.[63] We can challenge territorial borders as the definitive characteristic of international politics, the essential and unchanging dividing lines between the site of a potential politics and the site of an, at best, politically mute armed truce to be managed by law. This opens up the possibility of an international in-between. An Arendtian account of this can still retain her emphasis on community and diversity by portraying this kind of non-state international and global politics as being about the political flowering of types of communities that were and continue to be stifled by the state. It can also contain the responses of other sorts of communities seeking to resist the new, to restate the value of the state, the nation, and the traditional building blocks of the Westphalian system. The nonspecific direction of the true politics that Arendt describes—its lack of blueprints and fixed goals—seems also characteristic of the moves underway within an emerging international space that has the potential to be a space in-between.

Bounded politics, if not territorially bordered politics, can thus still continue and endure. The boundaries of communities, and a greater multiplicity of communities than before, can continue to identify places and spaces where diverse, rooted individuals can enjoy the company of familiar equals and engage in the politics of public dialogue.

The quintessentially political issue of freedom retains its centrality, even if the context of freedom moves from freedom within a state to freedom within a transnational or supra-territorial location.[64] "Freedom in a positive sense is possible only among equals, and equality itself, is by no means a universally valid principle but, again, applicable only with limitations and even within spatial limits."[65] Here Arendt hints, but only hints, at a weakening of, or possible alternative to, her territorially bounded politics, and one that a reformulation of the idea and ideal of a nascent global civil society can appeal to.

Politics across boundaries also becomes more plausible and plural if the boundaries of community are multiplied and moved away from a focus on the borders of states, with their Weberian monopoly on the legitimate use of violence. The possibility of multiple community memberships leads to increased potential for engagement in different in-betweens and for laying the foundations for new in-betweens of cross-community dialogue. Illegitimate violence and the exclusionist ideologies of racist and fundamentalist groups remain a problem, but what Arendt seems to have regarded as the irredeemable pollution of international relations by violence does not necessarily apply in an international in-between. Violence is a problem, but violence is a problem within states, too. The ability of states to maintain a near monopoly on it within the rules of international society may well be a positive thing for the development of an international in-between. So too may be the recourse by states, on occasion, to necessary violence to resist violent intolerance by non-state groups and communities.[66]

Thus the de-territorialization, and/or supra-territorialization of global politics in contrast to the territoriality of international relations may mean the decline of the overwhelming significance, indeed onto-logical primacy, of the sovereign territorial border, but it does not mean the end of bounded politics. A straightforward jump from an international society of states to a world society of a liberal, cosmopol-itan form does not automatically follow. It may, and it may well be desirable, but a turn to Arendt reminds us of a powerful case in the defense of a view of politics that stresses participation, engagement, and action within the context of community. This requires the space in-between and, whereas the space in-between has long been squeezed within the state, the potential for an in-between to emerge in the spaces opened by international and world societies, in the supra-territorial realms of globalization, should not be foreclosed. Rooted individuals, engaged with their communities and in an open-minded and open-ended dialogic politics of the unpredictable and the unlimited is a powerful normative vision. Partially de-linking community from citizenship of the state offers the potential for proper political action within and across a far more diverse range of communities, increasing the opportunities for and potential of political action in pursuit of freedom for essentially diverse and essentially social human beings.

CONCLUSION

The chapter has thus attempted to offer a summary of Arendt's ideas about the space in-between as the site of politics, stressing its ephemeral, intersubjective nature. This is rooted in a particular view of political action that stresses the Arisotelian idea of people as political and speaking animals. The Athenian *agora* as the paradigmatic expression of such a political space in-between offered the potential for change, preventing its respect for tradition becoming merely conservative. Arendt's account of the modern state as the inheritor of the *polis* tradition was also considered, making the state the potential site for the appearance of the space in-between. However, the expansion of what Arendt called the social world and the move away from a politics of engagement has stymied the potential for true politics.

The chapter then assessed Arendt's case against international relations, stressing her argument that it is sullied by violence and that violence is politically mute. One route to the possibility of an international in-between—the ideas of a pluralist international society—was considered and dismissed because of its reliance on an unsustainable individual analogy. However, Arendt's account of international politics was found wanting and that the potential for an international in-between may exist, partly as a result of the changing circumstances of international politics and partly through a more thorough consideration of the international than what Arendt offers.

Finally, the virtues of an international in-between were considered as providing an alternative account of the development of global civil society that retains Arendt's emphases on bounded communities and the importance of engagement and participation characteristic of the space in-between. There are virtues in an approach to politics emphasizing and valuing diversity and community, while retaining a transformative agenda rooted in the potential of natality actualized through the space in-between. It provides a way of responding to the problems of cultural relativism and cultural imperialism associated with a straightforwardly liberal, cosmopolitan account of an emerging global civil society. It enables the protection of a valuable diversity in human affairs, relations, and conduct. It reemphasizes the role of individuals as political actors in making and shaping the world around them, in a way that often seems increasingly lost in the modern world. It connects international and world societies.

Arendt's concept of the in-between, therefore, offers an important addition to the theoretical and normative agenda raised by the search to understand and to engage with the changing nature of place, space, community, and freedom in a developing post–Westphalian era. Her idea of the in-between as a site of politics offers a different and dynamic take on the development of global civil society, and one where diversity is not only protected, but promoted because it is the nature of the human condition. It offers a distinct vision of what an active and engaged public politics of dialogue, idea, and immanent potential could look like.

NOTES

I would like to acknowledge the generous financial support of the British Academy in enabling the presentation of an earlier version of this chapter at the 43rd Annual Convention of the International Studies Association, New Orleans.

1. There is a large literature in this area, but one influential instance of a liberal version of this is to be found in the idea of cosmopolitan democracy, exemplified in the work of David Held and Daniele Archibugi. For example, Daniele Archibugi and David Held (eds.), *Cosmopolitan Democracy* (Cambridge: Polity, 1995).
2. This comes most clearly in her account of the *vita activa* and the political nature of action. See Hannah Arendt, *The Human Condition* (Chicago, IL.: University of Chicago Press, 1958), 7–21, 175–247.
3. Hannah Arendt, *On Revolution* (London: Faber and Faber, 1963), especially 13–52. Also Philip Hansen, *Hannah Arendt: Politics, History and Citizenship* (Cambridge: Polity, 1993), 54–57.
4. Hannah Arendt, *Origins of Totalitarianism* (New Edition with Added Prefaces) (New York: Harcourt Brace Jovanovich, 1973), especially 389–391.
5. See the discussion of the *vita activa* and the meaning of action in *Human Condition*, 7–21, 175–247, and her approving comments on the basis for the success of the American Revolution in its engaged, active popular basis, *On Revolution*, 179–216.
6. For Arendt's definition, see *Human Condition*, 182–183.
7. This is summed up by her account of the dominance of "ruling," rather than "politics" in the Western tradition of political thought. Arendt, *Human Condition*, 28–50.
8. James Bohman, "The Moral Costs of Political Pluralism: the dilemmas of difference and equality in Arendt's 'Reflections on Little Rock,' " in

Larry May and Jerome Kohn (eds.), *Hannah Arendt: Twenty Years Later* (Cambridge, MA.: MIT Press, 1997), 68.

9. Arendt, *Human Condition*, 186–207.

10. For a useful summary of Arendt's thought here, see Jerome Kohn, "Freedom: the priority of the political," in Dana Villa (ed.), *Cambridge Companion to Hannah Arendt* (Cambridge: Cambridge University Press, 2000).

11. T. H. Marshall, *Class, Citizenship and Social Development* (Westport, CN.: Greenwood Press, 1973).

12. Hansen, *Hannah Arendt*, 89–128.

13. Arendt, *On Revolution*, 275.

14. See, e.g., her approving discussion of how the American Revolution recognized the need to build on the existing, local, political forms, rather than wiping them out. Arendt, *On Revolution*, 139–178, especially 164–178.

15. Arendt, *Origins of Totalitarianism*, 477.

16. For Arendt's critique of nationalism, see *Human Condition*, 256.

17. For example, "Plurality is the condition of human action because we are all the same, that is, human, in such a way that nobody is ever the same as anyone else who ever lived, lives or will live." Arendt, *Human Condition*, 8. Plurality and its consequences are one of the main themes of the book.

18. Arendt, *On Revolution*, 9. See also *Human Condition*, 3.

19. Arendt, *Human Condition*, 4.

20. Ibid., 186–187.

21. Ibid., 236–243.

22. Arendt, *On Revolution*, 139.

23. Margaret Canovan, *The Political Thought of Hannah Arendt* (London: J. M. Dent, 1974), 68.

24. For a discussion of the potential for "true" politics, see Arendt, *On Revolution*, 217–286.

25. Arendt, *Human Condition*, 234.

26. Hannah Arendt (ed.), "On Humanity in Dark Times: Thoughts about Lessing," *Men in Dark Times* (London: Jonathan Cape, 1970), 18.

27. For example, see her critique of the absolutism of the French Revolution and its role in its failure. *On Revolution*, especially 154–159. For a general discussion of her view of political communities, see Bikhu Parekh, *Hannah Arendt and the Search for a New Political Philosophy* (London: Macmillan, 1981), 131–172.

28. On the world as artifice, see Hansen, *Hannah Arendt*, 65–66. For the necessity of the state, see Arendt, *On Revolution*.

29. Arendt, *On Revolution*, 1–11.

30. For the classical Greek origins of such a view, see Arendt, *On Revolution*, 2, "since for the Greeks political life *by definition* did not

extend beyond the walls of the polis in the realm of what we today call foreign affairs or international relations" (emphasis added).

31. She sums up the Greek view of international relations, and thus, in many ways, her own, with Thucydides' famous aphorism, "the strong did what they could, and the weak suffered what they must." Arendt, *On Revolution*, 3.

32. Arendt, *On Revolution*, 279.

33. Ibid.

34. For example, Hedley Bull, *The Anarchical Society: A Study of Order in World Politics* (London: Macmillan, 1977); Robert H. Jackson, *The Global Covenant: Human Conduct in a World of States* (Oxford: Oxford University Press, 2000).

35. This summary definition of an international society reflects the fuller definition given in Hedley Bull and Adam Watson (eds.), *The Expansion of International Society* (Oxford: Clarendon Press, 1984), 1.

36. John Williams, "Territorial Borders, Toleration and the English School," *Review of International Studies*, 28, no. 4 (2002).

37. Hannah Arendt (ed.), "Tradition and the Modern Age," *Between Past and Future: Six Essays in Political Thought* (London: Faber and Faber, 1961), 22.

38. For a discussion of the link between international and world society, see Richard Little, "The English School's Contribution to International Relations," *European Journal of International Relations*, 6, no. 3 (2000). For an account focusing on Arendt, see chapter 7 by Anthony Lang in this volume.

39. See "Introduction" (chapter 1) to this volume for a more detailed exposition of this point.

40. Jackson, *The Global Covenant*.

41. For example, Bull, *Anarchical Society*; Hedley Bull (ed.), "The Concept of Justice in International Relations," *Justice in International Relations: The Hagey Lectures* (Waterloo: University of Waterloo Press, 1984). Hedley Bull, "The State's Positive Role in World Affairs," *Daedalus*, 108, no. 4 (1979); Jackson, *Global Covenant*.

42. Bull, *Anarchical Society*, 7.

43. John Williams, "The Ethics of Borders and the Borders of Ethics: International Society and Rights and Duties of Special Beneficence," *Global Society*, 13, no. 4 (1999); Williams, "Territorial Borders, Toleration and the English School."

44. "For political freedom . . . means the right 'to be a participator in government' or it means nothing." Arendt, *On Revolution*, 221 (she is quoting Thomas Jefferson).

45. The literature here is very substantial. For a critical summary of its main claims and ideas, see Chris Brown, "Cosmopolitanism, World Citizenship and Global Civil Society," in Simon Caney and Peter Jones (eds.), *Human Rights and Global Diversity* (London: Frank Cass, 2001).

46. For a critique of such claims, see Friedrich Kratochwil, "The Embarrassment of Changes: Neo-Realism as the Science of *Realpolitik* without Politics," *Review of International Studies*, 19, no. 1 (1993).

47. For example, Alexander Wendt, *Social Theory of International Relations* (Cambridge: Cambridge University Press, 1999).

48. See chapter 7 in this volume.

49. Probably the best introductory, general survey of globalization is Jan Aart Scholte, *Globalization: A Critical Introduction* (Basingstoke: Macmillan, 2000).

50. I cannot hope to do full justice to the complexity of this work here. A useful starting point is the prolific work of David Held. For example, Held, *Democracy and the Global Order: From the Modern State to Cosmopolitan Governance* (Stanford, CA: Stanford University Press, 1995).

51. For example, Barry K. Gills (ed.), *Globalization and the Politics of Resistance* (Basingstoke: Macmillan, 2000).

52. For example, Nigel Dower, *World Ethics: The New Agenda* (Edinburgh: Edinburgh University Press, 1998).

53. For example, Nigel Dower and John Williams (eds.), *Global Citizenship: A Critical Reader* (Edinburgh: Edinburgh University Press, 2002).

54. Arendt, *On Revolution*, 283.

55. Williams, "The Ethics of Borders and the Borders of Ethics."

56. "Human dignity needs a new guarantee which can be found only in a new political principle, in a new law on earth, whose validity this time must comprehend the whole of humanity while its power must remain strictly limited, rooted in and controlled by newly defined territorial entities." Arendt, *Origins of Totalitarianism*, ix.

57. For a discussion of contemporary debates about the nature of territorial borders, see David Newman and Anssi Paasi, "Fences and Neighbours in the Postmodern World: Boundary Narratives in Political Geography," *Progress in Human Geography*, 22, no. 2 (1998).

58. For Arendt's discussion of the dilemma of institutionalizing action and the space in-between in post-revolutionary America, see *On Revolution*, 234–242.

59. For a discussion of the social world, see Hannah Pitkin, *The Attack of the Blob: Hannah Arendt's Conception of the Social* (Chicago, IL.: University of Chicago Press, 1998).

60. See, e.g., her critique of representative democracy and particularly the party system in *On Revolution*, 275–279.

61. See chapter 5 by Bridget Cotter in this volume for a discussion of this point.

62. Bernard Crick, "Hannah Arendt and the Burden of Our Times," *Political Quarterly*, 68, no. 1 (1997): 82–83.

63. The link between the in-between and the potential for limitless change is rooted in her concept of "natality"—the potential for

something new inherent in every human birth. See Arendt, *Human Condition*, 9 for a definition of natality and its importance.

64. For "supra-territoriality" as the defining characteristic of globalization, see Scholte, *Globalization*, chapter 2.

65. Arendt, *On Revolution*, 279.

66. Williams, "Territorial Borders, Toleration and the English School," 754–756.

CHAPTER 9

BETWEEN INTERNATIONAL POLITICS AND INTERNATIONAL ETHICS

Anthony F. Lang, Jr. with John Williams

When the original manuscript of this volume was sent to a series of outside readers, one critique came back from them all: The book does not adequately explain what Arendt says about international affairs. We agree with this assessment, at least in part. This is not a book that "finds" in Arendt answers to questions in international relations. Indeed some of the most pressing debates in the discipline would appear rather strange to Arendt. As noted in the introductory essay, this disconnect of standard IR theory from Arendt's concerns results, in part, from her refusal to see politics as a matter of "ruling" but rather as a form of political action. In a world defined by sovereign states that compete on a global stage with military and economic tools, a focus on individual political action makes little sense.

Instead, the contributors to this volume have found in Arendt some inspiration for asking different questions, questions that do not dominate the discipline. As Jerome Kohn states in his most recent introduction to some of Arendt's work: "It is not theoretical solutions she advances but an abundance of incentives to think for oneself."[1] We are not striving to find the real IR Arendt; rather, we, along with our contributors, have used Arendt's writings to provoke some new ideas about international affairs.

Is such an enterprise justified? Can the new questions being asked by these contributors and others in the discipline of IR help us to understand international affairs better? In this concluding chapter, we suggest that turning to Arendt and the questions raised in this volume will, hopefully, help reorient the discipline in new directions. In the introductory chapter, we demonstrated how Arendt helps move the discipline away from a focus on politics as a form of ruling and from solidified identities. Building on these insights, this chapter suggests how Arendt can help us think anew about agency and responsibility, two topics of importance in the area sometimes called international political theory—the study of rights and justice in a world of sovereign states.[2] That is, Arendt might help us think within the space between international politics and international ethics.

Agency

Agency is an important topic in international relations. When Alexander Wendt published his article in 1987 on agency and structure in international relations, IR theorists saw the importance of what had traditionally been a sociological debate—Does individual agency or social structure shape outcomes?[3] Wendt argued that both neorealism and Marxist inspired critical theory have an underdeveloped notion of the relationship between agents and structures. Without developing a better understanding of the relationship between these two elements of social theory, IR theory will be incapable of truly advancing.[4] Wendt's work has been broadly accepted as an important counter to neorealism and neoliberalism, but based on a methodology and ontology that most positivist social scientists can accept.

Critical theory has also opened up our notions of agency, primarily through reconsiderations of citizenship and community. Andrew Linklater is a leading figure here, one whose works have sought to rethink the relationship between the individual and the community in which she lives. As opposed to a state agent that subsumes the individual, Linklater proposes opening up the community and seeing how it functions as a device for exclusion rather than political action.[5]

Adopting a post-structuralist approach, David Campbell has highlighted how practices of U.S. foreign policy have led to the construction of a particular type of state agent—one that is surrounded by enemies and must establish its identity in relation to those enemies.[6] Drawing on feminist theories of identity formation, Campbell points to the largely unsettled nature of state identity. Much of the poststructuralist literature has been built upon the concept of identity rather than agency, although the terms function in similar ways. Identity formation, in these formulations, is the process by which, through continued performances, states enact themselves as stable entities, a stability that turns to quicksilver once subject to the deconstructive tactics of these theories.

Wendt, Linklater, and Campbell, along with many others, have opened up an important avenue of investigation for IR theorists. Rather than uncritically accepting the state as an agent that can be perceived and theorized about, they have pointed to the highly contingent nature of state agency. These theories have produced important contributions to our understanding of practices such as military intervention, foreign policy planning, diplomacy, and structural change.

What does Arendt offer as an alternative notion of agency, one that might have more critical or explanatory power? Unlike Wendt's theory of agency, Arendt does not rely on a binary notion of agency and structure. Her aversion to sociological approaches, what Hannah Pitkin identifies as the "blob" in her work, results in a focus on how individuals act in unexpected and nondeterministic ways.[7] While Linklater's critical theory may be close to some Arendtian formulations, it does not theorize agency directly, but only understands it as part of a relationship to a political community, especially in his focus on citizenship. In fact, his notions of citizenship seem closer to the Roman conception, derived from rights, rather than the Greek one, derived from obligations to engage in public action.[8] For Campbell and other poststructuralists, Arendt provides a challenge to their work by presenting a theory in which individuals enact themselves through their participation in the political, rather than being subject to constructions of their identity in ways they cannot control. Arendt provides purpose to the agency of individuals where post-structuralist theories tend to undermine that purpose by placing identity and agency beyond the control of the individual (indeed, some post-structural formulations deny the existence of agency altogether).

Arendt's political model is the Athenian *agora* and it is the *agora*'s virtues of participation and political debate that she wishes to protect and promote in a more properly political, and more properly human, world.[9] This is an account of political agency that challenges IR, an arena where it seems especially out of place, given the obvious impossibility of recreating the *agora* on an international scale. This is too simplistic, though. The *agora* is not just a particular political institution from a particular time and place, but a metaphor for a form of political agency whose challenge is not defeated by the impracticality of recreating an institution. Arendt argues against ". . . our common emphasis on government as an inevitable feature of politics [and] our usual assumption that politics is essentially a matter of the working of political institutions."[10] Institutions are important only in so far as they can guarantee access to the political world: "Political equality requires a minimum threshold: that all must have access to the political world."[11]

The political world is therefore both much more and much less than constitutions, parliaments, bureaucracies, elections, dictatorships, and ideologies. It is less because Arendt argues that concern with these misses the wood for the trees.[12] Politics is much more than institutions because it is, or ought to be, more widely pervasive than conventional institutional processes and is regarded as the highest form of human action.

Rather than great leaders and institutional building projects, politics for Arendt is fragile and transitory and it is the product of human discourse as human action.[13] Permanence is politically undesirable because it fails to fulfill Arendt's understanding of the vital role played by unpredictability in politics. The homogenizing effects of the expansion of capitalism, for example, are not only closing down the opportunities for political action by expanding the social world of work and labor, but they also contribute to the sclerosis of political institutions. Politics becomes the successful management of the economy and the provision of the social goods necessary to make capitalism run effectively and without serious disruption.[14]

Real politics, for Arendt, exists not among institutions but in the space "in-between" individuals and communities, a space that is created and re-created by political action manifested in dialogue, which forms a web of human relationships.

> Action and speech go on between men, as they are directed toward them, and they retain their agent-revealing capacity even if their content is exclusively "objective," concerned with the matters of the world of things in which men move, which physically lies between them and out of which arise their specific, worldly interests. These interests constitute, in the word's most literal significance, something which *inter-est*, which lies between people and therefore can relate and bind them together. Most action and speech is concerned with this in-between, which varies with each group of people, so that most words and deeds are *about* some worldly objective reality in addition to being a disclosure of the acting and speaking agent. Since this disclosure of the subject is an integral part of all, even the most "objective" inter-course, the physical, worldly in-between along with its interests is overlaid and, as it were, overgrown with an altogether different in-between which consists of deeds and words and owes its origin exclusively to men's acting and speaking directly *to* one another.

This second, subjective in-between, is not tangible . . . the process of acting and speaking can leave behind no such results and end products. But for all its intangibility, this in-between is no less real than the world of things we visibly have in common.[15]

Arendt emphasizes that this revelatory act is "heroic" in that it demonstrates the courage to be one's self and to reveal this self to others, revealing truly human character and initiating sequences of action with unpredictable outcomes.[16] The political arena is the "space of appearance" existing "in-between" individuals engaged in discourse.[17]

Therefore Arendt reacts against the idea of sovereign individuals as the essence of agency.[18] One must have someone to talk to, to engage with and with whom to exercise the political virtues of promising and forgiveness.[19] It is these virtues that enable humans to cope with the unpredictability and irreversibility of action. "The two faculties belong together in so far as the one of them, forgiving, serves to undo the deeds of the past . . . and the other, binding oneself through promises, serves to set up in the ocean of uncertainty, which the future is by definition, islands of security . . . in the relationships between men."[20] IR is particularly hostile to such a conception of politics because of its traditional state-centrism, resulting in little room for individuals, something exacerbated by the pursuit of system-level explanation, whether via neorealism or Marxist-inspired Dependency Theory. Also important is the skepticism much of IR has about promising and forgiving as meaningful in the face of security and power maximizing imperatives with power understood as dominance—the ability to get others to do our will—rather than as the co-operative ability to achieve goals.

Arendt's passion for the *agora* as the paradigmatic example of real political activity where people can be real political agents means that she reduces the applicability of her ideas, arguably unnecessarily. By casting so much of what we usually regard as political activity into the categories of the social world, Arendt leaves little to which she can apply her approach. Examples of true political activity are few and far between, exacerbated by Arendt's seeming unwillingness to search outside the categories of conventional politics with which she is so dissatisfied. While one may argue that this is a reflection of her commitment to studying politics as it is really experienced in real lives, it is nevertheless surprising. As a result, Arendt shows little interest in, or knowledge of, any non-Western approaches to political theory or philosophy. The Western tradition is assumed to encompass all possible political experience and thought. While discussing institutions such as factories and universities, she does not, in the search for elements of genuine politics, cast her net beyond the usual locations within a liberal, capitalist political system.

Arendt can thus be a frustrating theorist in that her originality and insights are not developed in concrete examples. This may in part be put down to the conventions and structures of the time. It would certainly have been unusual for a political philosopher to look to the international political environment for examples at a time of near absolute Realist hegemony.[21] Equally, within U.S. Political Science in the 1950s and 1960s, the Behaviorist methodological dominance focused attention on areas unhelpful to a theorist such as Arendt. However, aspects of contemporary international relations, particularly the efforts to understand an international or global public sphere and debates over the development of a global civil society, point to areas in which an Arendtian notion of political agency can gain purchase, as Owens, Lang, and Williams demonstrate in their chapters.

Arendt's ideas of agency can give us greater critical purchase on human rights. Cotter has provided some important insights into how Arendt can help rethink rights. An alternative approach to Arendt on this question is to highlight a right that rarely finds its way into international instruments on human rights—the right to democratic governance. The International Covenant on Civil and Political Rights (1966) enumerates a right to "participate in public affairs," but not until Article 25, after delineating the ways in which individual's rights must be protected from the state. While the right does exist in this document, its location as one of the last civil rights suggests that other rights remain paramount.

Recently, international lawyers have begun to examine more critically the right to democracy. Brad Roth argues that the "democratic entitlement" thesis remains underdeveloped in international law, while Gregory Fox and Thomas Franck see it as arising naturally from developments in the law over the last 50 years.[22] Do individuals have a right to participate in public affairs? For Arendt, this right arises not from treaties but from the very nature of the human condition. Her theorization of agency provides a much stronger basis on which to assert that there is a right to democracy. Moreover, her notion of agency fleshes out that right in ways left undefined by the international legal instruments. It is not simply that one has a right to vote or serve on a jury, the standard Anglo-American manifestations of political action. Rather, individuals have the right to voice their views, to engage in public protest, to agitate for causes and issues in which they believe.

A danger with this notion of democratic entitlement is that it could lead to the sorts of military intervention the U.S. has undertaken in Iraq. While most certainly undertaken for a wide variety of reasons, the 2003 U.S. intervention in Iraq included an attempt to create a "democratic" Iraq. Would Arendt support such attempts at forcefully creating democracy? If we turn to her theories of violence and power, it is highly unlikely that she would support such forms of violent imposition of democracy. Power comes from individuals acting together, not from imposing political order on a community. Moreover, the attempts by American policy-makers at the time of this writing (May 2004) to structure an Iraqi democracy such that it will produce oil for the Western market and establish positive relations with Israel denies the very agency that Arendt finds so important. Even the motives that supposedly underlie the democratic peace thesis—that democracies will not go to war—are too instrumental for an Arendtian conception of democratic agency. If democracy is set up only to accomplish certain policy objectives defined by the intervener, democracy is denied its "natality," the element of unpredictability that makes agency so distinctly human.

RESPONSIBILITY

The study of moral agency leads one to moral responsibility. If individuals can be considered agents who are held to certain standards of behavior and can be causally effective in the world around them, they can be considered responsible agents. Responsibility has become an important locus of analysis in international relations. A number of scholars have turned their attention to the question of whether or not institutions, or corporate entities such as states, multinational corporations, and intergovernmental organizations, can be considered responsible for outcomes in the international system.[23] This work draws on older literature in philosophy that has sought to locate responsibility in the will and in interactions within a community.[24]

Arendt has much to tell us about responsibility. One way to approach Arendt on these questions is to examine her writing on evil, which draws on two different approaches.[25] In *The Origins of Totalitarianism*, Arendt found anti-Semitism, imperialism, and totalitarianism to be three instances of "radical evil," institutional structures and ways of thinking that progressively degraded human dignity until they resulted in large scale slaughter in the pursuit of ideological ends. Especially in totalitarianism, the individual human person loses the ability to think and judge as a system of government seeks to privilege the "masses" above citizens. Without the ability to participate in the deliberations and debates that constitute politics, Arendt argued that mass political behavior leads to slavish adherence to ideals that demean the human person.

In *Eichmann in Jerusalem*, Arendt coined the phrase "banality of evil" to describe the inability of Eichmann, and many others, to think clearly about what they were doing. While critics saw this as a refusal to hold individuals responsible for their actions, Arendt believed that Eichmann demonstrated a lack of judgment, the concept that she had begun to explore in her last years.[26]

These two different interpretations of evil suggest two ways of evaluating global politics. In the *Origins* approach, Arendt focuses on institutional and governmental structures that prevent the individual from partaking in political actions. These structures, while perhaps pursuing a noble end (e.g., the emancipation of man in Marxist ideology), undermine the inherent worth of the human person. They turn human persons into tools, exactly the outcome that Immanuel Kant sought to prevent in the categorical imperative. In this interpretation, evil is not an inherent characteristic of the human person, but a systemic element of an institution. This interpretation suggests that more sustained critical engagement with institutions is necessary for developing alternatives in global politics. Rather than holding individuals to account for war, for example, perhaps we need to see how various institutions, such as great powers, international organizations, and even capitalist structures of production might need to be reconfigured to bring about peace in the international system.

While institutions can be characterized as evil, Arendt also explores the evil that individuals can do in the Eichmann approach. Like Plato, Arendt sees evil as the result of failing to think. Arendt, however, adds the additional criterion of judging, or the ability to differentiate between right and wrong in situations where rules do not exist. The moral failing of Eichmann was that in a situation where the rules quickly collapsed, he was unable to think and make judgments that would allow him to resist the orders he was receiving from his superiors. Arendt was amazed at his failure, both during the trail and at his execution, to understand the crimes he had committed and why he was being held responsible for them. The international community has moved in this direction in the last 20 years with the creation of war crimes tribunals in Rwanda, Yugoslavia and Sierra Leone, along with the International Criminal Court. These new institutions in the international system are designed to hold individuals responsible for war, genocide and crimes against humanity. Arendt concluded

Eichmann by calling for the creation of international courts, perhaps because of the ways in which the Israeli political system, especially David Ben Gurion, used the Eichmann trial as a show rather than an institution to pin down the responsibility of the individual sitting in the dock.

Arendt also addressed the question of responsibility more directly, particularly in her writings on collective responsibility and moral philosophy. In a colloquium sponsored by the American Philosophical Association in 1968, Arendt presented an argument concerning collective responsibility. She begins by distinguishing between guilt and responsibility: "Guilt, unlike responsibility, always singles out; it is strictly personal."[27] But while guilt is individual, responsibility can be corporate. She notes that for collective responsibility to make sense two conditions must apply:

> I must be held responsible for something I have not done, and the reason for my responsibility must be my membership in a group (a collective), which no voluntary act of mine can dissolve, that is, a membership which is utterly unlike a business partnership which I can dissolve at will.[28]

Collective responsibility applies most clearly, according to this conception, in cases where individuals are held responsible for what their governments do. The context of her argument (she was responding to a paper which was not reprinted in this collection) seems to be an attempt to locate the responsibility of individuals who do not support the actions of their government but who are being held responsible for that government's actions. In light of the time of the writing, one might guess that she is responding to those who were dissenting from the war in Vietnam, although this is only a conjecture.[29]

Arendt takes this point even further, however. Rather than simply stating that collective responsibility is possible in these situations, she argues that simply by living in the current world, one in which we are automatically bound up in a community, we can never avoid responsibility for the actions of our states. To clarify this, she notes that only refugees are innocent of this collective responsibility, precisely because they are outside the boundaries of any community. Arendt claims that political nonparticipation, as a sign of political protest, does not alleviate this responsibility. Simply by the fact that we live in a community, we are responsible for its collective actions.

> This vicarious responsibility for things we have not done, this taking upon ourselves the consequences for things we are entirely innocent of,

is the price we pay for the fact that we live our lives not by ourselves but among our fellow men, and that the faculty of action which, after all, is the political faculty par excellence, can be actualized only in one of the many and manifold forms of human community.[30]

This is a strong claim, one that implicates every person in the acts of their government. The justifications of this argument are rather weak in the short essay from which I am quoting here. One could argue that they result from Arendt's writings on power, in which she argues that power only results from people acting together. At the same time, it is not compatible with her writing on agency, which states that in the moment of acting, individuals differentiate themselves from all others. One of the criticisms of Arendt is her nonsystematic corpus of work, of which the fit between this essay and her other writings is perhaps a good example.

Nevertheless, the argument here is certainly germane to international relations. The U.S. war against Iraq (2003) and the results of that war, especially the revelations about how U.S. soldiers treated Iraqi (and perhaps Afghani) prisoners of war might be interpreted through Arendt's argument. In attempting to respond to the egregious violations of the prisoners' rights, the Bush administration sought to locate the responsibility on a "few" soldiers who acted outside the boundaries of what it means to be an "American." In so doing, the political leadership sought to distance not only itself but the entire American polity from responsibility for these actions. According to Arendt, perhaps such distancing is not possible. While individual Americans (other than the soldiers involved) cannot be found guilty of abusing the prisoners, they do have a certain political responsibility for what happened. One might argue that the war on Iraq is the culmination of a 25-year process by which American foreign policy has engaged the Islamic and Arab world, a process justified in terms of creating a constructed other who is so unlike an American that he/she does not deserve the same treatment.[31] Thus, rather than implicating this particular administration, or these particular soldiers, perhaps the culmination of various discourses has resulted in this particular set of abuses.

The line of argument here is only suggestive. In moving Arendt's essay in this direction, we are suggesting how she might be used to deflate certain debates in international ethics. Moral justifications for the war on terrorism and the manifestations of it in Afghanistan and Iraq have been infused with moral bases, especially as the leaders of the United States and United Kingdom have articulated them.

While we do not wish to make the claim that moral argument is irrelevant to international affairs, it is important to recognize the consequences of using such arguments. This conclusion, and the entire volume, is only an attempt to "think what we are doing"—a call that applies not just to domestic but to international politics as well.

NOTES

1. Jerome Kohn, "Introduction," in Hannah Arendt, *Responsibility and Judgment*, edited with an introduction by Jerome Kohn (New York: Schocken Books, 2003), xi.
2. See Chris Brown, *Sovereignty, Rights and Justice: International Political Theory Today* (Cambridge: Polity Press, 2002).
3. Alexander Wendt, "The Agent-Structure Problem in International Relations," *International Organization*, 41 (1987): 335–370.
4. He has continued to explore these themes in various articles since that time, culminating in his *Social Theory of International Politics* (Cambridge: Cambridge University Press, 1999).
5. Andrew Linklater, *The Transformation of Political Community* (Columbia, SC: University of South Carolina Press, 1998), 2.
6. David Campbell, *Writing Security: United States Foreign Policy and the Politics of Identity* (Minneapolis: University of Minnesota Press, 1992).
7. Hannah Pitkin, *The Attack of the Blob: Hannah Arendt's Concept of the Social* (Chicago, IL: University of Chicago Press, 1998).
8. These two ideas—Greek and Roman notions of citizenship—should be seen only as shorthand. Arendt, in fact, presents both Greek and Roman models as similar in her theory of agency. For a version of the distinction between the two, see J. G. A. Pocock, "The Ideal of Citizenship Since Classical Times," in Roland Beiner (ed.), *Theorizing Citizenship* (Albany, NY: SUNY Press, 1995), 29–52.
9. See Philip Hansen, *Hannah Arendt: Politics, History and Citizenship* (Cambridge: Polity Press, 1993), 50–54.
10. Margaret Canovan, *The Political Thought of Hannah Arendt* (New York: Harcourt, Brace Jovanovich, 1974), 68.
11. James Bohman, "The Moral Costs of Political Pluralism: The Dilemmas of Difference and Equality in Arendt's 'Reflections on Little Rock,' " in Larry May and Jerome Kohn (eds.), *Hannah Arendt: Twenty Years Later* (Cambridge, MA: MIT Press, 1996), 60.
12. See the discussion of her emphasis on ruling in the Introduction.
13. See Arendt, *The Human Condition* (Chicago, IL: University of Chicago Press, 1956), 175–247.
14. This is rather how Arendt portrays the lot of humans in capitalist modernity. See Arendt, *Human Condition*, 248–326.
15. Arendt, *Human Condition*, 182–183. Emphases in original.
16. Ibid., 186–187.

17. Arendt, *Human Condition*, 199–207.
18. Ibid., 234.
19. Ibid., 236–243.
20. Ibid., 237.
21. For example, her brief discussion of international relations at the start of *On Revolution* casts it as being encompassed by the strategic discourse of nuclear strategy—unpromising territory for "proper" politics. *On Revolution*, 1–11.
22. See these essays, along with others, in Gregory H. Fox and Brad R. Roth (eds.), *Democratic Governance and International Law* (Cambridge: Cambridge University Press, 2000).
23. One of the leading figures in this area is Toni Erskine; see "Assigning Responsibilities to Institutional Moral Agents: The Case of States and Quasi-States," *Ethics & International Affairs*, 15, no. 2 (2001): 67–85; " 'Blood on the UN's Hands?' Assigning Responsibilities to an Intergovernmental Organization," *Global Society*, 18 (2004): 21–42; and Toni Erskine, (ed.), *Can Institutions Have Responsibilities? Collective Moral Agency and International Relations* (London: Palgrave Publishers, 2003). See also, Anthony F. Lang, Jr. "Responsibility in the International System: Reading U. S. Foreign Policy in the Middle East," *European Journal of International Relations*, 5, no. 1 (March 1999): 67–107.
24. See John Martin Fischer and Mark Ravizza (eds.), *Perspectives on Moral Responsibility* (Ithaca, NY: Cornell University Press, 1993) for a small sample of some of this literature.
25. For a different treatment of Arendt on the question of evil, especially as it has been employed in foreign policy rhetoric, see Douglas Klusmeyer and Astri Suhrke, "Comprehending Evil: Challenges for Law and Policy," *Ethics & International Affairs*, 16, no. 1 (2002): 27–42.
26. See Hannah Arendt, *Lectures on Kant's Political Philosophy*, edited by Ronald Beiner (Chicago: University of Chicago Press, 1982).
27. Hannah Arendt, "Collective Responsibility," in *Responsibility and Judgment*, 147.
28. Ibid., 149.
29. Toni Erskine has suggested that this reference may have come from Arendt's correspondence with Karl Jaspers concerning German guilt; see Lotte Kohler and Hans Saner (eds.), *Hannah Arendt Karl Jaspers; Correspondence 1926–1969*, trans. from German by Robert and Rita Kimber (New York: Harcourt Brace, 1992).
30. Arendt, "Collective Responsibility," 157–158.
31. For further elaboration of this point, but from two different perspectives, see Edward Said, *Covering Islam: How the Media and Experts Determine How We See the Rest of the World* (London: Routledge, 1981) and Fawaz Gerges, *America and Islam: Clash of Cultures or Clash of Interests?* (Cambridge: Cambridge University Press, 1999).

LIST OF CONTRIBUTORS

Bridget Cotter teaches at the Centre for the Study of Democracy, University of Westminster.

Douglas Klusmeyer is Assistant Professor in the Department of Justice, Law and Society at American University.

Anthony F. Lang, Jr. is Lecturer in the School of International Relations at the University of St Andrews.

Patricia Owens is Lecturer in Strategic Studies in the Department of Politics and International Relations and Seton-Watson Research Fellow in International Relations at Oriel College, University of Oxford.

Andrew Schapp is a Research Fellow in the Centre for Applied Philosophy and Public Ethics at the University of Melbourne.

John Williams is Lecturer in the School of Government and International Affairs at the University of Durham.

INDEX